Norihiro Yagi won the 32nd Akatsuka Award for his debut work, *UNDEADMAN*, which appeared in *Monthly Shonen Jump* magazine and produced two sequels. His first serialized manga was his comedy *Angel Densetsu* (Angel Legend), which appeared in *Monthly Shonen Jump* from 1992 to 2000. His epic saga, *CLAYMORE*, has been running in the magazine since 2001.

In his spare time, Yagi enjoys things like the Japanese comedic duo Downtown, martial arts, games, driving, and hard rock music, but he doesn't consider these actual hobbies.

CLAYMORE VOL. 2
SHONEN JUMP ADVANCED Manga Edition

STORY AND ART BY
NORIHIRO YAGI

English Adaptation & Translation/Jonathan Tarbox
Touch-up Art & Lettering/Sabrina Heep
Design/Izumi Evers
Editor/Yuki Takagaki

CLAYMORE © 2001 by Norihiro Yagi. All rights reserved. First
published in Japan in 2001 by SHUEISHA Inc., Tokyo. English
translation rights arranged by SHUEISHA Inc.

The rights of the author(s) of the work(s) in this publication to
be so identified have been asserted in accordance with the
Copyright, Designs and Patents Act 1988. A CIP catalogue record
for this book is available from the British Library.

Some scenes containing nudity have been modified from the
original Japanese edition.

The stories, characters and incidents mentioned in this
publication are entirely fictional.

No portion of this book may be reproduced or transmitted in
any form or by any means without written permission from the
copyright holders.

Printed in the U.S.A.

Published by VIZ Media, LLC
P.O. Box 77010
San Francisco, CA 94107

10 9
First printing, June 2006
Ninth printing, October 2011

THE WORLD'S MOST
CUTTING-EDGE MANGA

SHONEN JUMP ADVANCED Manga Edition

Claymore

クレイモア

Vol. 2
Darkness in Paradise

Story and Art by **Norihiro Yagi**

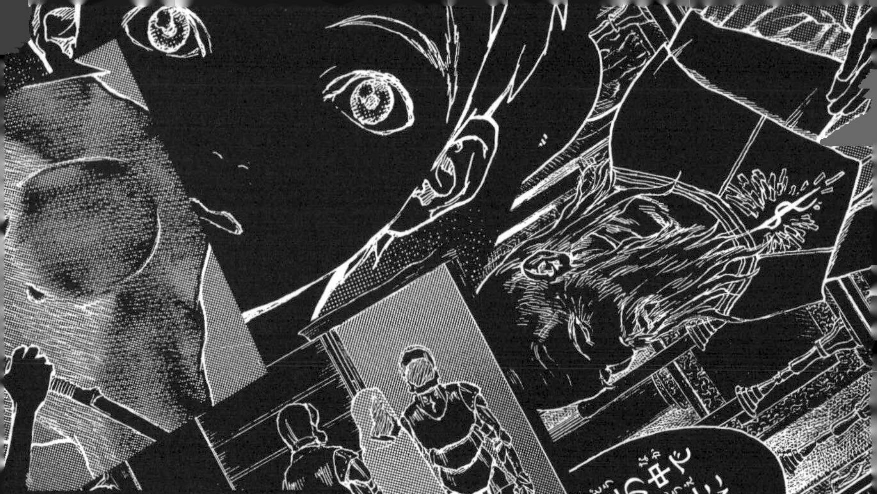

"Claymores" after the immense broadswords that they carried.

During her travels, a Claymore named Clare meets Raki, a boy whose family has been wiped out by Yoma, and together they begin a journey...

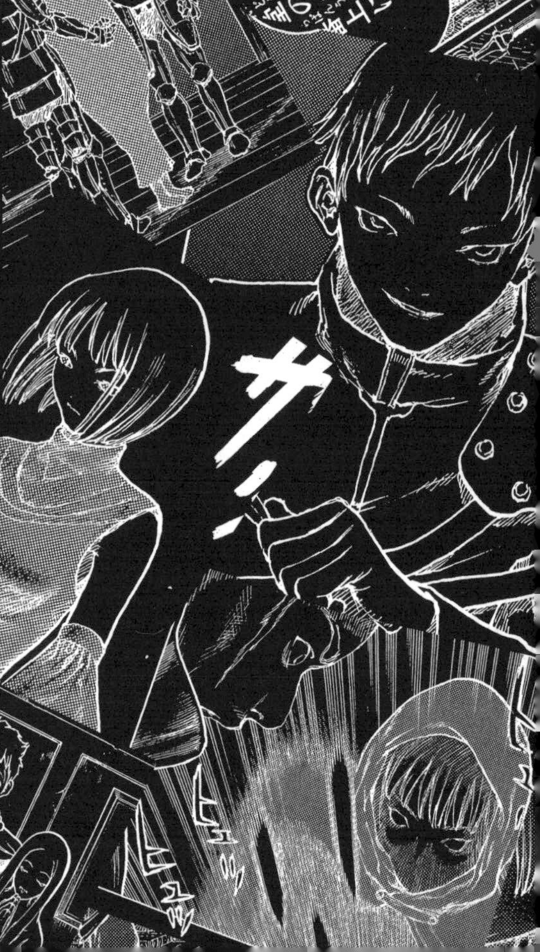

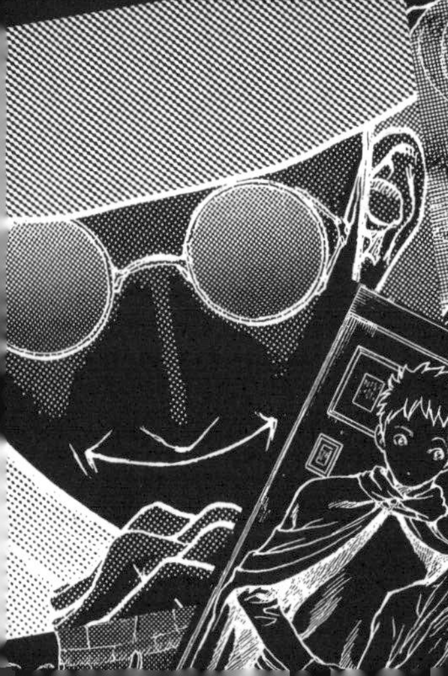

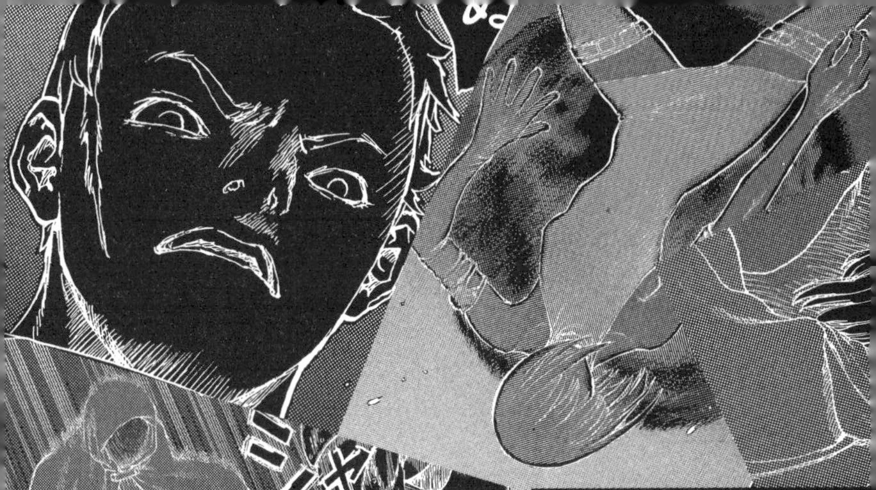

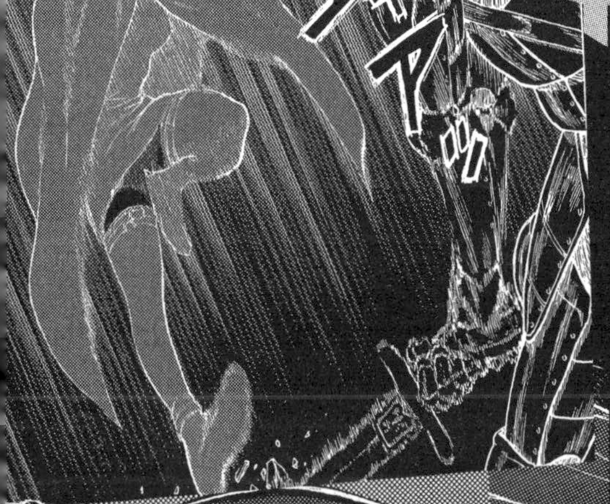

The Story Thus Far

Creatures known as Yoma have long preyed on humans, who were once powerless against their predators. But now they've developed female warriors who are half human and half monster, with silver eyes that can see the monsters' true form. These warriors came to be called

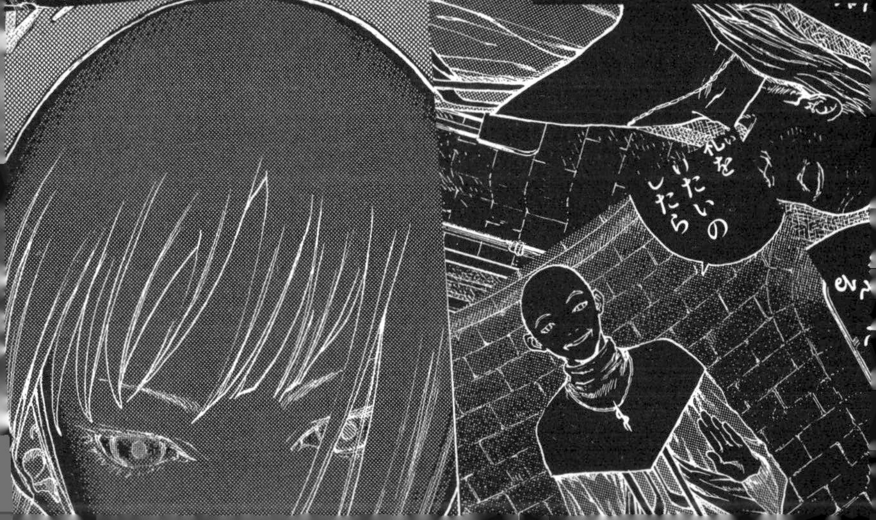

Claymore

クレイモア

Vol. 2

CONTENTS

Scene 5: Darkness in Paradise, Part 1

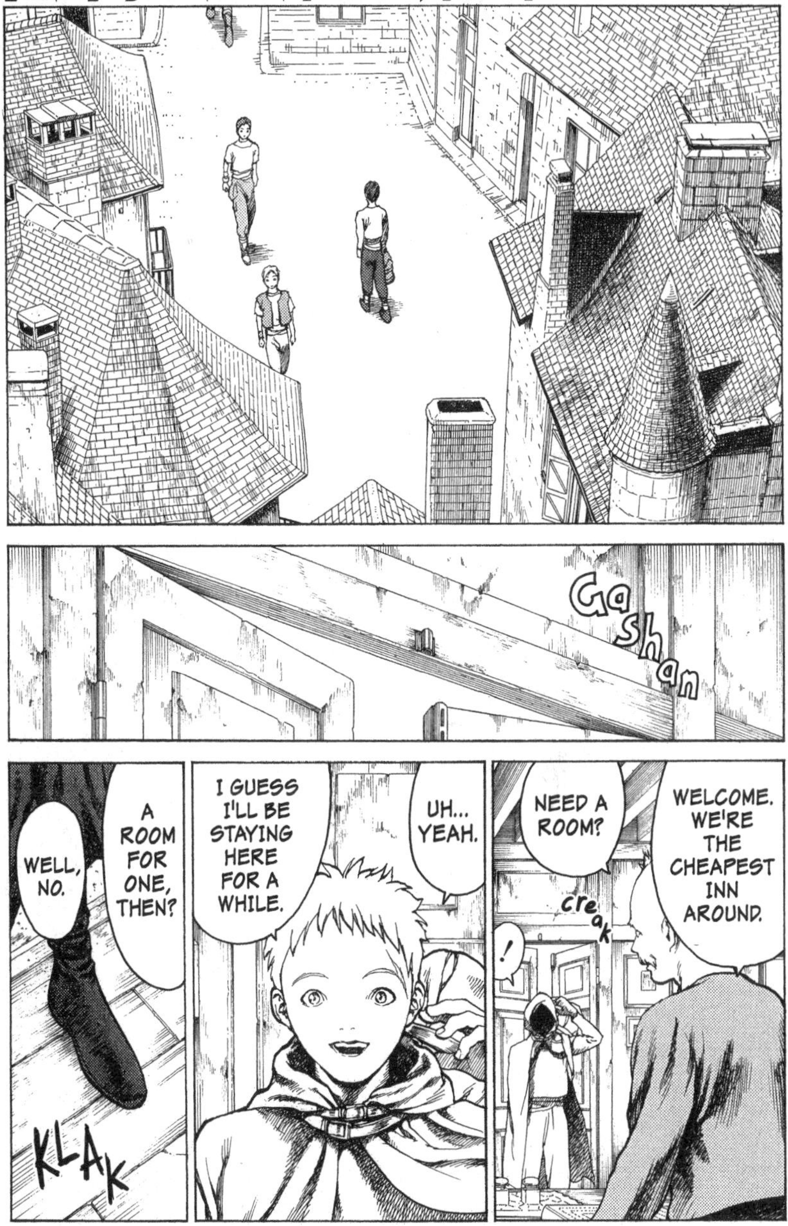
Gashan
Welcome. We're the cheapest inn around.
Need a room?
creak
!
Uh... yeah.
I guess I'll be staying here for a while.
A room for one, then?
Well, no.
KLAK

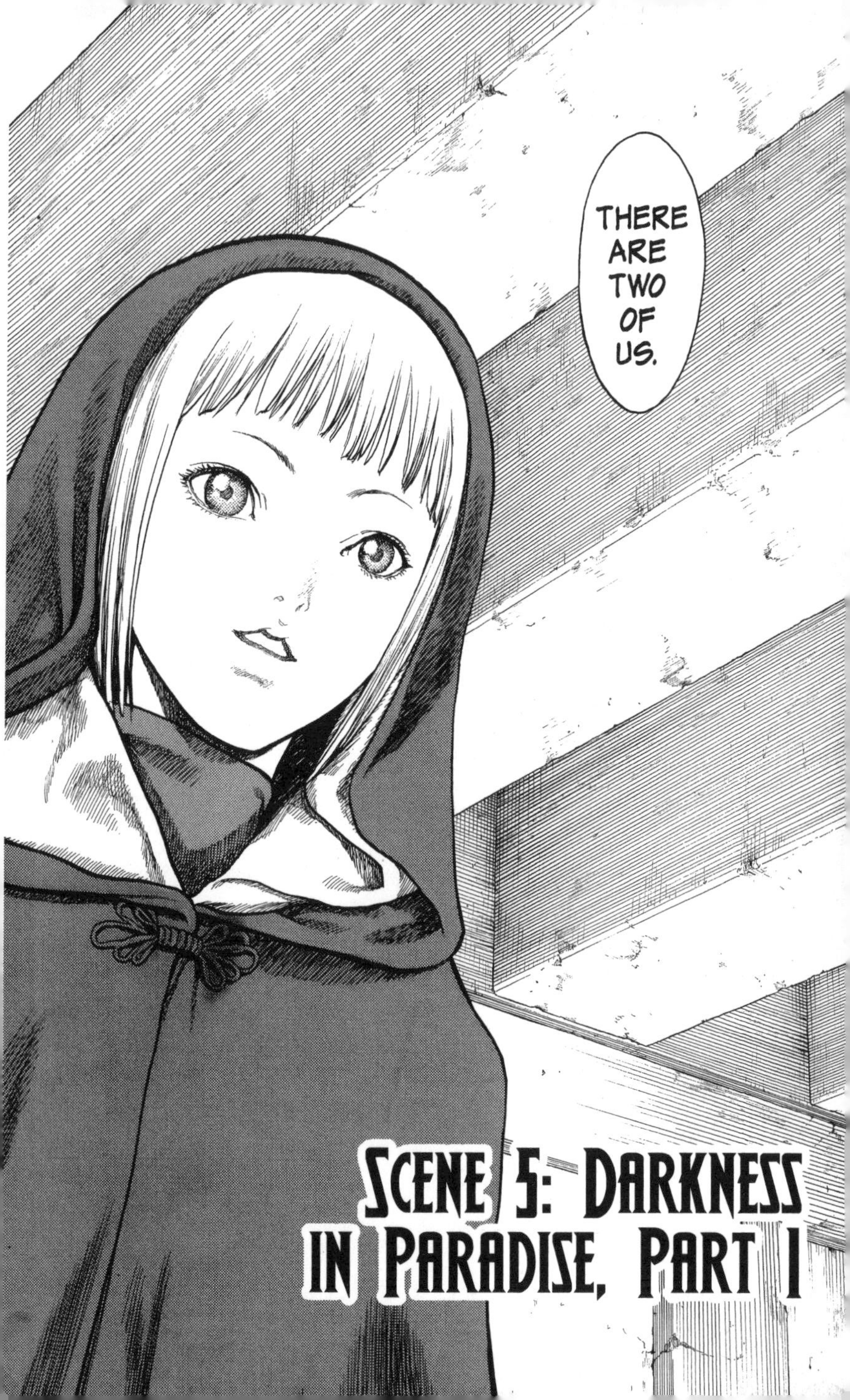
THERE ARE TWO OF US.
SCENE 5: DARKNESS IN PARADISE, PART 1

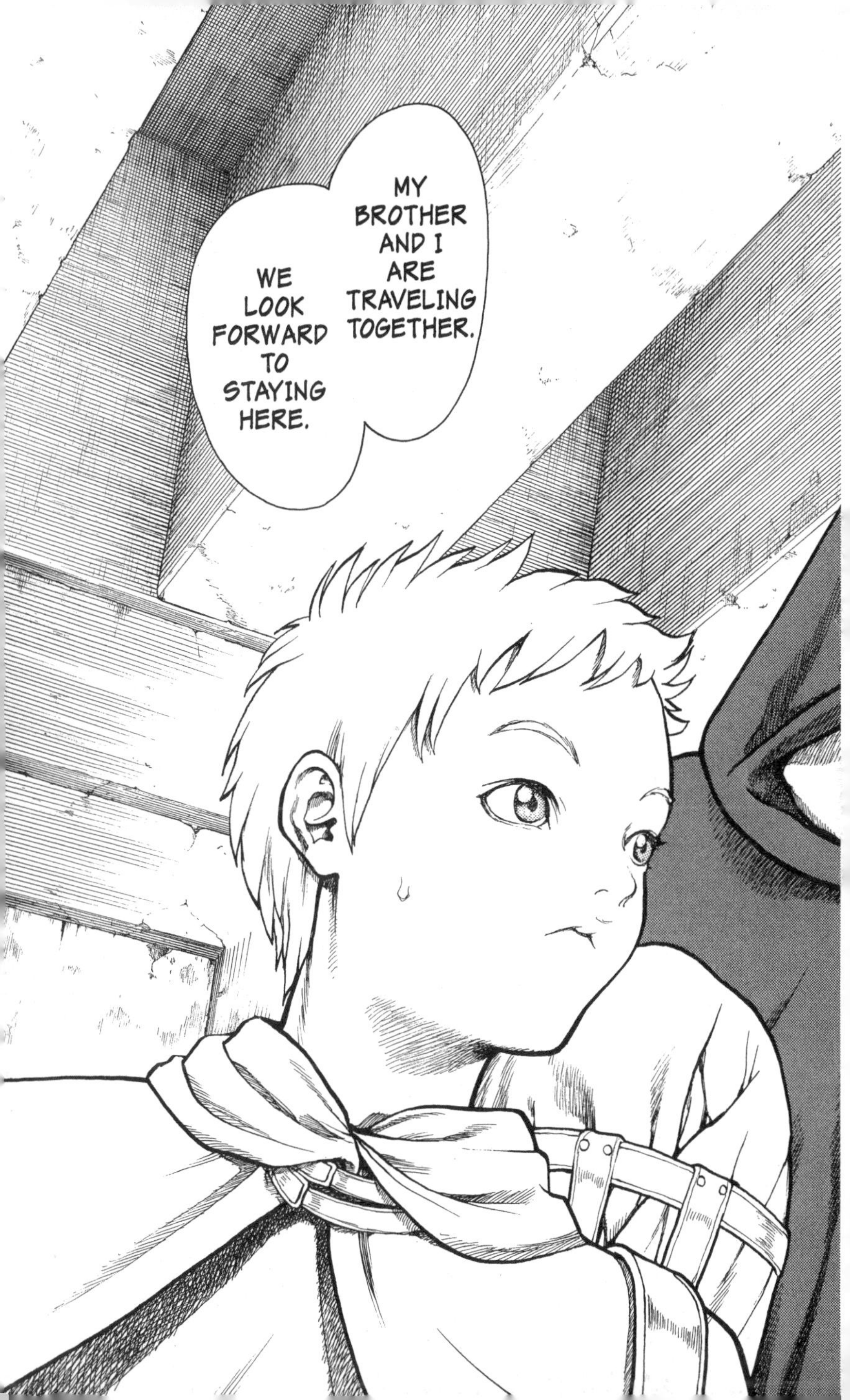
MY BROTHER AND I ARE TRAVELING TOGETHER.
WE LOOK FORWARD TO STAYING HERE.

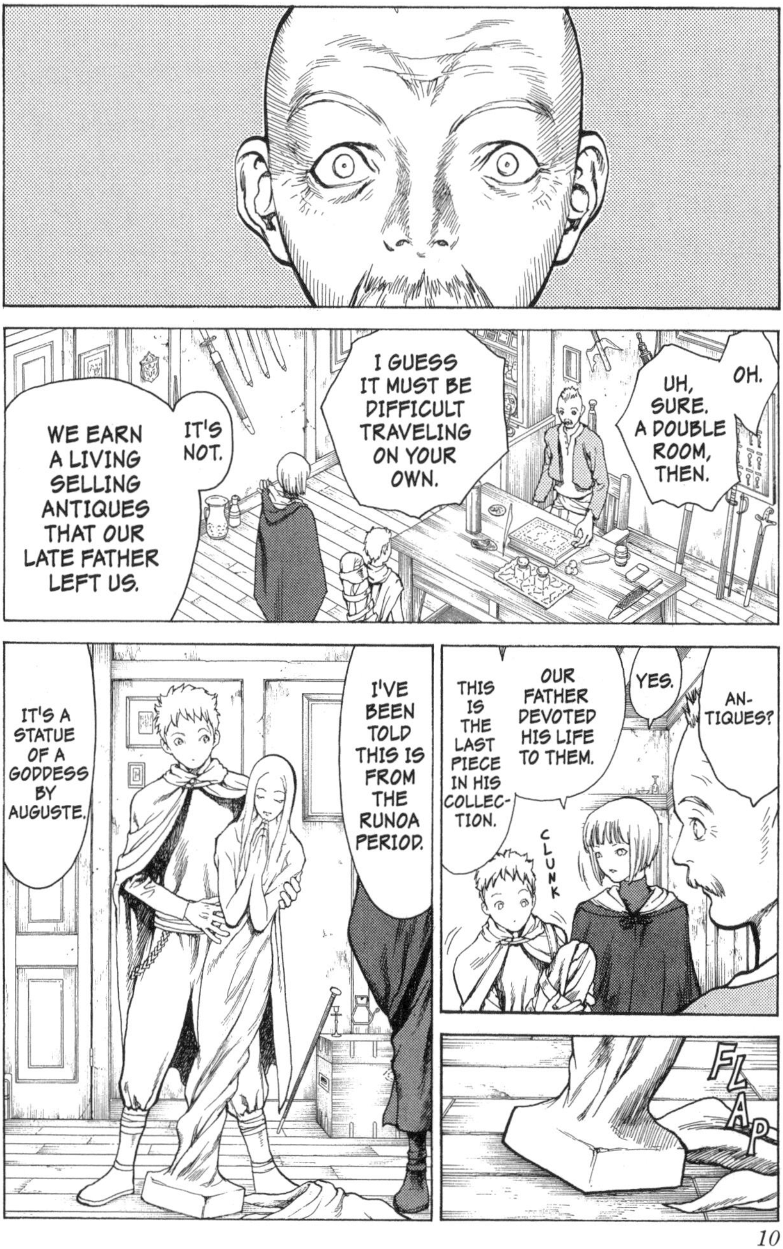
OH.
UH, SURE. A DOUBLE ROOM, THEN.
I GUESS IT MUST BE DIFFICULT TRAVELING ON YOUR OWN.
IT'S NOT.
WE EARN A LIVING SELLING ANTIQUES THAT OUR LATE FATHER LEFT US.
ANTIQUES?
YES.
OUR FATHER DEVOTED HIS LIFE TO THEM.
THIS IS THE LAST PIECE IN HIS COLLECTION.
CLUNK
FLAP
I'VE BEEN TOLD THIS IS FROM THE RUNOA PERIOD.
IT'S A STATUE OF A GODDESS BY AUGUSTE.

READ THIS WAY

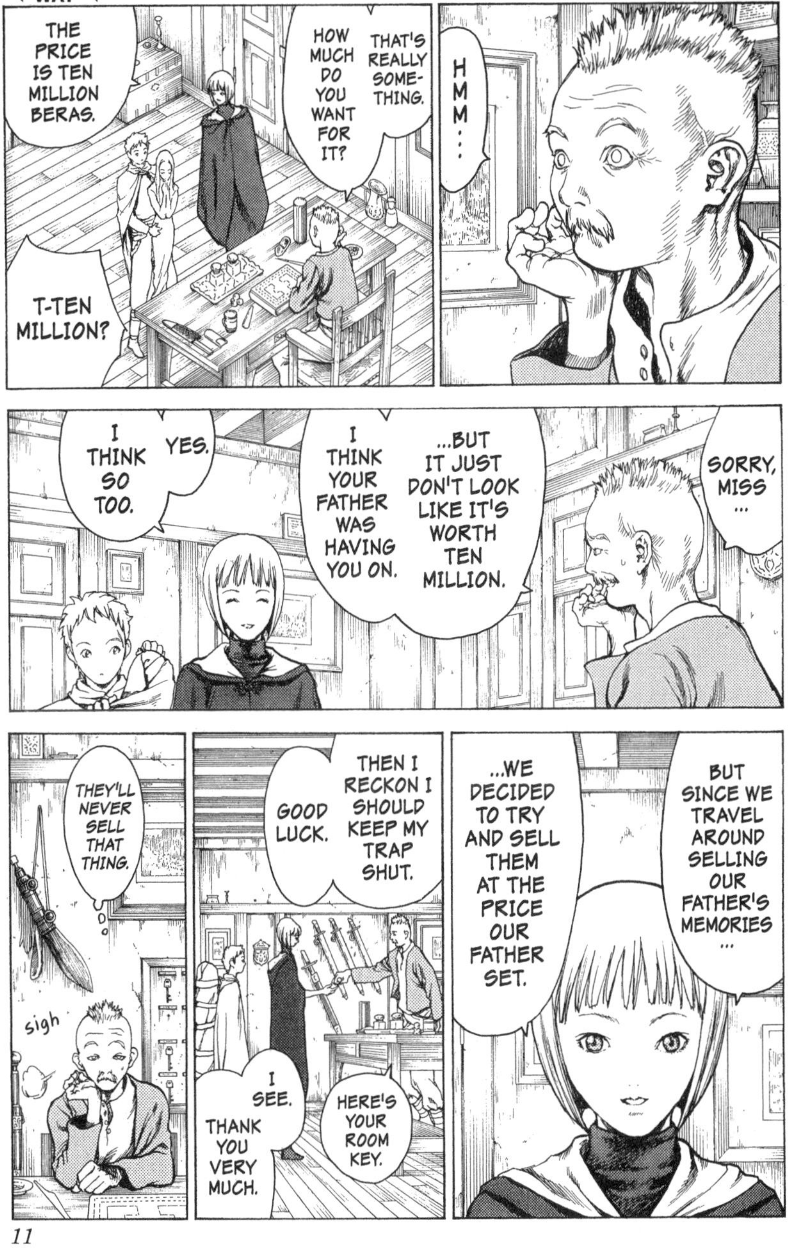
HMM...
THAT'S REALLY SOMETHING.
HOW MUCH DO YOU WANT FOR IT?
THE PRICE IS TEN MILLION BERAS.
T-TEN MILLION?
SORRY, MISS...
...BUT IT JUST DON'T LOOK LIKE IT'S WORTH TEN MILLION.
I THINK YOUR FATHER WAS HAVING YOU ON.
YES.
I THINK SO TOO.
BUT SINCE WE TRAVEL AROUND SELLING OUR FATHER'S MEMORIES...
...WE DECIDED TO TRY AND SELL THEM AT THE PRICE OUR FATHER SET.
THEN I RECKON I SHOULD KEEP MY TRAP SHUT.
GOOD LUCK.
HERE'S YOUR ROOM KEY.
I SEE.
THANK YOU VERY MUCH.
THEY'LL NEVER SELL THAT THING.
sigh

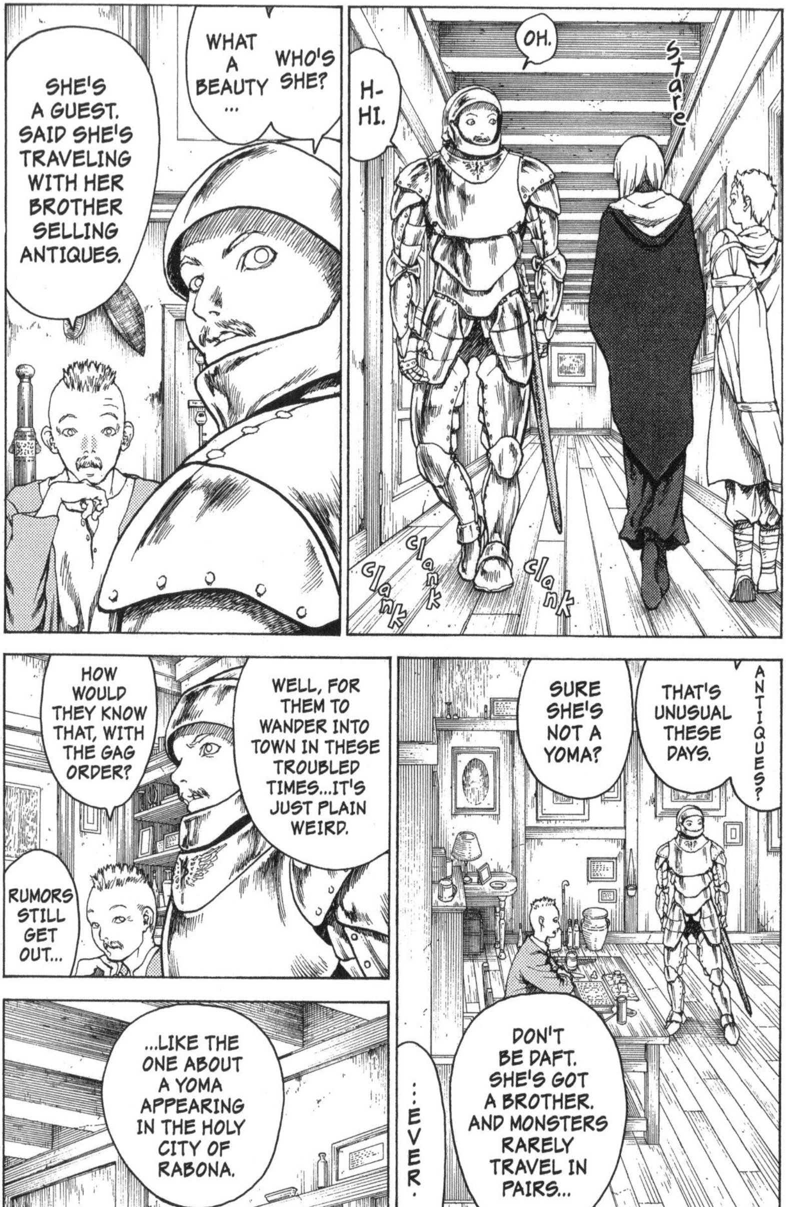
Stare
OH.
H-HI.
clank
clank
clank
WHO'S SHE?
WHAT A BEAUTY ...
SHE'S A GUEST. SAID SHE'S TRAVELING WITH HER BROTHER SELLING ANTIQUES.
ANTIQUES?
THAT'S UNUSUAL THESE DAYS.
SURE SHE'S NOT A YOMA?
DON'T BE DAFT. SHE'S GOT A BROTHER. AND MONSTERS RARELY TRAVEL IN PAIRS...
...EVER.
WELL, FOR THEM TO WANDER INTO TOWN IN THESE TROUBLED TIMES...IT'S JUST PLAIN WEIRD.
HOW WOULD THEY KNOW THAT, WITH THE GAG ORDER?
RUMORS STILL GET OUT...
...LIKE THE ONE ABOUT A YOMA APPEARING IN THE HOLY CITY OF RABONA.

READ THIS WAY

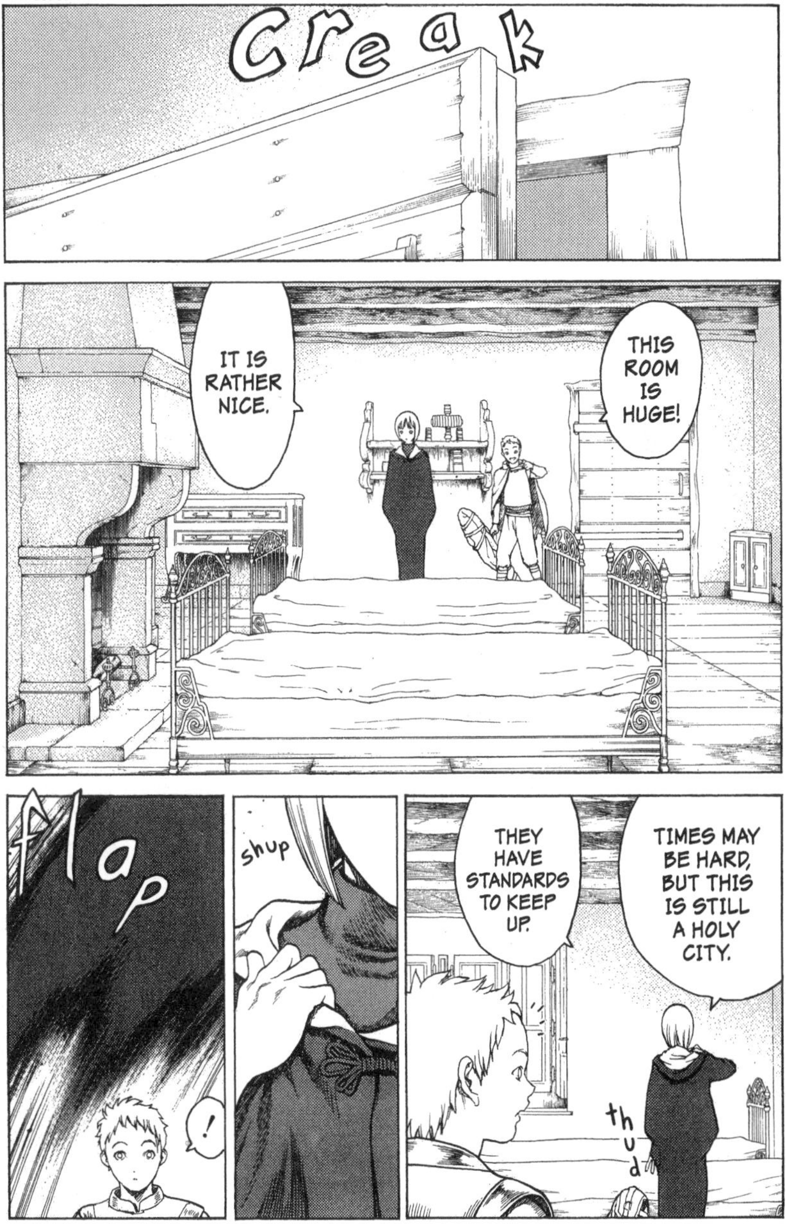
Creak
THIS ROOM IS HUGE!
IT IS RATHER NICE.
TIMES MAY BE HARD, BUT THIS IS STILL A HOLY CITY.
THEY HAVE STANDARDS TO KEEP UP.
thud
shup
flap
!

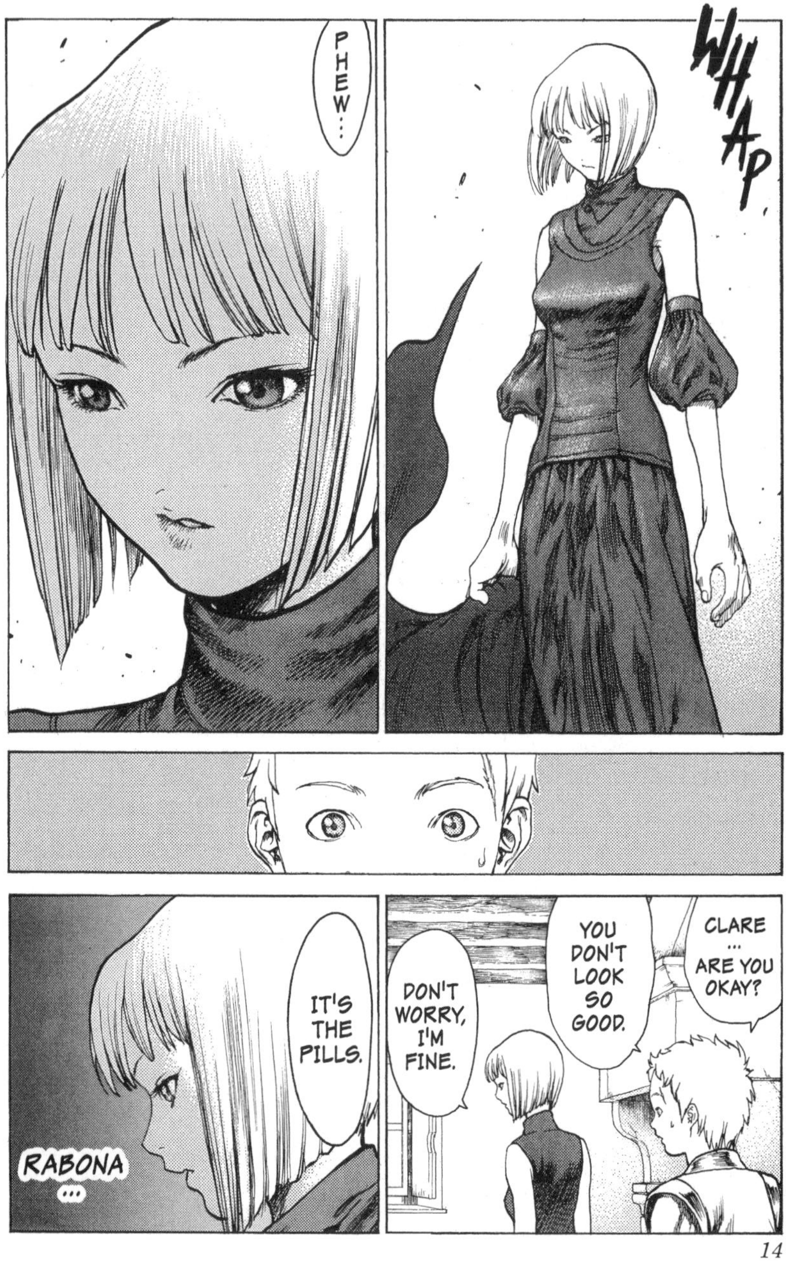
WHAP
PHEW...
CLARE ... ARE YOU OKAY?
YOU DON'T LOOK SO GOOD.
DON'T WORRY, I'M FINE.
IT'S THE PILLS.
RABONA ...

READ THIS WAY

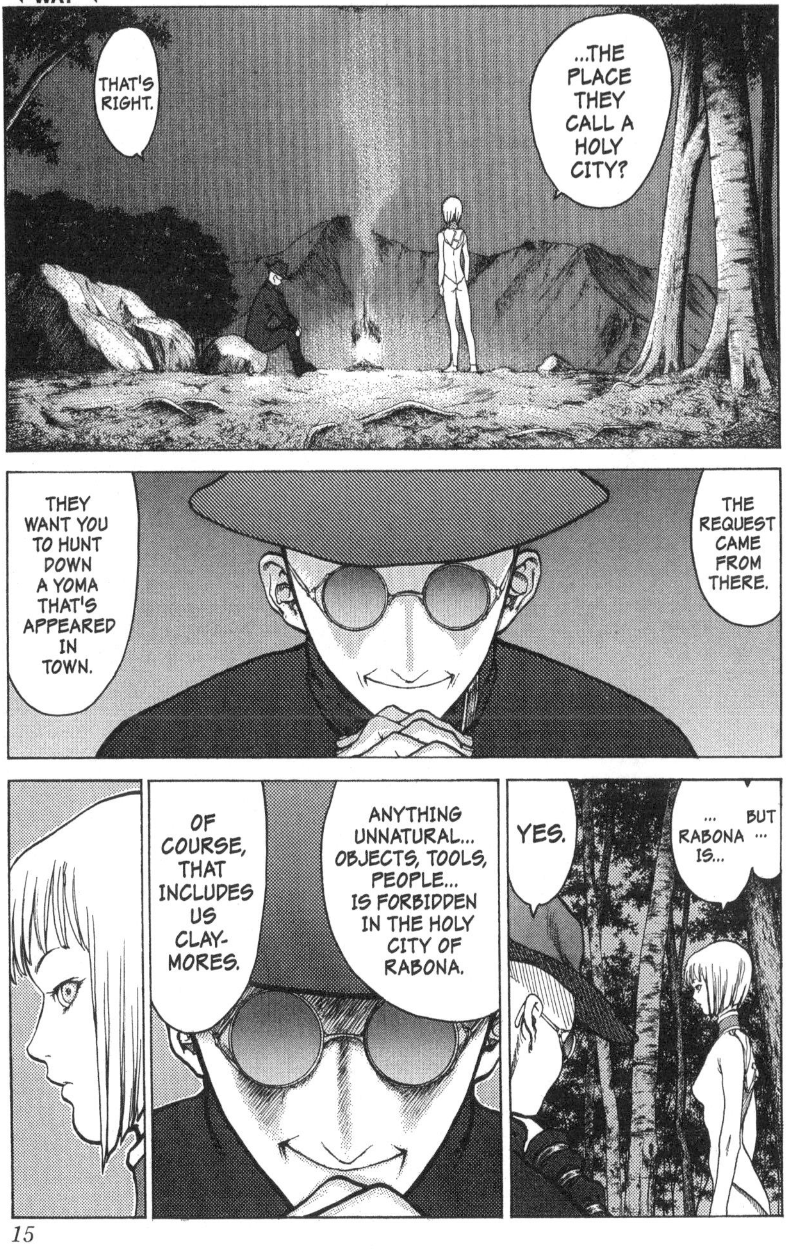
...THE PLACE THEY CALL A HOLY CITY?
THAT'S RIGHT.
THE REQUEST CAME FROM THERE.
THEY WANT YOU TO HUNT DOWN A YOMA THAT'S APPEARED IN TOWN.
... BUT ... RABONA IS...
YES.
ANYTHING UNNATURAL... OBJECTS, TOOLS, PEOPLE... IS FORBIDDEN IN THE HOLY CITY OF RABONA.
OF COURSE, THAT INCLUDES US CLAY-MORES.

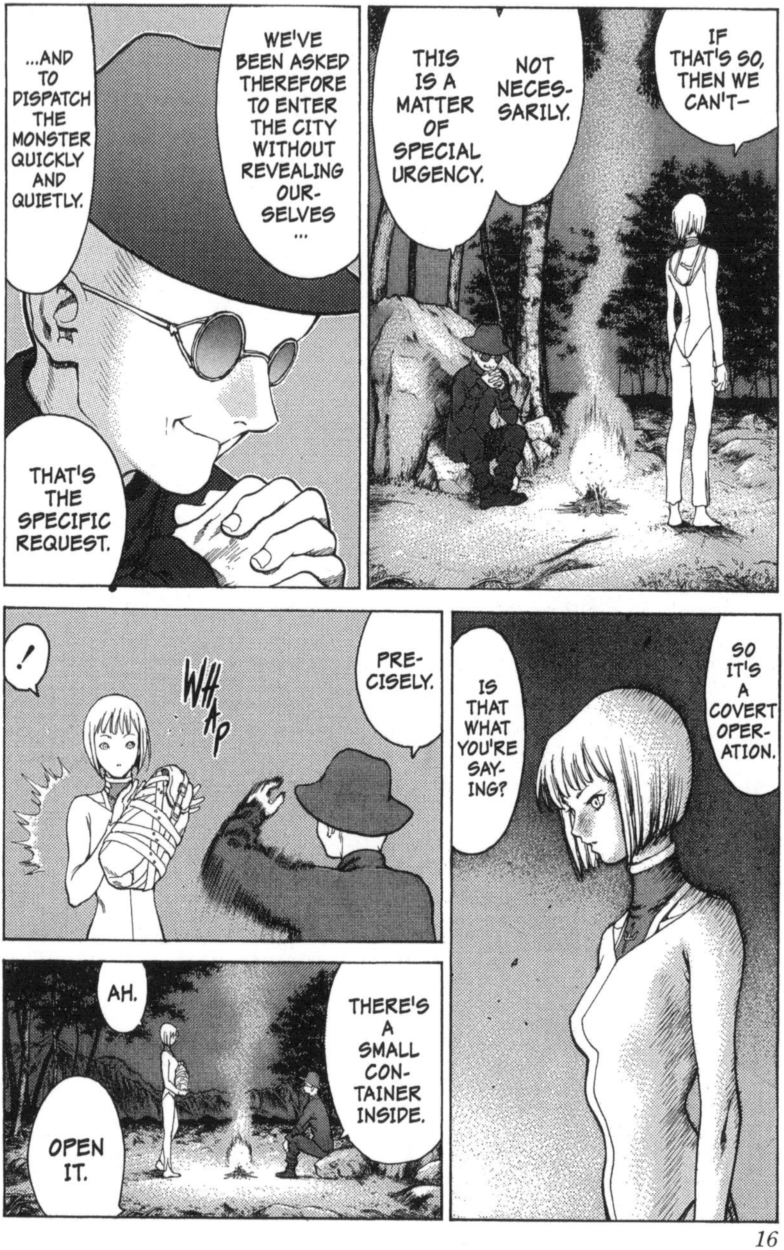
IF THAT'S SO, THEN WE CAN'T—
NOT NECES-SARILY.
THIS IS A MATTER OF SPECIAL URGENCY.
WE'VE BEEN ASKED THEREFORE TO ENTER THE CITY WITHOUT REVEALING OUR-SELVES ...
...AND TO DISPATCH THE MONSTER QUICKLY AND QUIETLY.
THAT'S THE SPECIFIC REQUEST.
SO IT'S A COVERT OPER-ATION.
IS THAT WHAT YOU'RE SAY-ING?
PRE-CISELY.
WHAP
!
THERE'S A SMALL CON-TAINER INSIDE.
AH.
OPEN IT.

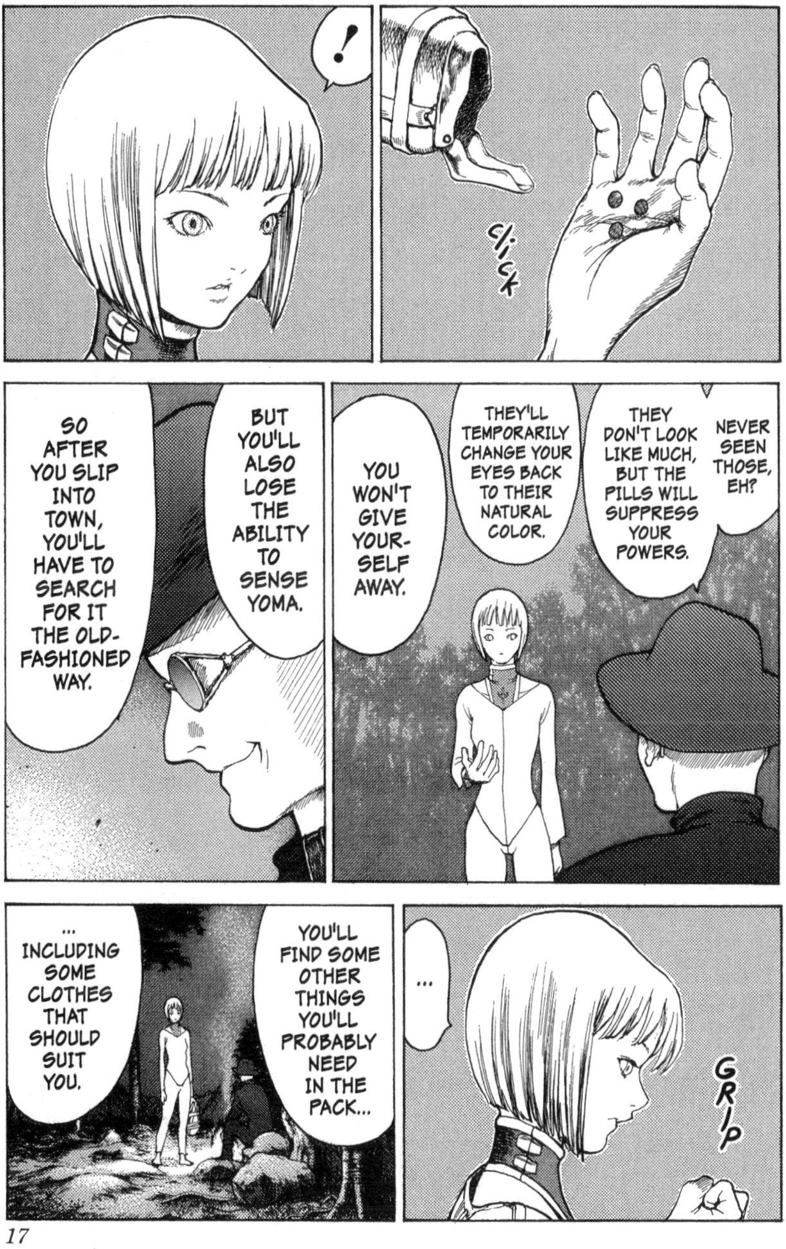
CLICK
!
NEVER SEEN THOSE, EH?
THEY DON'T LOOK LIKE MUCH, BUT THE PILLS WILL SUPPRESS YOUR POWERS.
THEY'LL TEMPORARILY CHANGE YOUR EYES BACK TO THEIR NATURAL COLOR.
YOU WON'T GIVE YOURSELF AWAY.
BUT YOU'LL ALSO LOSE THE ABILITY TO SENSE YOMA.
SO AFTER YOU SLIP INTO TOWN, YOU'LL HAVE TO SEARCH FOR IT THE OLD-FASHIONED WAY.
...
GRIP
YOU'LL FIND SOME OTHER THINGS YOU'LL PROBABLY NEED IN THE PACK...
...INCLUDING SOME CLOTHES THAT SHOULD SUIT YOU.

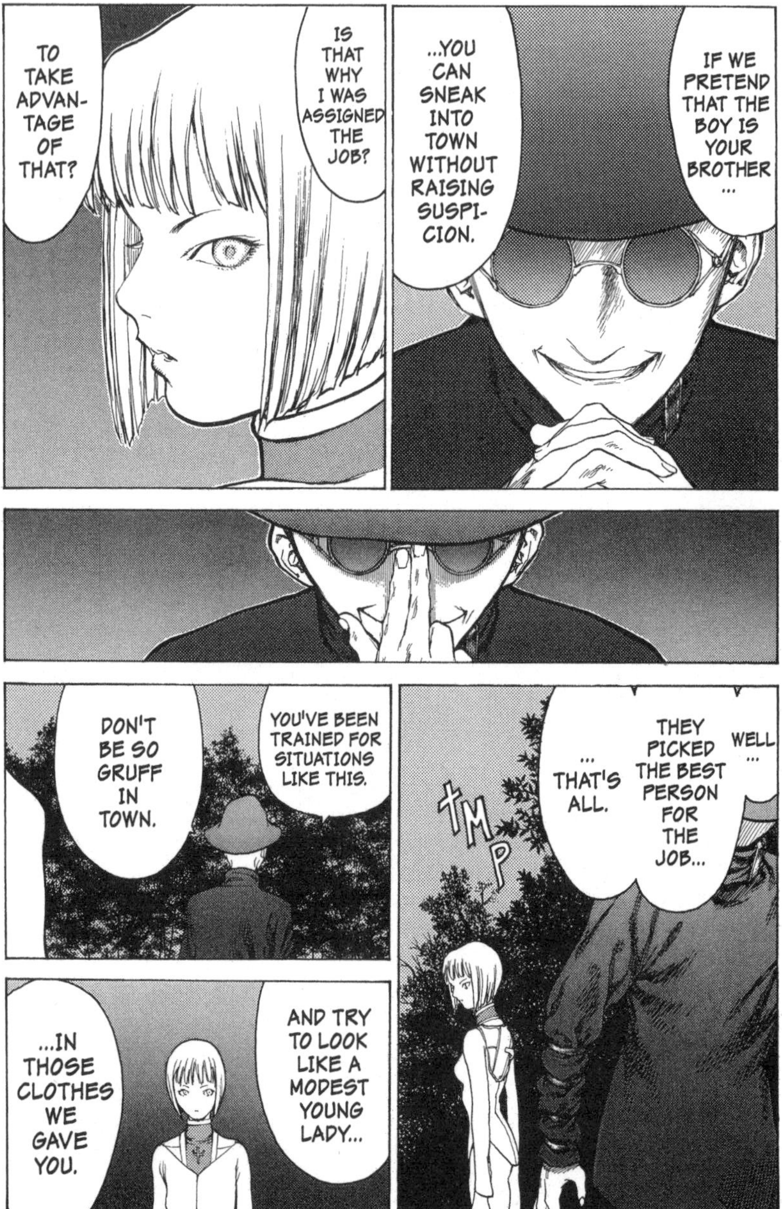
IF WE PRETEND THAT THE BOY IS YOUR BROTHER ...
...YOU CAN SNEAK INTO TOWN WITHOUT RAISING SUSPICION.
IS THAT WHY I WAS ASSIGNED THE JOB?
TO TAKE ADVANTAGE OF THAT?
WELL ...
THEY PICKED THE BEST PERSON FOR THE JOB...
... THAT'S ALL.
TMP
YOU'VE BEEN TRAINED FOR SITUATIONS LIKE THIS.
DON'T BE SO GRUFF IN TOWN.
AND TRY TO LOOK LIKE A MODEST YOUNG LADY...
...IN THOSE CLOTHES WE GAVE YOU.

READ THIS WAY

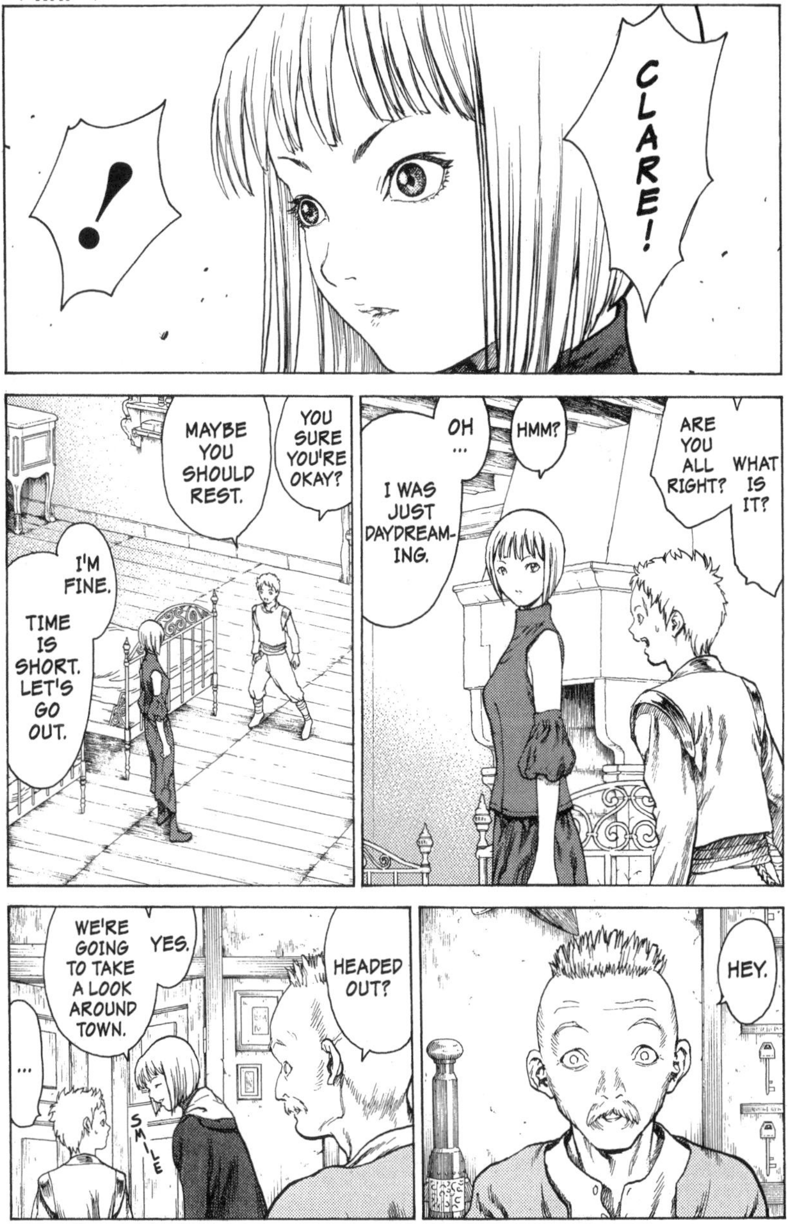

CLARE!
!
WHAT IS IT?
ARE YOU ALL RIGHT?
HMM?
OH ...
I WAS JUST DAYDREAMING.
YOU SURE YOU'RE OKAY?
MAYBE YOU SHOULD REST.
I'M FINE.
TIME IS SHORT. LET'S GO OUT.
HEY.
HEADED OUT?
YES.
WE'RE GOING TO TAKE A LOOK AROUND TOWN.
SMILE
...

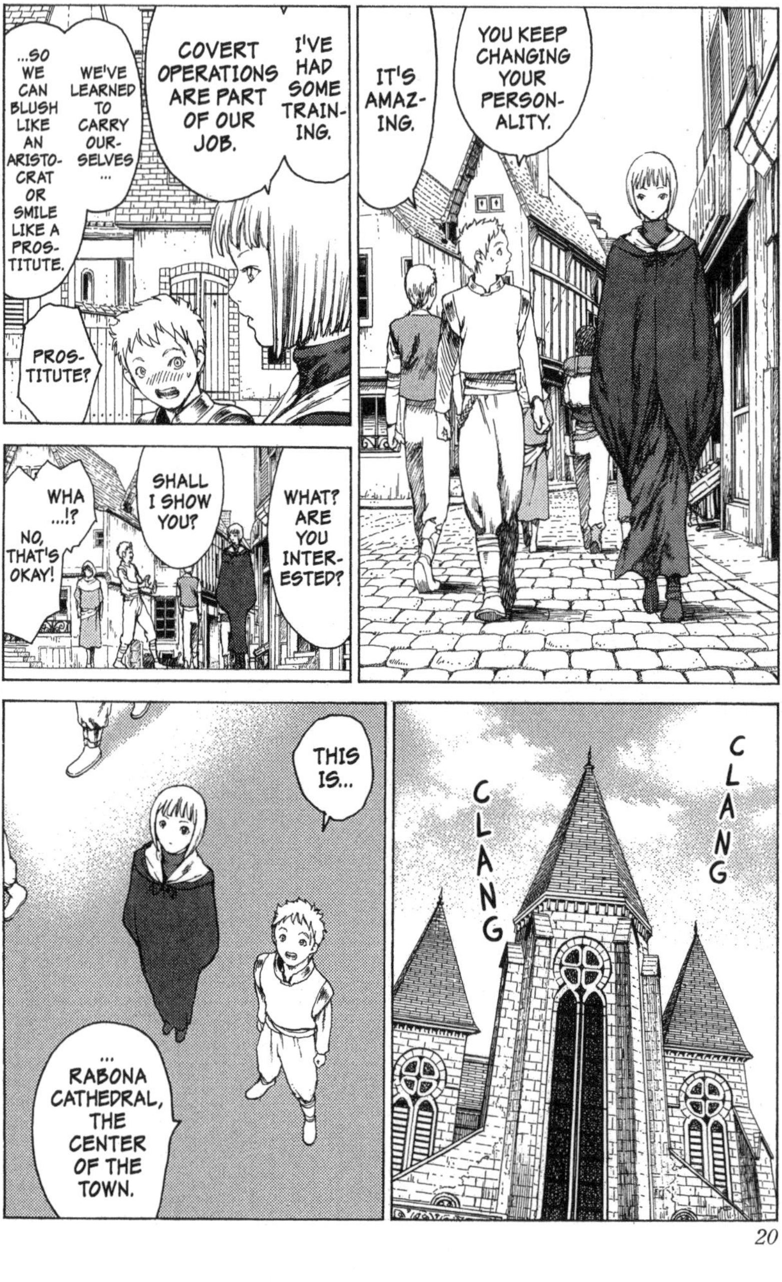
YOU KEEP CHANGING YOUR PERSONALITY.
IT'S AMAZING.
I'VE HAD SOME TRAINING.
COVERT OPERATIONS ARE PART OF OUR JOB.
WE'VE LEARNED TO CARRY OURSELVES...
...SO WE CAN BLUSH LIKE AN ARISTOCRAT OR SMILE LIKE A PROSTITUTE.
PROSTITUTE?
WHAT? ARE YOU INTERESTED?
SHALL I SHOW YOU?
WHA...!?
NO, THAT'S OKAY!
CLANG
CLANG
THIS IS...
...RABONA CATHEDRAL, THE CENTER OF THE TOWN.

READ THIS WAY

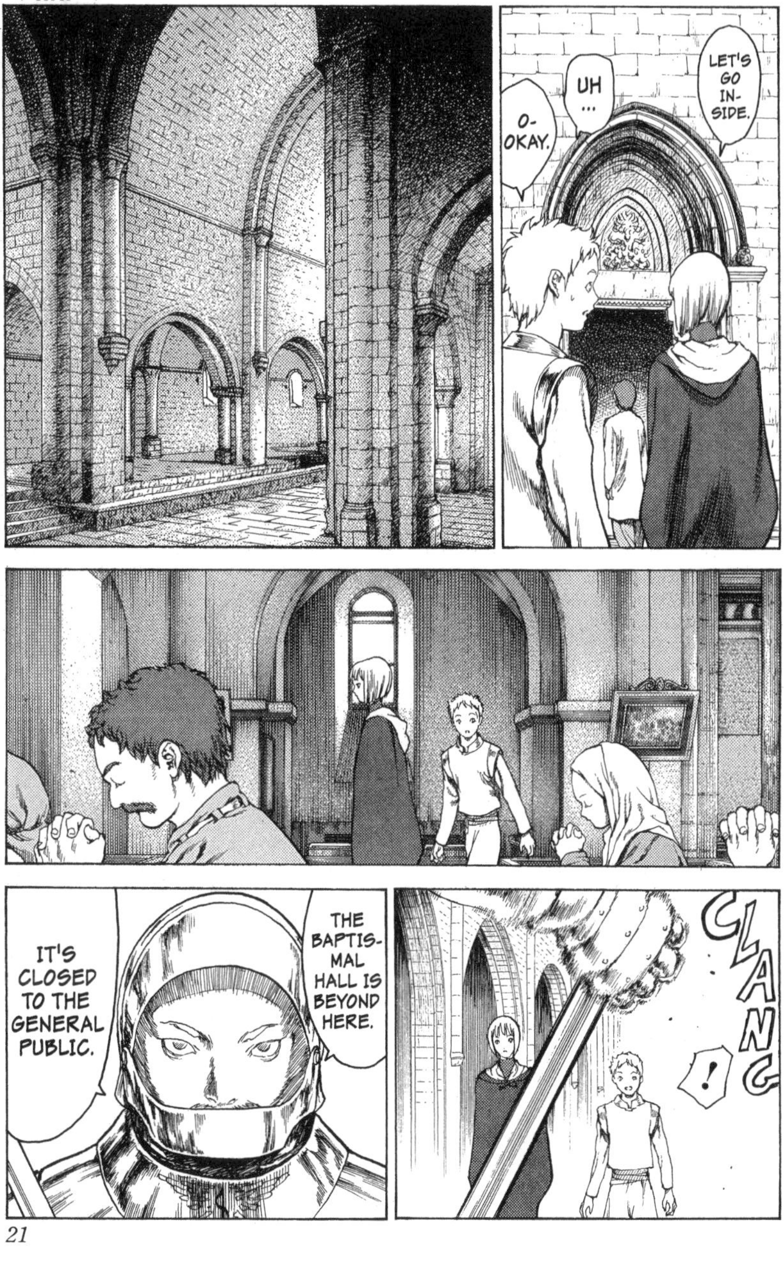
LET'S GO IN-SIDE.
UH ...
O-OKAY.
CLANG
!
THE BAPTIS-MAL HALL IS BEYOND HERE.
IT'S CLOSED TO THE GENERAL PUBLIC.

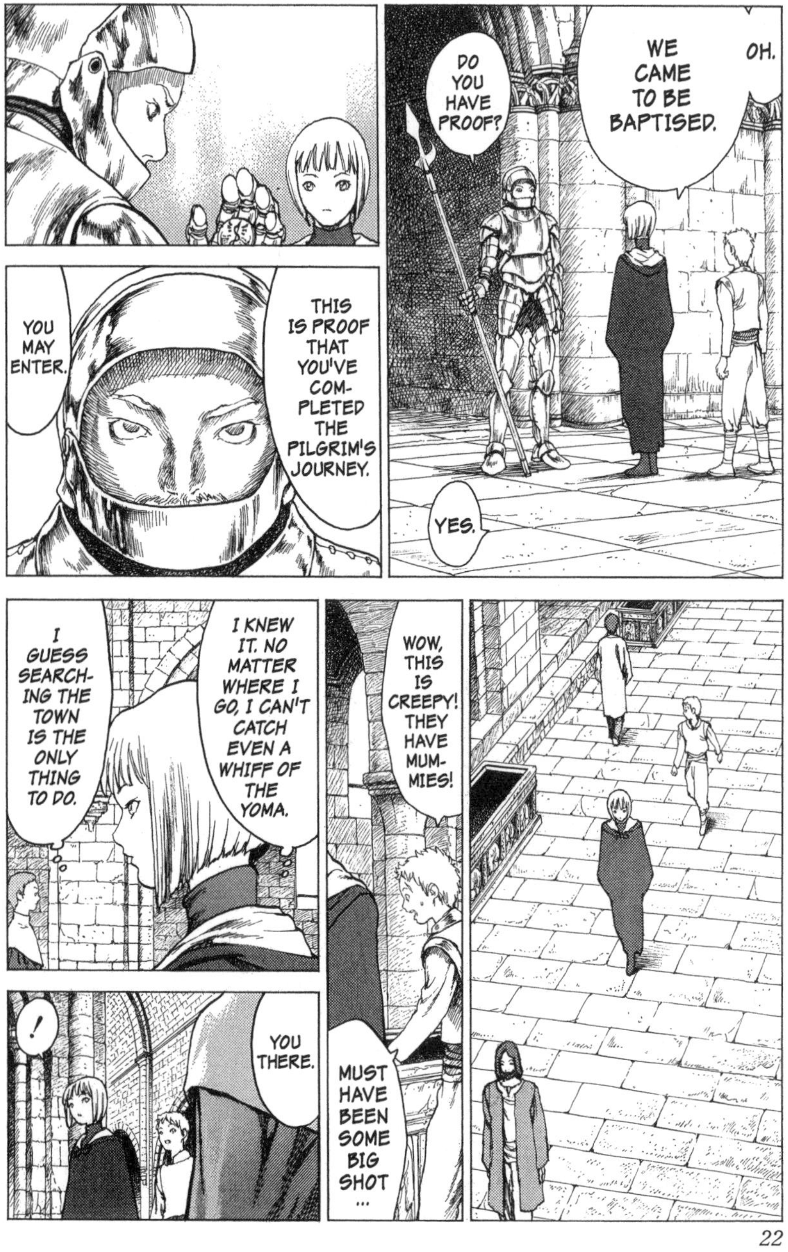
OH.
WE CAME TO BE BAPTISED.
DO YOU HAVE PROOF?
YES.
THIS IS PROOF THAT YOU'VE COMPLETED THE PILGRIM'S JOURNEY.
YOU MAY ENTER.
WOW, THIS IS CREEPY! THEY HAVE MUMMIES!
MUST HAVE BEEN SOME BIG SHOT...
I KNEW IT. NO MATTER WHERE I GO, I CAN'T CATCH EVEN A WHIFF OF THE YOMA.
I GUESS SEARCHING THE TOWN IS THE ONLY THING TO DO.
YOU THERE.
!

READ THIS WAY

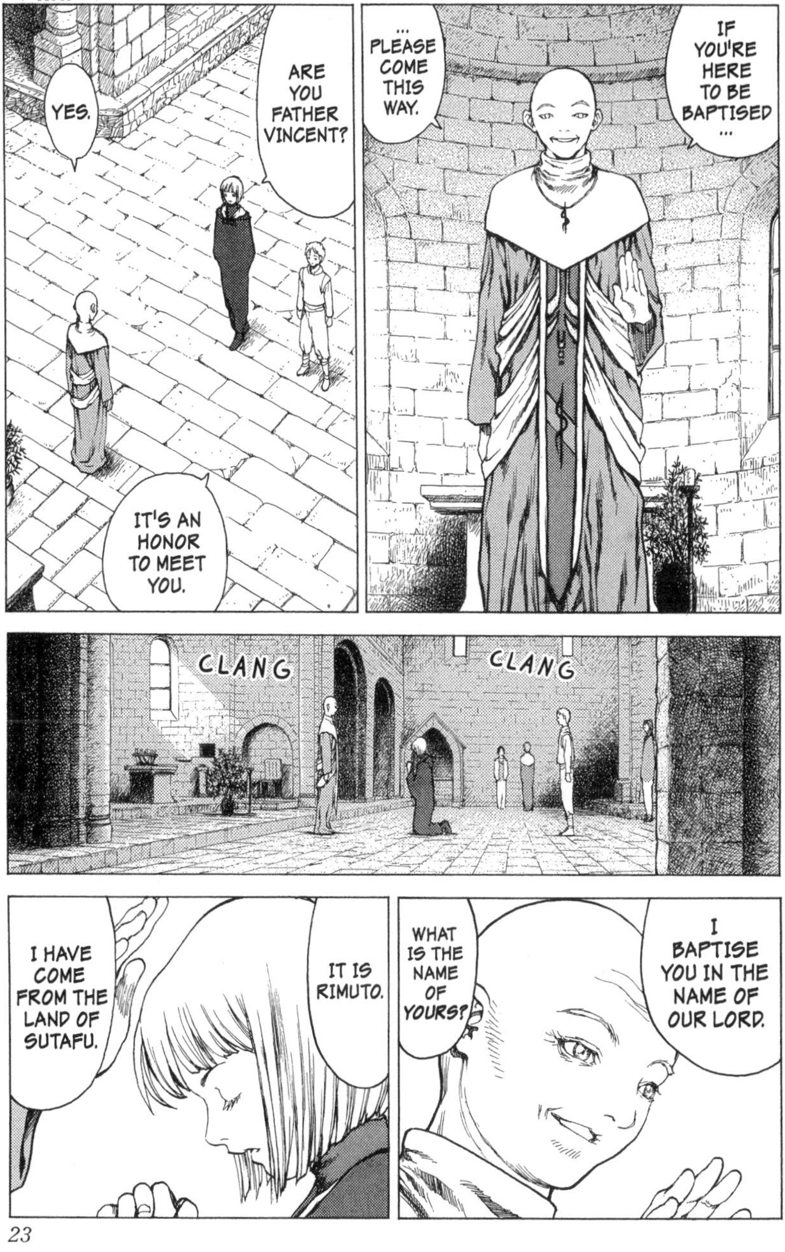
IF YOU'RE HERE TO BE BAPTISED ...
... PLEASE COME THIS WAY.
ARE YOU FATHER VINCENT?
YES.
IT'S AN HONOR TO MEET YOU.
CLANG
CLANG
I BAPTISE YOU IN THE NAME OF OUR LORD.
WHAT IS THE NAME OF YOURS?
IT IS RIMUTO.
I HAVE COME FROM THE LAND OF SUTAFU.

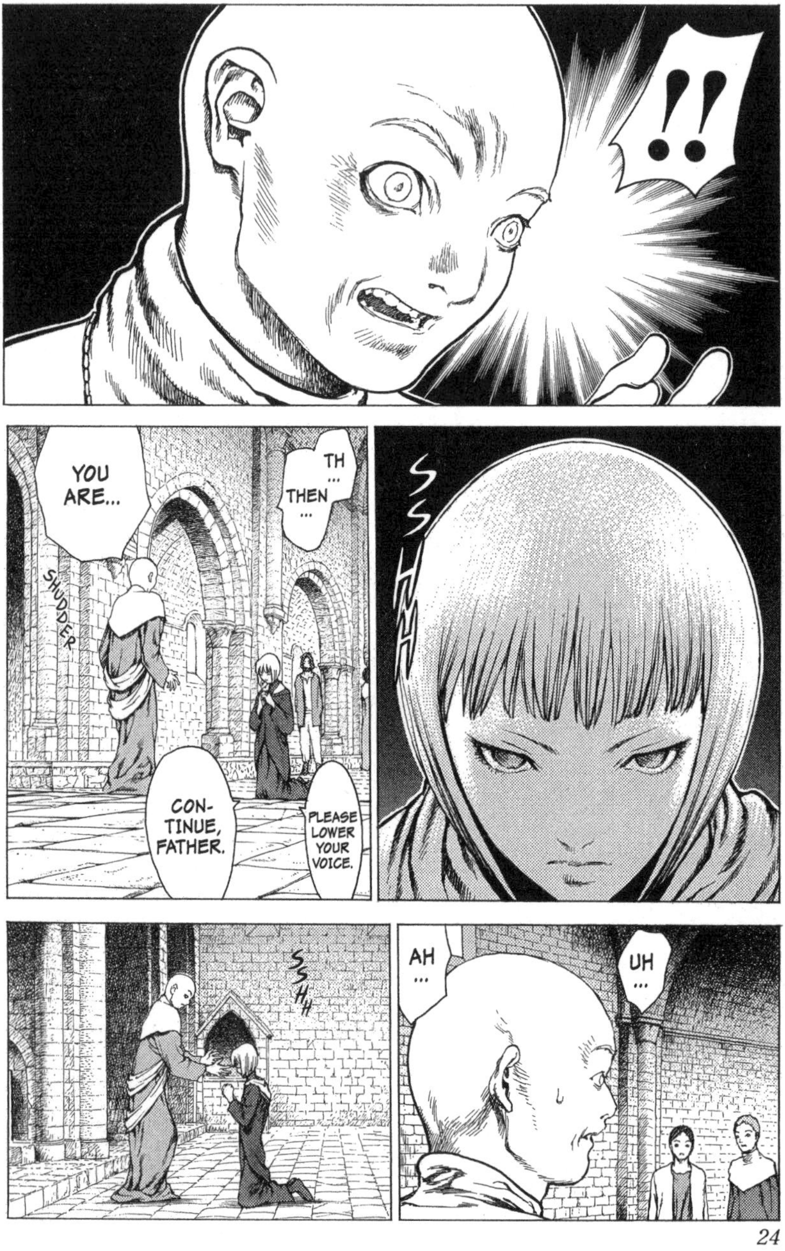
!!
SSHHH
TH... THEN...
YOU ARE...
SHUDDER
PLEASE LOWER YOUR VOICE.
CON-TINUE, FATHER.
UH...
AH...
SSHH

READ THIS WAY

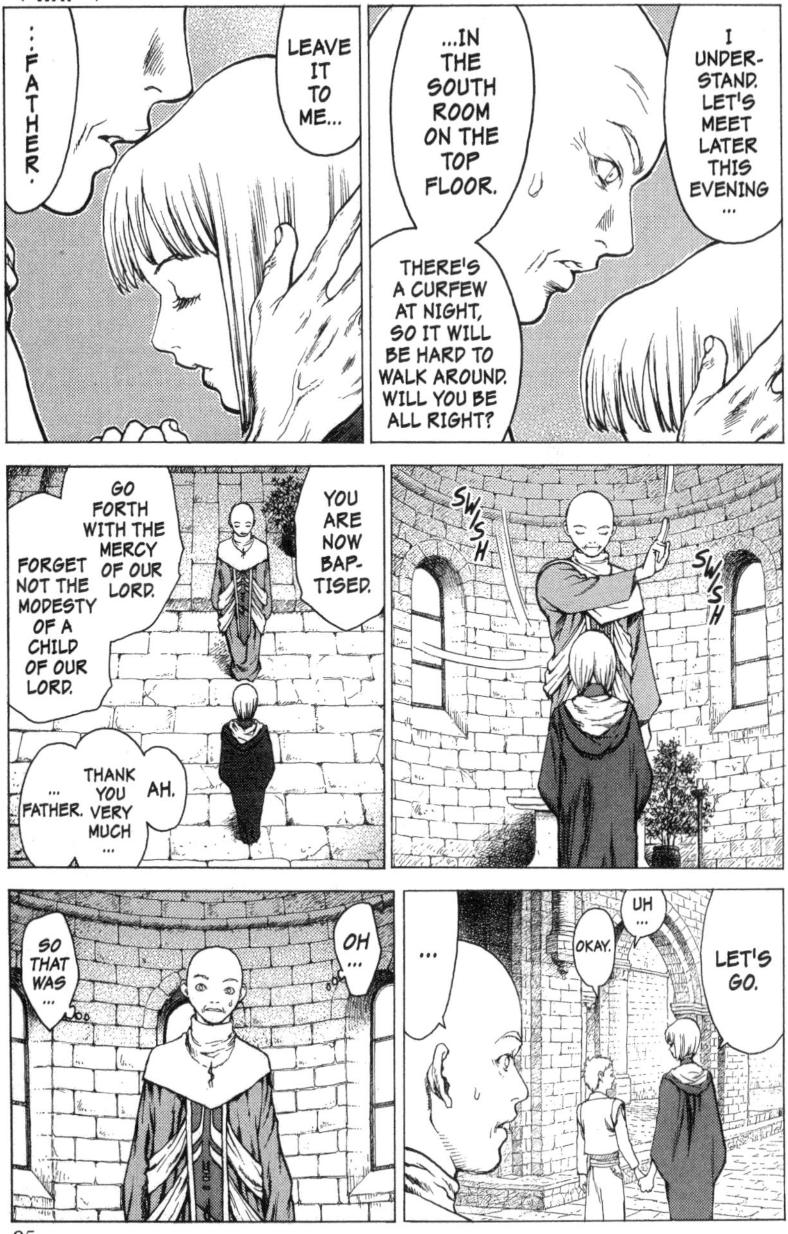

I UNDERSTAND. LET'S MEET LATER THIS EVENING...
...IN THE SOUTH ROOM ON THE TOP FLOOR.
THERE'S A CURFEW AT NIGHT, SO IT WILL BE HARD TO WALK AROUND. WILL YOU BE ALL RIGHT?
LEAVE IT TO ME...
...FATHER.
SWISH
SWISH
YOU ARE NOW BAPTISED.
GO FORTH WITH THE MERCY OF OUR LORD.
FORGET NOT THE MODESTY OF A CHILD OF OUR LORD.
AH.
THANK YOU VERY MUCH...
...FATHER.
LET'S GO.
UH...
OKAY.
...
OH...
SO THAT WAS...

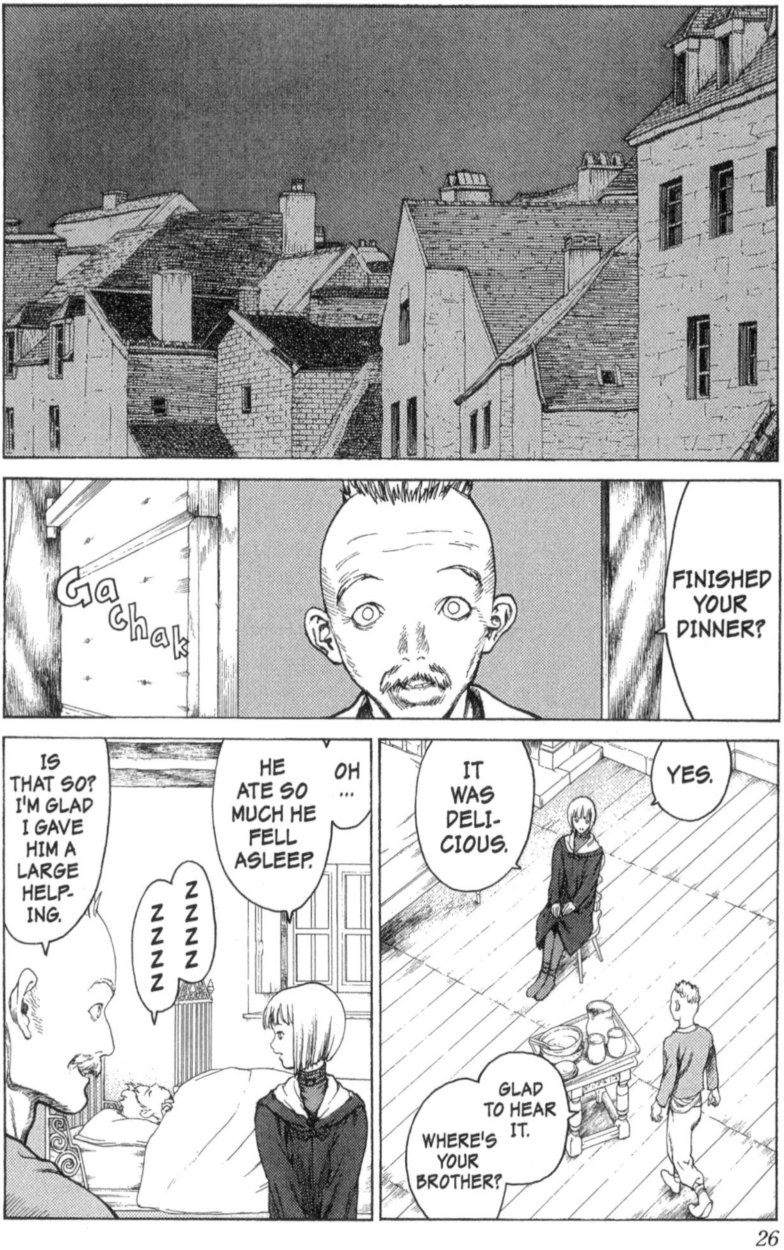
FINISHED YOUR DINNER?
Gachak
YES.
IT WAS DELICIOUS.
GLAD TO HEAR IT.
WHERE'S YOUR BROTHER?
OH ...
HE ATE SO MUCH HE FELL ASLEEP.
ZZZZ ZZZZ
IS THAT SO? I'M GLAD I GAVE HIM A LARGE HELPING.

READ THIS WAY

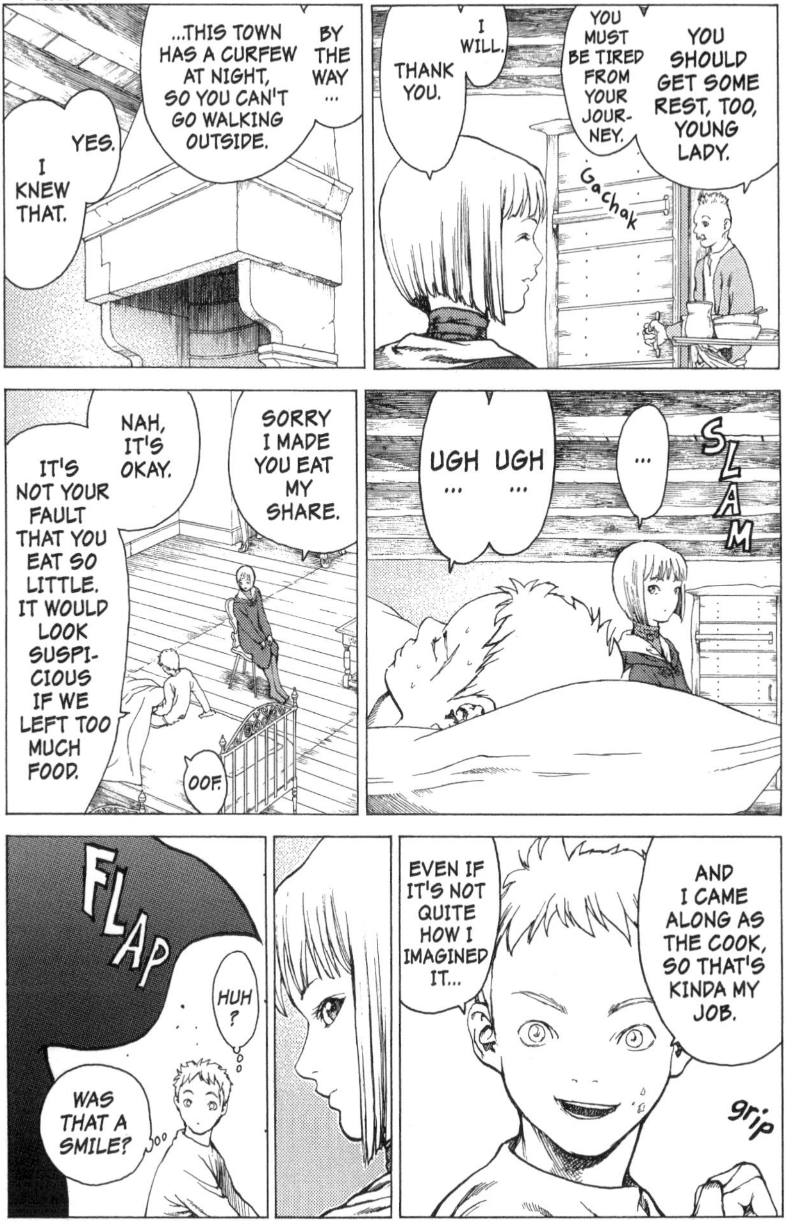
YOU SHOULD GET SOME REST, TOO, YOUNG LADY.
YOU MUST BE TIRED FROM YOUR JOURNEY.
I WILL.
THANK YOU.
Gachak
BY THE WAY ...
...THIS TOWN HAS A CURFEW AT NIGHT, SO YOU CAN'T GO WALKING OUTSIDE.
YES.
I KNEW THAT.
SLAM
...
UGH UGH ... ...
SORRY I MADE YOU EAT MY SHARE.
NAH, IT'S OKAY.
IT'S NOT YOUR FAULT THAT YOU EAT SO LITTLE. IT WOULD LOOK SUSPICIOUS IF WE LEFT TOO MUCH FOOD.
OOF.
AND I CAME ALONG AS THE COOK, SO THAT'S KINDA MY JOB.
EVEN IF IT'S NOT QUITE HOW I IMAGINED IT...
grip
FLAP
HUH ?
WAS THAT A SMILE?

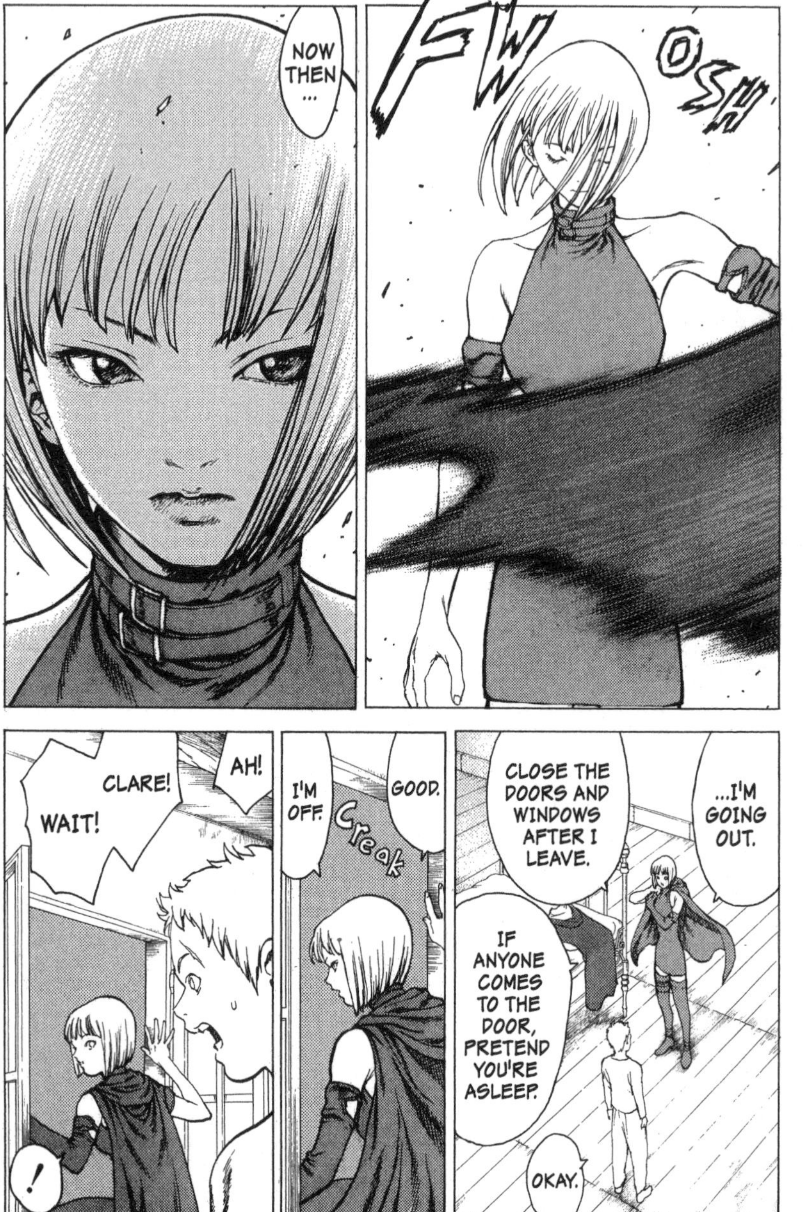
FWOSH
NOW THEN ...
...I'M GOING OUT.
CLOSE THE DOORS AND WINDOWS AFTER I LEAVE.
IF ANYONE COMES TO THE DOOR, PRETEND YOU'RE ASLEEP.
OKAY.
GOOD.
I'M OFF.
Creak
AH!
CLARE! WAIT!
!

READ THIS WAY

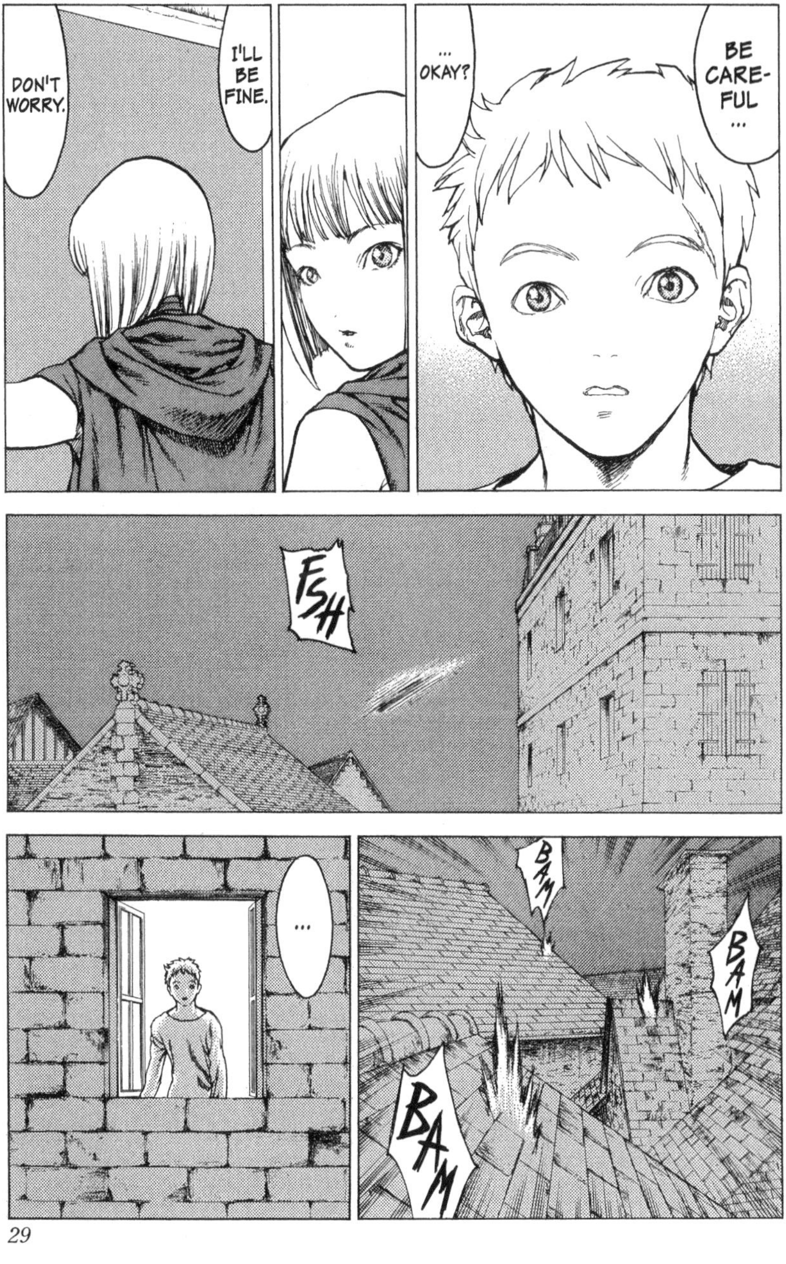

BE CARE-FUL ...
... OKAY?
I'LL BE FINE.
DON'T WORRY.
FSH
BAM
BAM
BAM
...

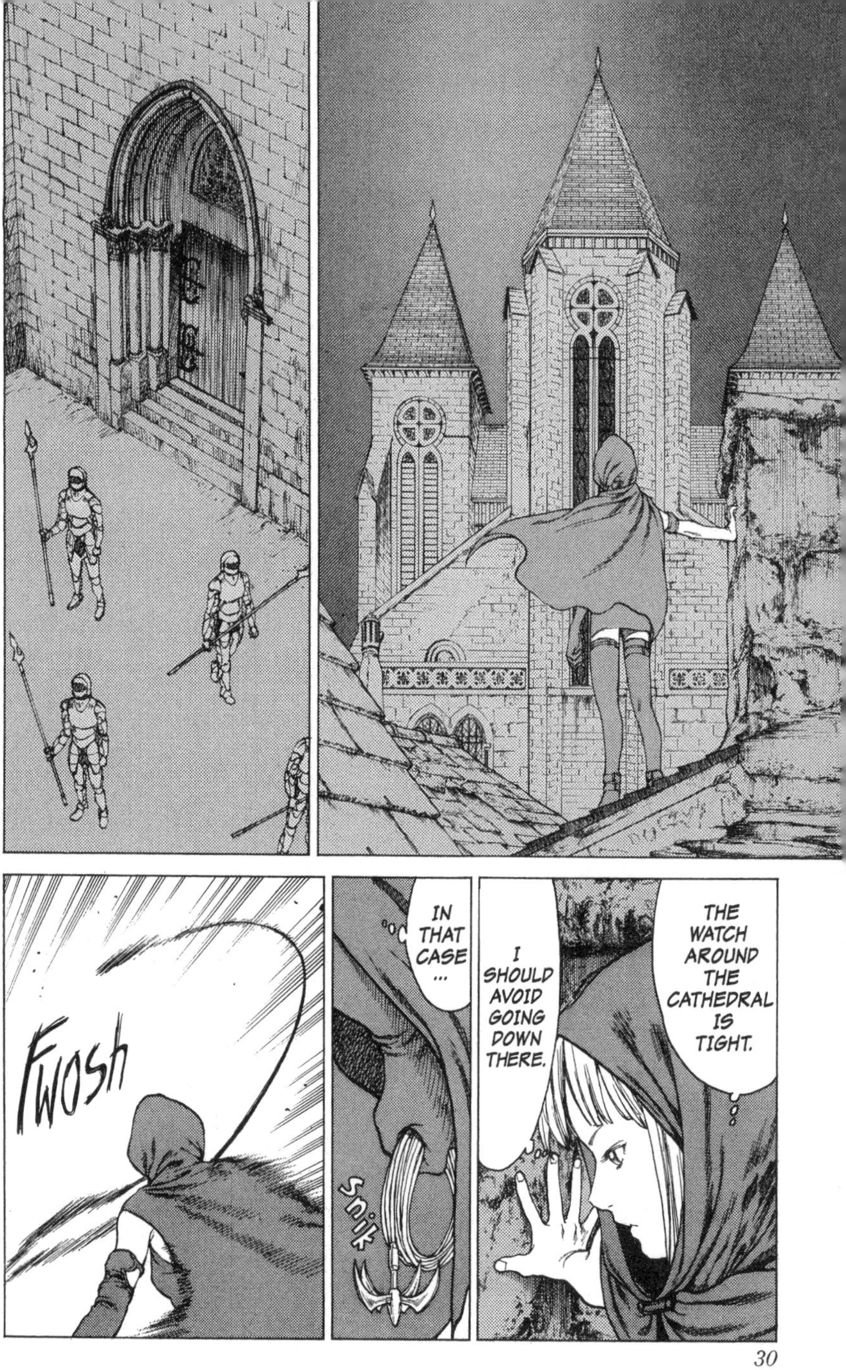
THE WATCH AROUND THE CATHEDRAL IS TIGHT.
I SHOULD AVOID GOING DOWN THERE.
IN THAT CASE ...
Snik
Fwosh

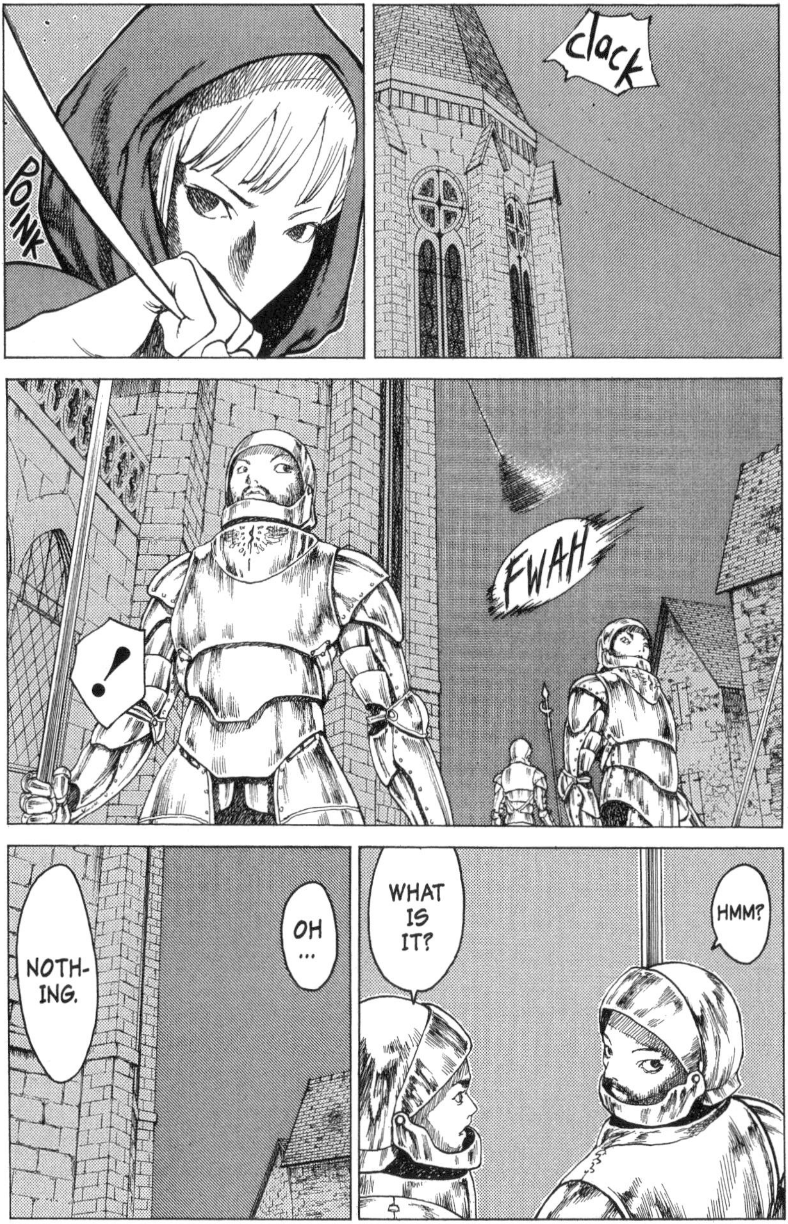
clack
POINK
FWAH
!
HMM?
WHAT IS IT?
OH ...
NOTH-ING.

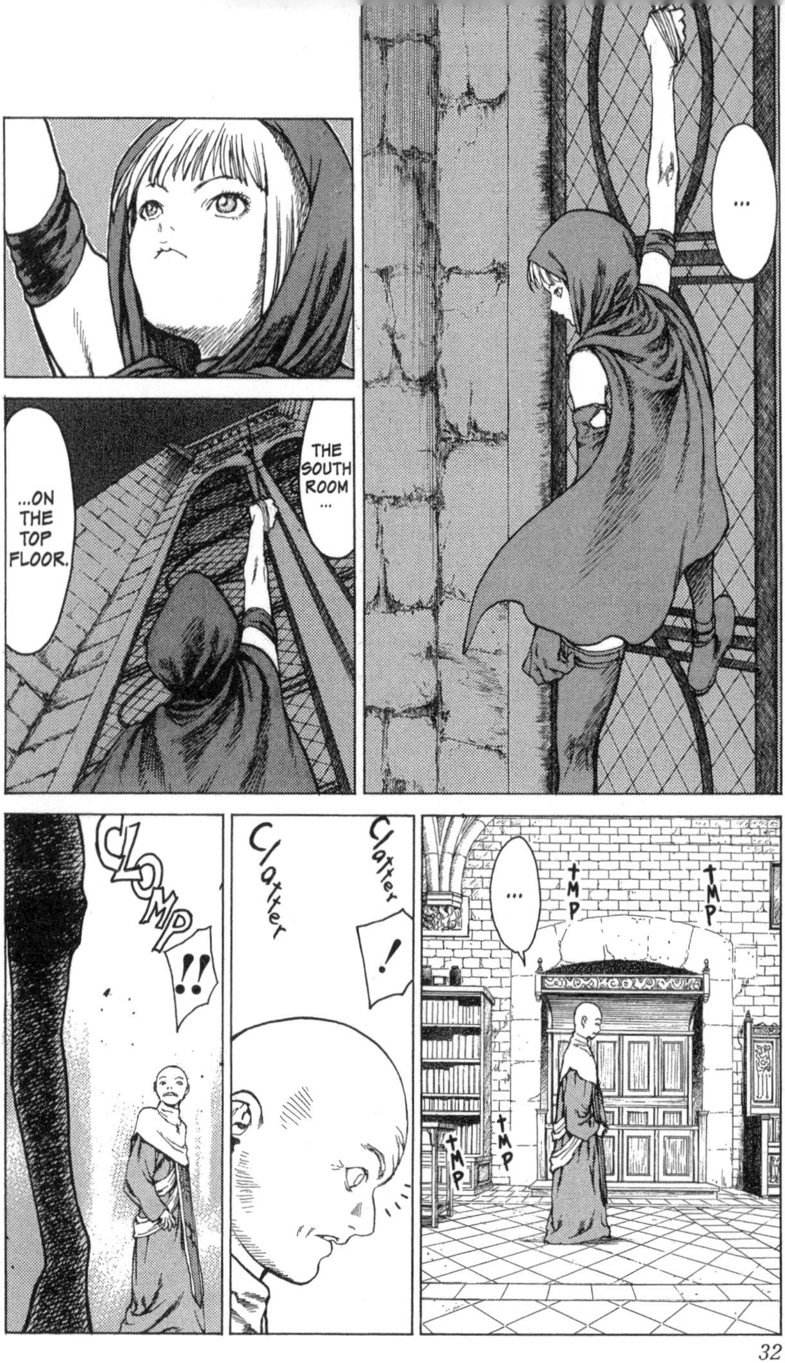
...
THE SOUTH ROOM ...
...ON THE TOP FLOOR.
...
TMP
TMP
TMP
TMP
Clatter
!
Clatter
CLOMP!!

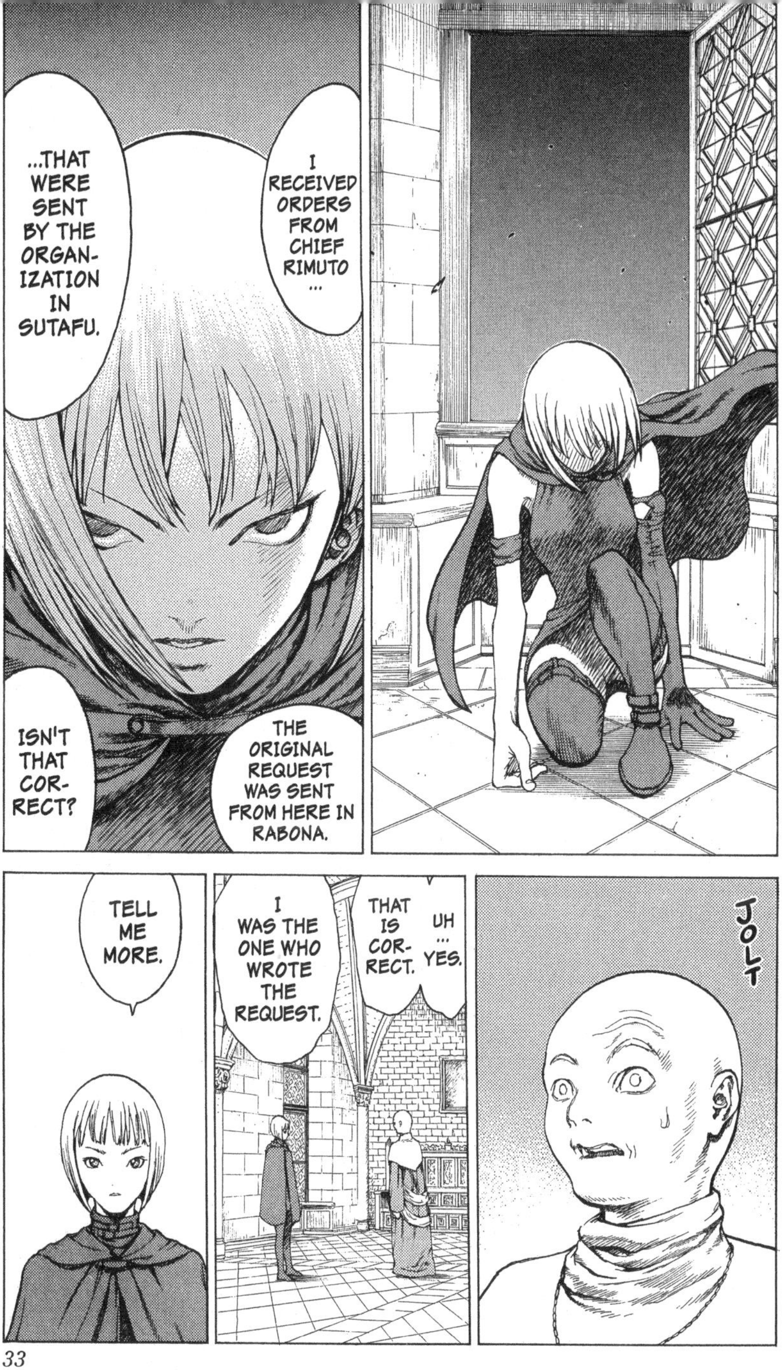
I RECEIVED ORDERS FROM CHIEF RIMUTO ...
...THAT WERE SENT BY THE ORGAN-IZATION IN SUTAFU.
THE ORIGINAL REQUEST WAS SENT FROM HERE IN RABONA.
ISN'T THAT COR-RECT?
JOLT
UH ... YES.
THAT IS COR-RECT.
I WAS THE ONE WHO WROTE THE REQUEST.
TELL ME MORE.

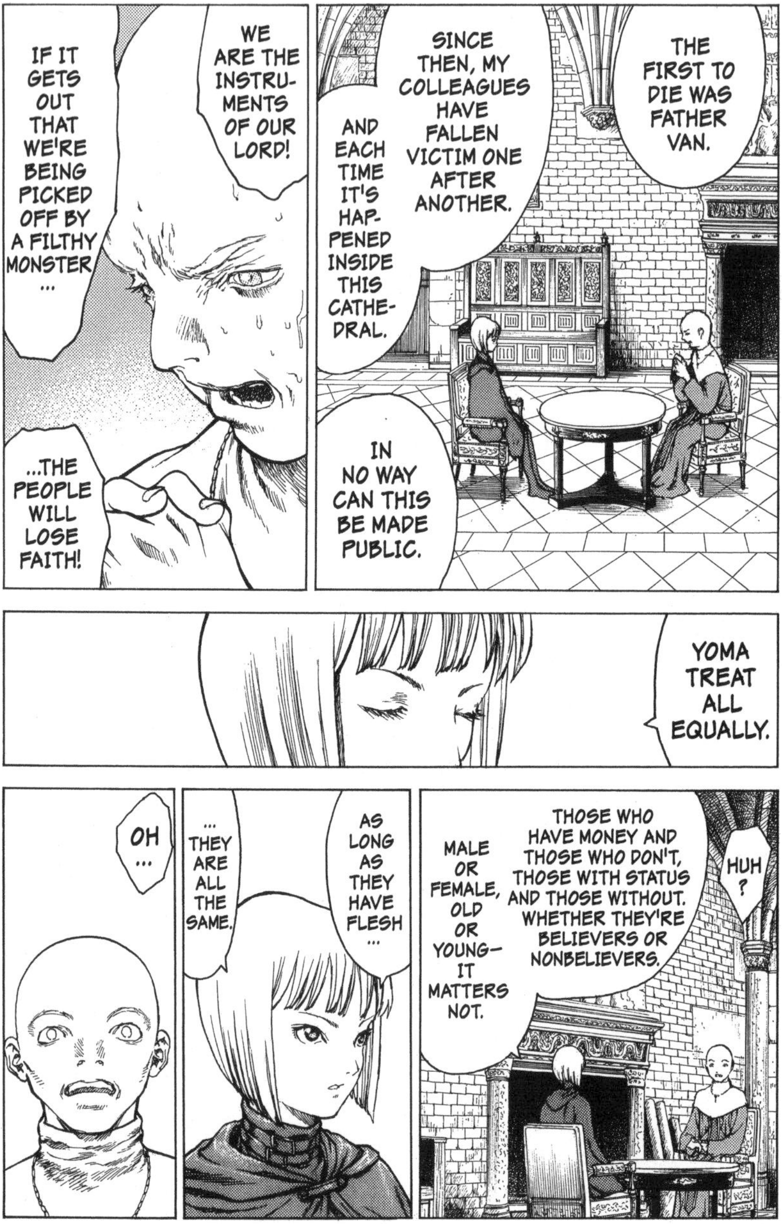
THE FIRST TO DIE WAS FATHER VAN.
SINCE THEN, MY COLLEAGUES HAVE FALLEN VICTIM ONE AFTER ANOTHER.
AND EACH TIME IT'S HAPPENED INSIDE THIS CATHEDRAL.
IN NO WAY CAN THIS BE MADE PUBLIC.
WE ARE THE INSTRUMENTS OF OUR LORD!
IF IT GETS OUT THAT WE'RE BEING PICKED OFF BY A FILTHY MONSTER...
...THE PEOPLE WILL LOSE FAITH!
YOMA TREAT ALL EQUALLY.
HUH?
THOSE WHO HAVE MONEY AND THOSE WHO DON'T, THOSE WITH STATUS AND THOSE WITHOUT. WHETHER THEY'RE BELIEVERS OR NONBELIEVERS.
MALE OR FEMALE, OLD OR YOUNG—IT MATTERS NOT.
AS LONG AS THEY HAVE FLESH...
...THEY ARE ALL THE SAME.
OH...

READ THIS WAY

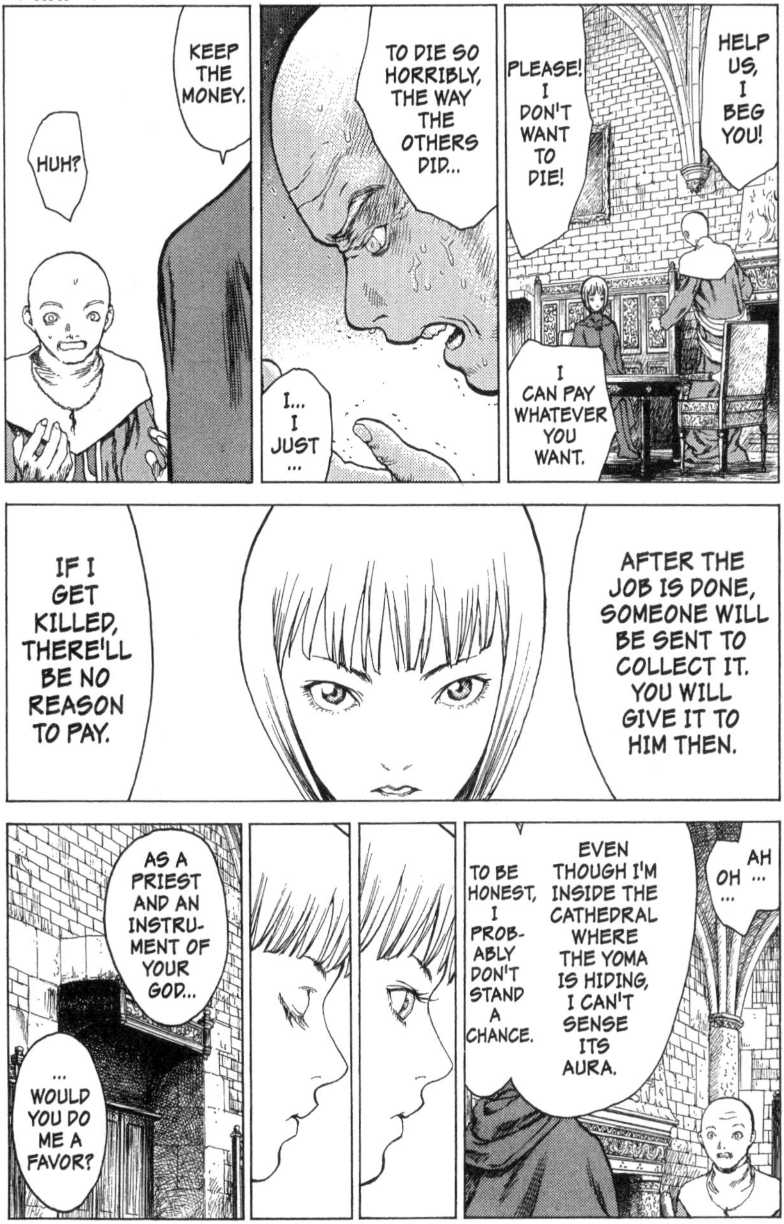
HELP US, I BEG YOU!
PLEASE! I DON'T WANT TO DIE!
I CAN PAY WHATEVER YOU WANT.
TO DIE SO HORRIBLY, THE WAY THE OTHERS DID...
I... I JUST ...
KEEP THE MONEY.
HUH?
AFTER THE JOB IS DONE, SOMEONE WILL BE SENT TO COLLECT IT. YOU WILL GIVE IT TO HIM THEN.
IF I GET KILLED, THERE'LL BE NO REASON TO PAY.
AH ...
OH ...
EVEN THOUGH I'M INSIDE THE CATHEDRAL WHERE THE YOMA IS HIDING, I CAN'T SENSE ITS AURA.
TO BE HONEST, I PROBABLY DON'T STAND A CHANCE.
AS A PRIEST AND AN INSTRUMENT OF YOUR GOD...
... WOULD YOU DO ME A FAVOR?

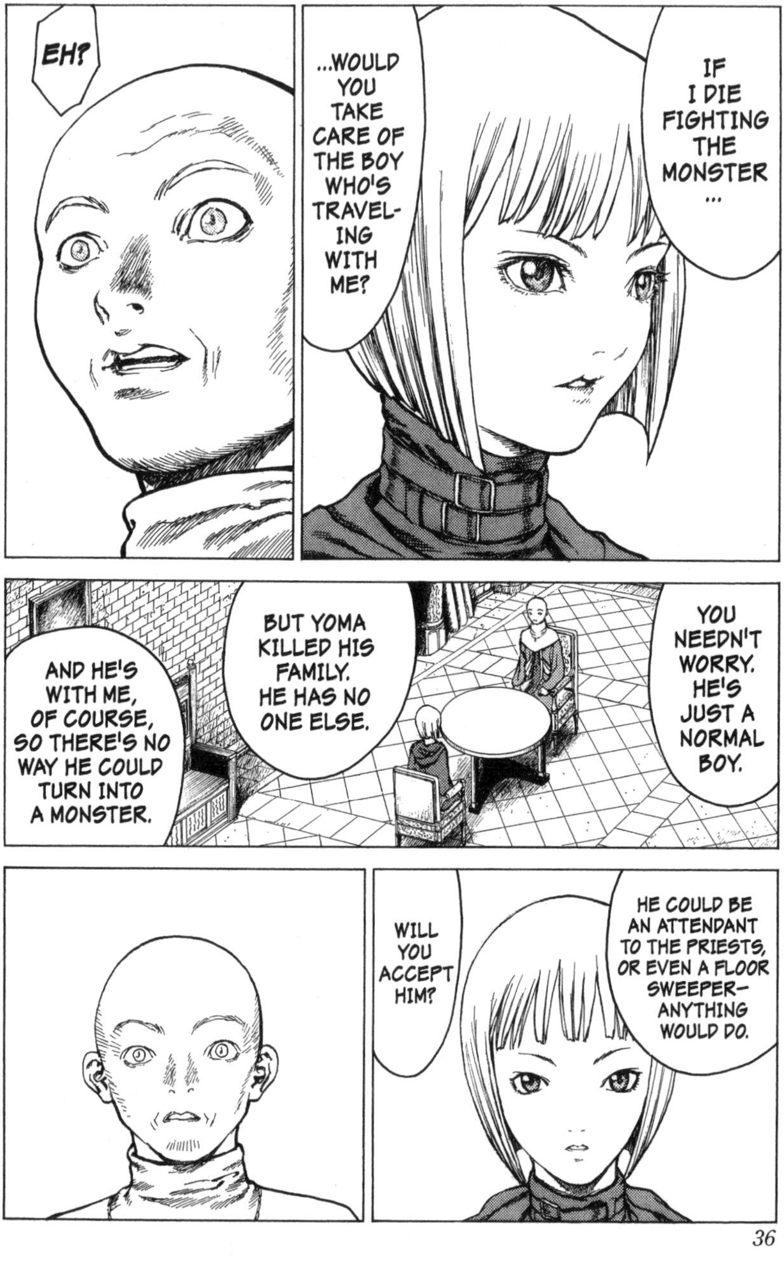
IF I DIE FIGHTING THE MONSTER ...
...WOULD YOU TAKE CARE OF THE BOY WHO'S TRAVELING WITH ME?
EH?
YOU NEEDN'T WORRY. HE'S JUST A NORMAL BOY.
BUT YOMA KILLED HIS FAMILY. HE HAS NO ONE ELSE.
AND HE'S WITH ME, OF COURSE, SO THERE'S NO WAY HE COULD TURN INTO A MONSTER.
HE COULD BE AN ATTENDANT TO THE PRIESTS, OR EVEN A FLOOR SWEEPER— ANYTHING WOULD DO.
WILL YOU ACCEPT HIM?

READ THIS WAY

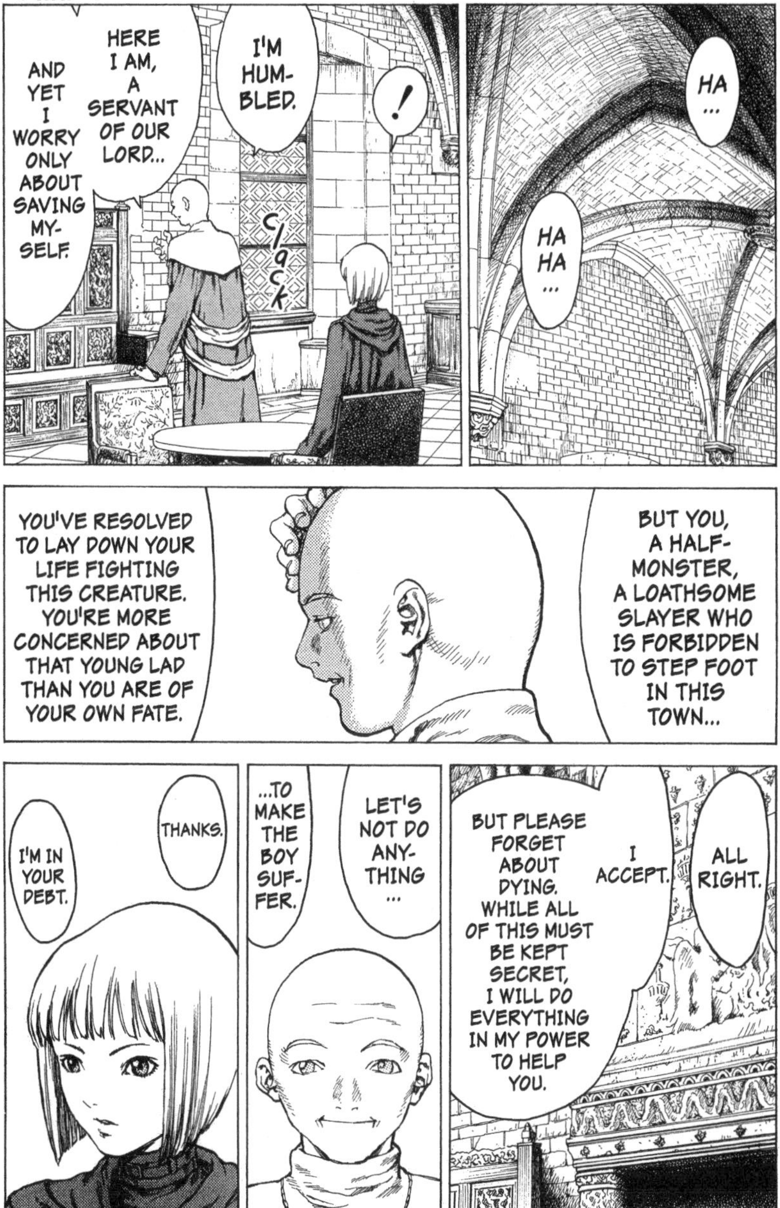
HA ...
HA HA ...
!
I'M HUMBLED.
HERE I AM, A SERVANT OF OUR LORD...
AND YET I WORRY ONLY ABOUT SAVING MYSELF.
Clack
BUT YOU, A HALF-MONSTER, A LOATHSOME SLAYER WHO IS FORBIDDEN TO STEP FOOT IN THIS TOWN...
YOU'VE RESOLVED TO LAY DOWN YOUR LIFE FIGHTING THIS CREATURE. YOU'RE MORE CONCERNED ABOUT THAT YOUNG LAD THAN YOU ARE OF YOUR OWN FATE.
ALL RIGHT.
I ACCEPT.
BUT PLEASE FORGET ABOUT DYING. WHILE ALL OF THIS MUST BE KEPT SECRET, I WILL DO EVERYTHING IN MY POWER TO HELP YOU.
LET'S NOT DO ANYTHING ...
...TO MAKE THE BOY SUFFER.
THANKS.
I'M IN YOUR DEBT.

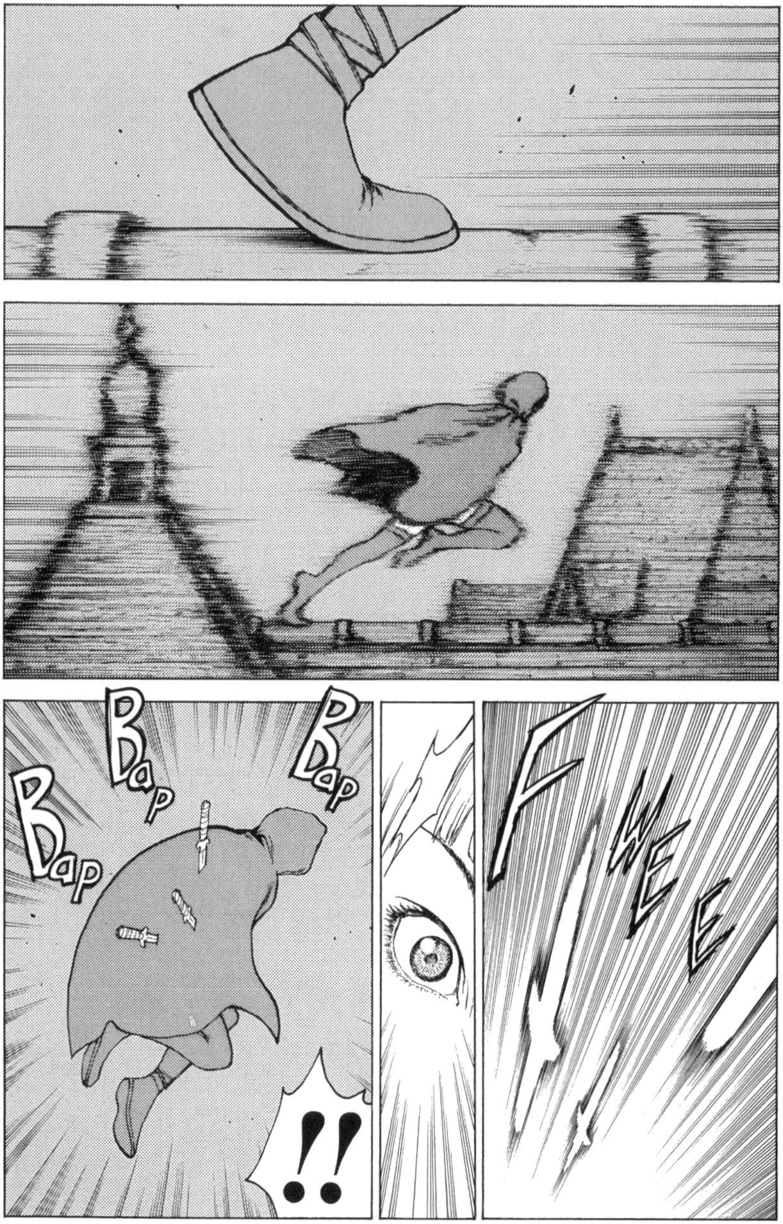
FWEE
Bap
Bap
Bap
!!

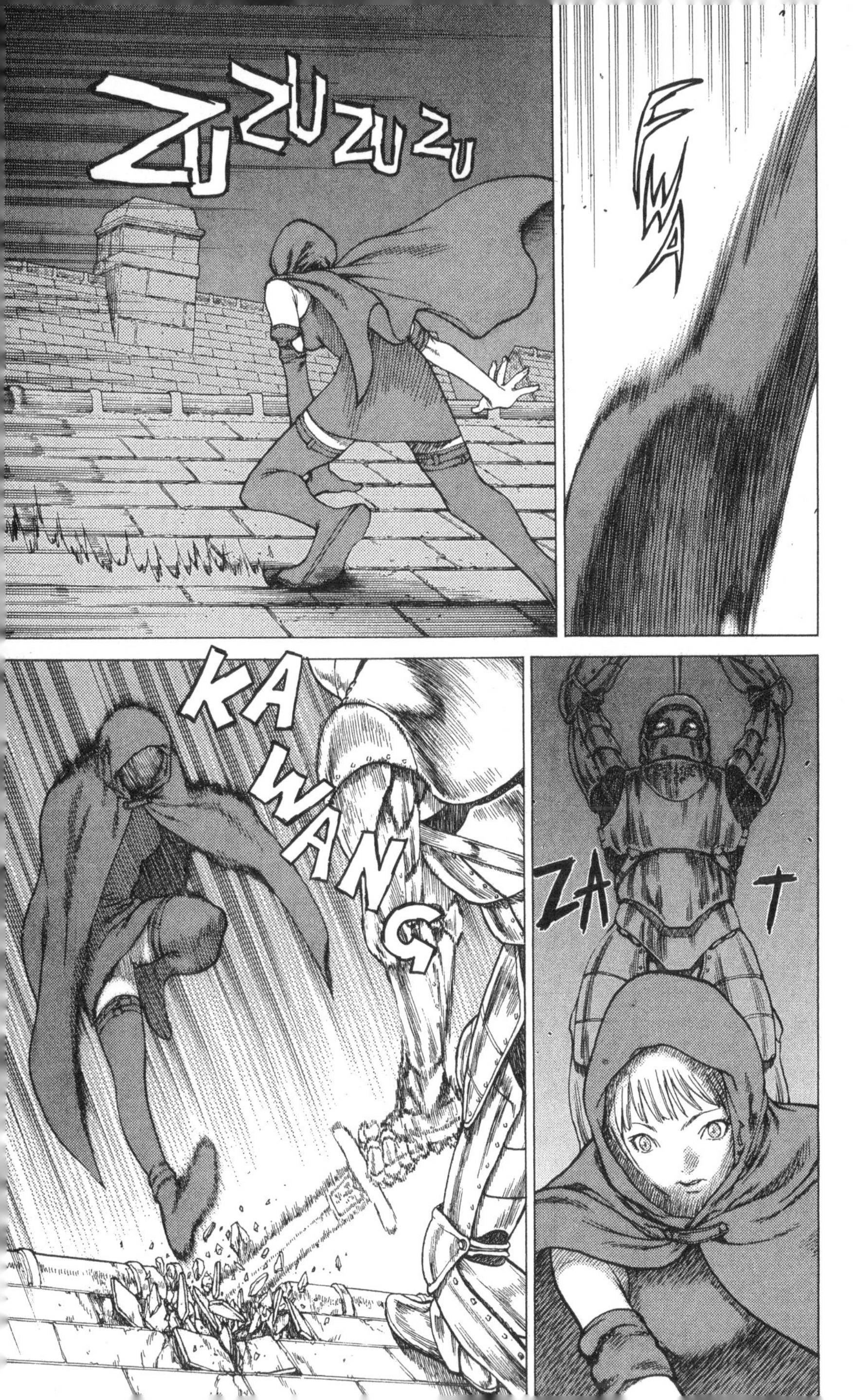
FWA
ZUZUZUZUZU
ZAT
KAWANG

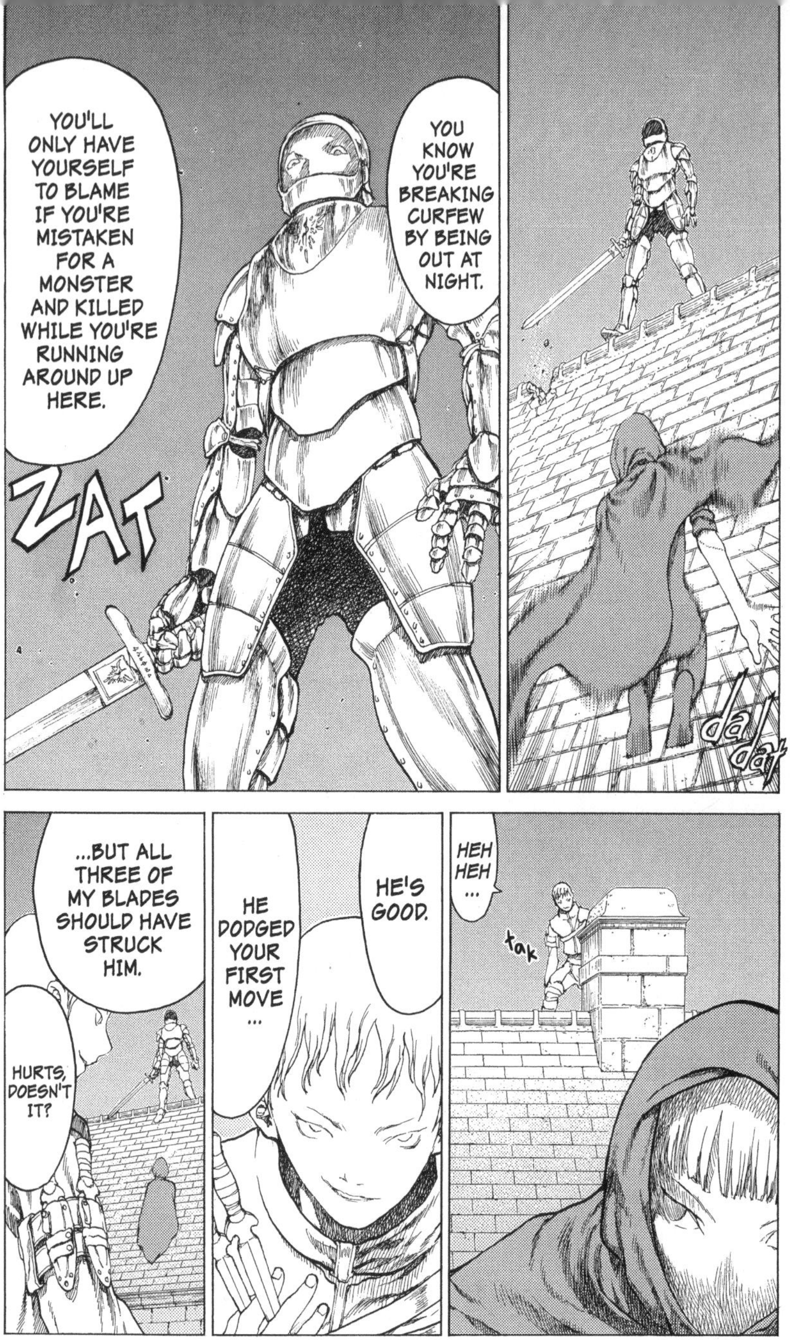
dadat
YOU KNOW YOU'RE BREAKING CURFEW BY BEING OUT AT NIGHT.
YOU'LL ONLY HAVE YOURSELF TO BLAME IF YOU'RE MISTAKEN FOR A MONSTER AND KILLED WHILE YOU'RE RUNNING AROUND UP HERE.
ZAT
HEH HEH ...
tak
HE'S GOOD.
HE DODGED YOUR FIRST MOVE ...
...BUT ALL THREE OF MY BLADES SHOULD HAVE STRUCK HIM.
HURTS, DOESN'T IT?

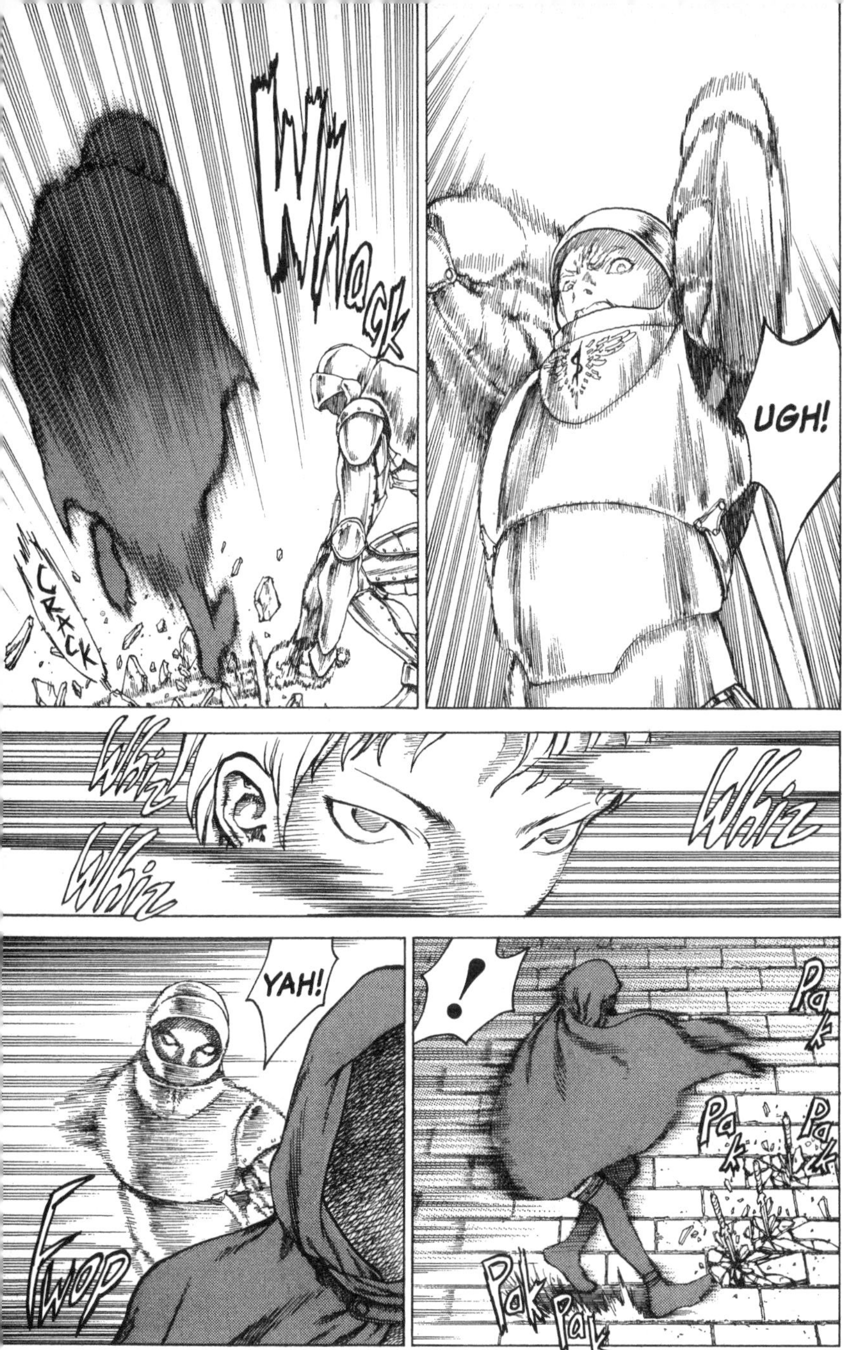
UGH!
Whack
CRACK
Whiz
Whiz
Whiz
!
Pak
Pak
Pak
Pak
Pak
YAH!
Fwop

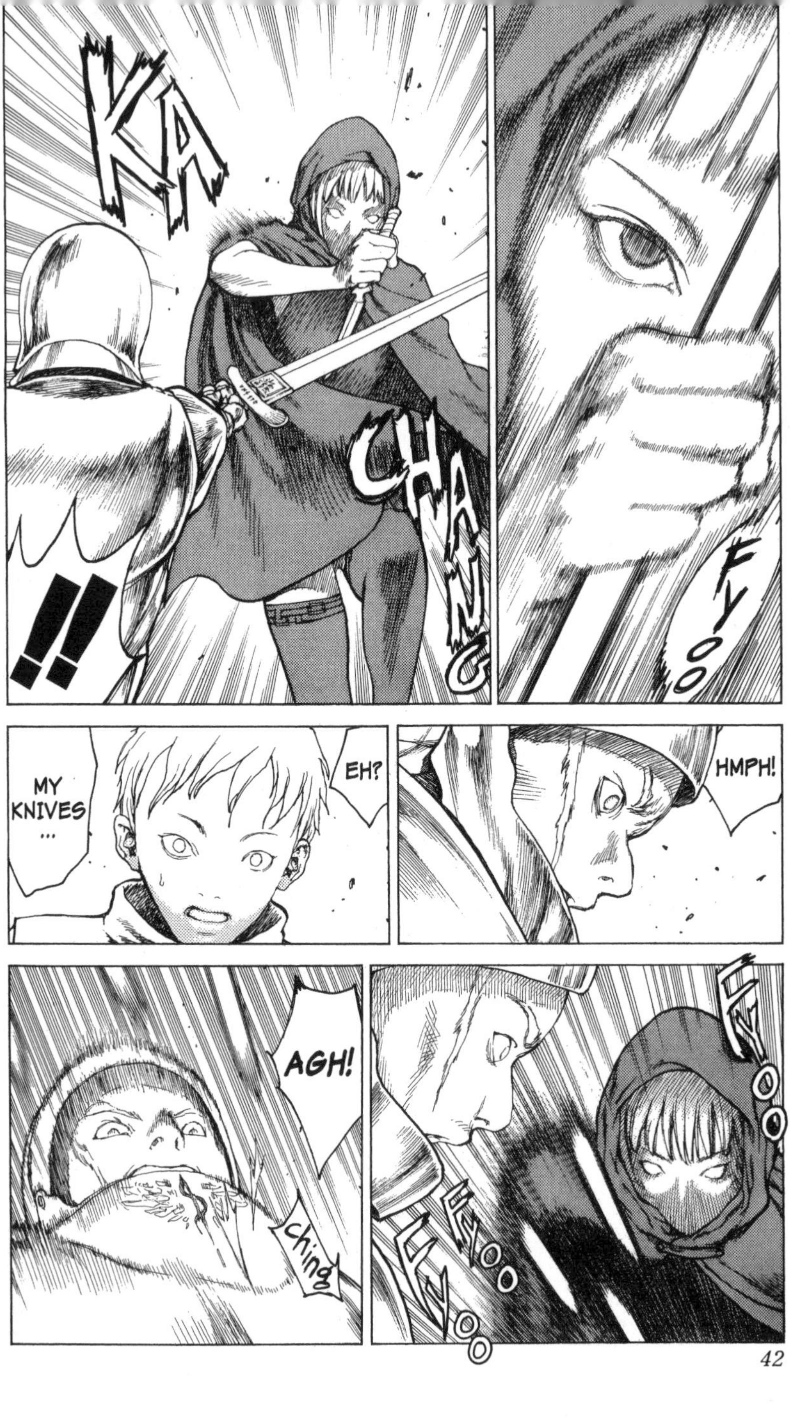
FYOO
KA
CHANNG
!!
HMPH!
EH?
MY KNIVES ...
FYOO
FYOO
FYOO
AGH!
ching

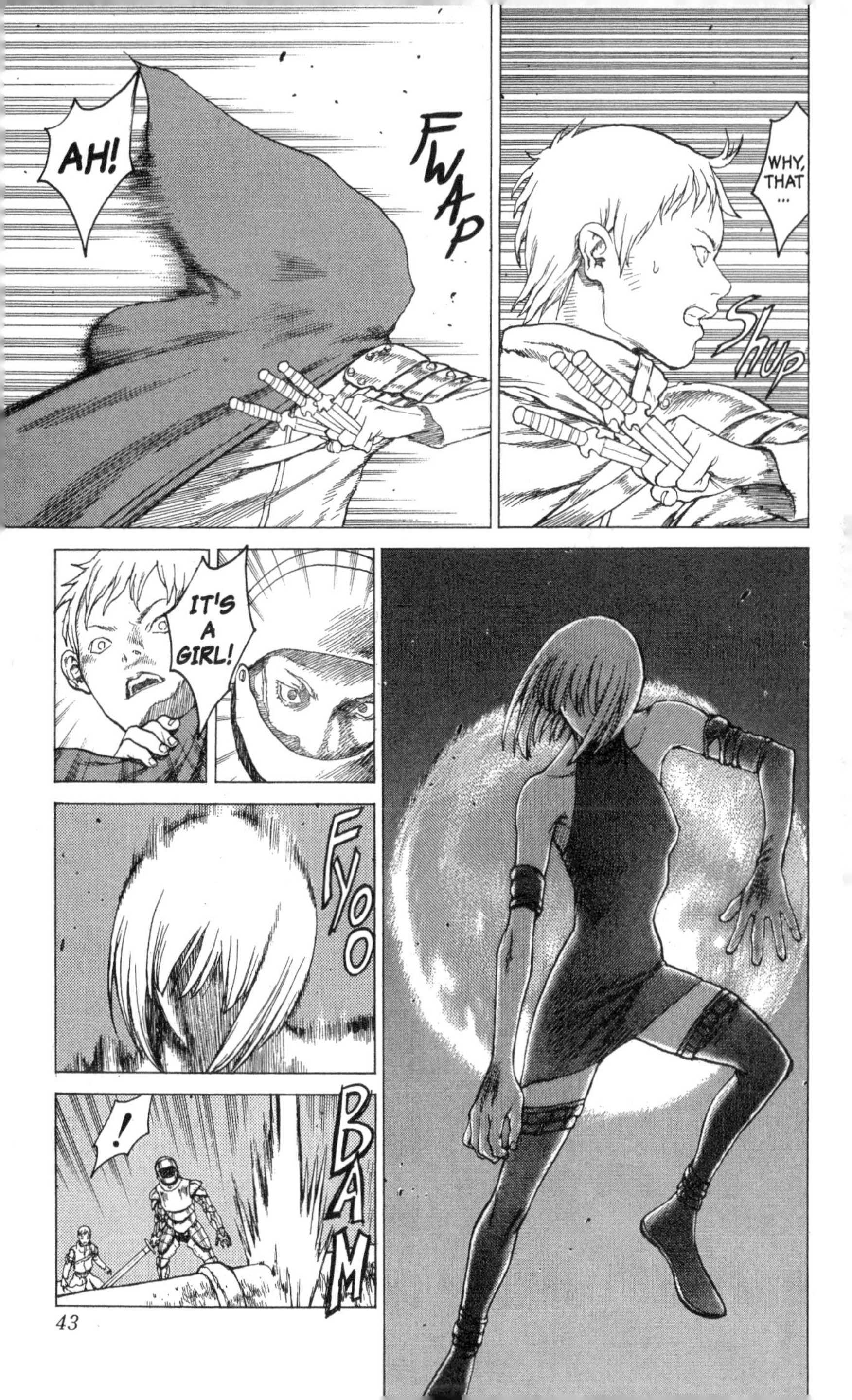
WHY, THAT ...
SHUP
AH!
FWAP
IT'S A GIRL!
FYOO
!
BLAM

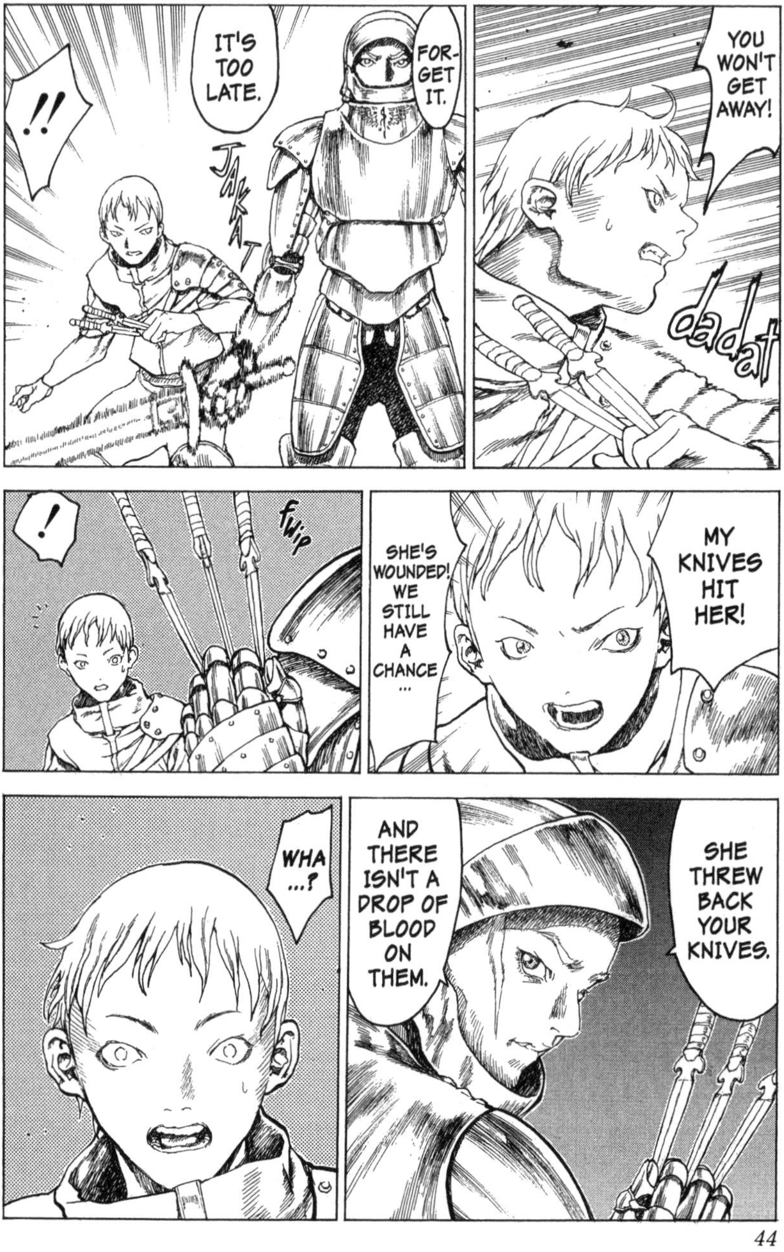
YOU WON'T GET AWAY!
dadat
FOR-GET IT.
IT'S TOO LATE.
!!
JAKAT
MY KNIVES HIT HER!
SHE'S WOUNDED! WE STILL HAVE A CHANCE ...
fwip
!
SHE THREW BACK YOUR KNIVES.
AND THERE ISN'T A DROP OF BLOOD ON THEM.
WHA ...?

READ THIS WAY

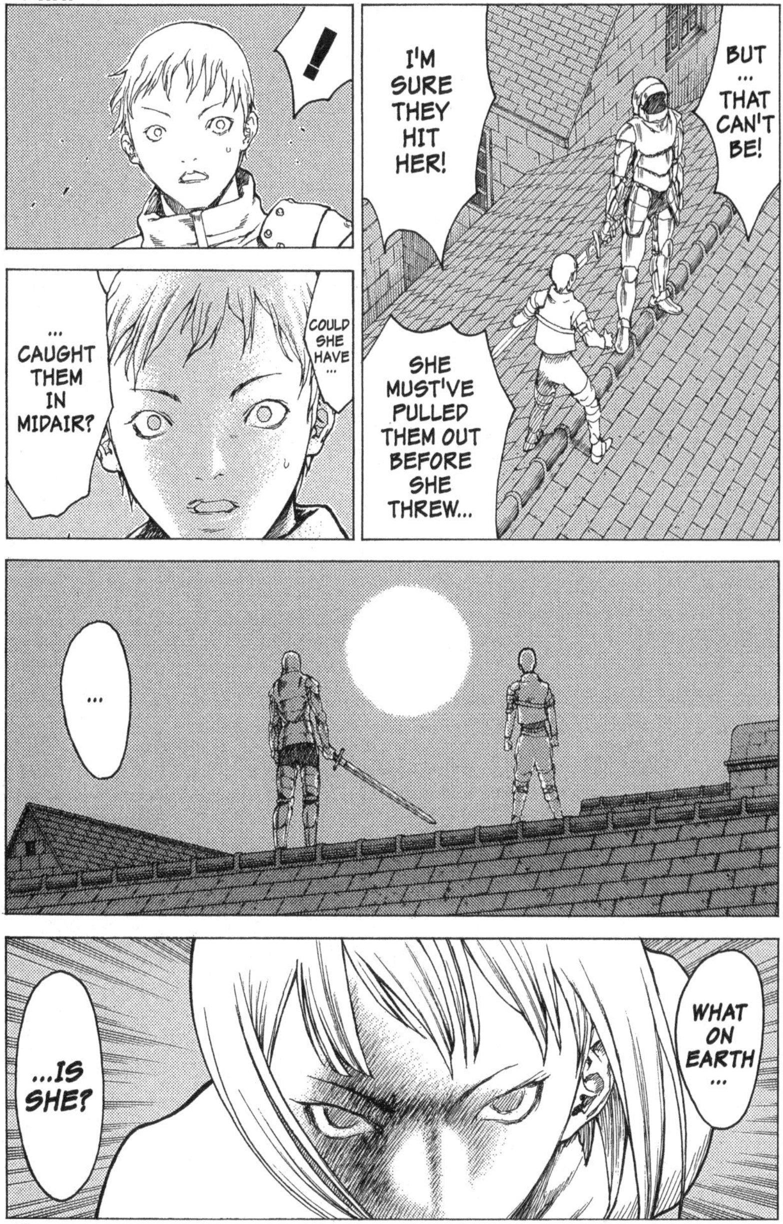
BUT ... THAT CAN'T BE!
I'M SURE THEY HIT HER!
SHE MUST'VE PULLED THEM OUT BEFORE SHE THREW...
!
COULD SHE HAVE ...
... CAUGHT THEM IN MIDAIR?
...
WHAT ON EARTH ...
...IS SHE?

クレイモア

Claymore™

Scene 6: Darkness in Paradise, Part 2

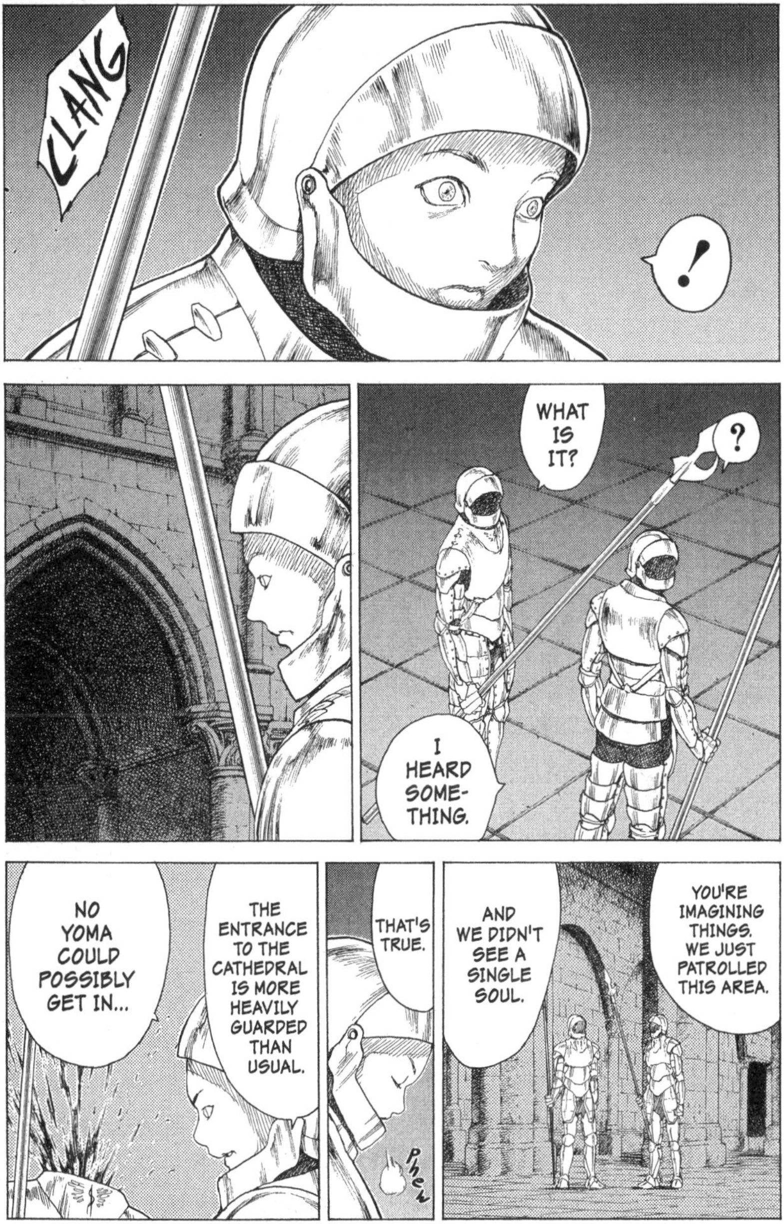
CLANG
!
WHAT IS IT?
?
I HEARD SOMETHING.
YOU'RE IMAGINING THINGS. WE JUST PATROLLED THIS AREA.
AND WE DIDN'T SEE A SINGLE SOUL.
THAT'S TRUE.
Phew
THE ENTRANCE TO THE CATHEDRAL IS MORE HEAVILY GUARDED THAN USUAL.
NO YOMA COULD POSSIBLY GET IN...

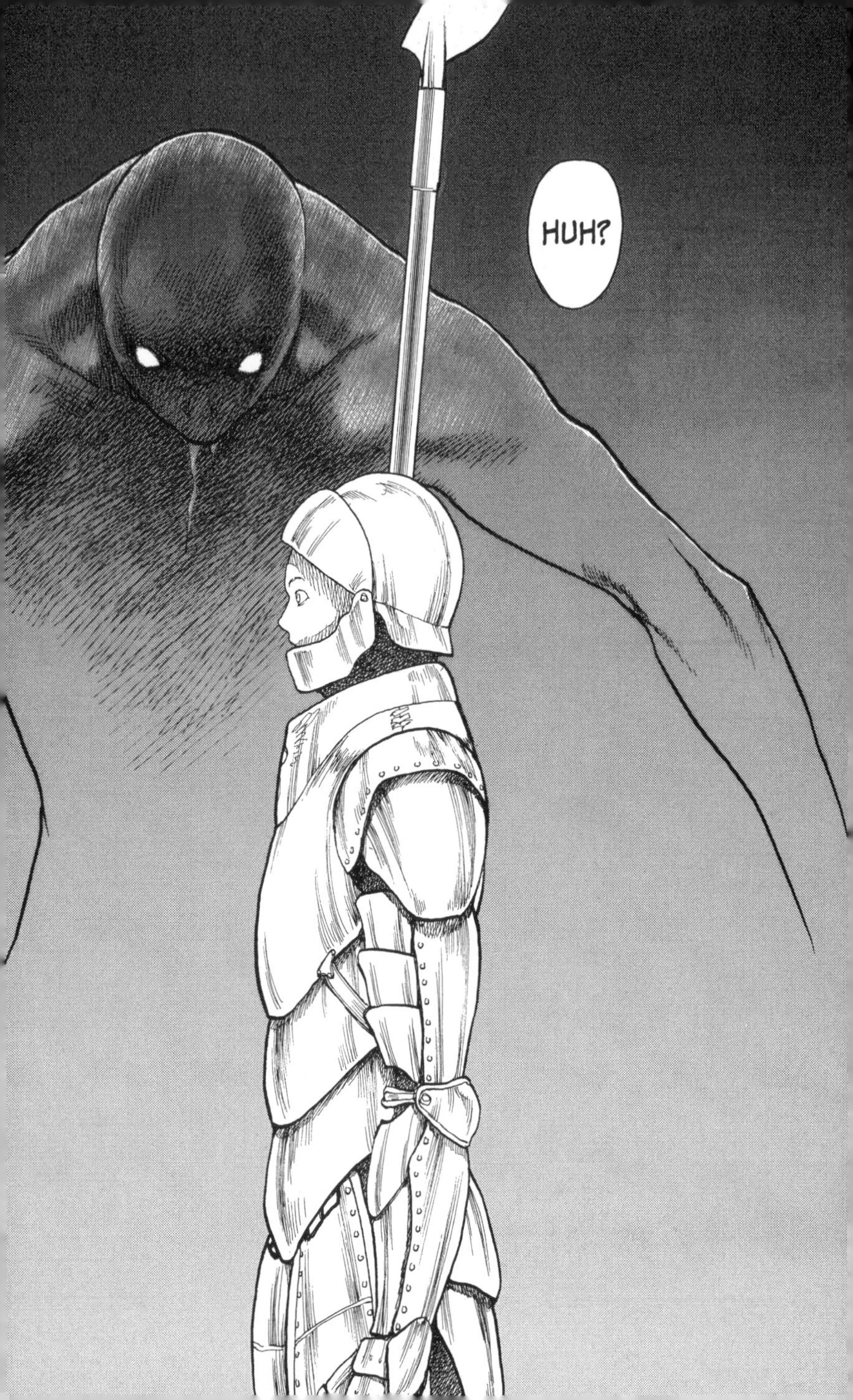
HUH?

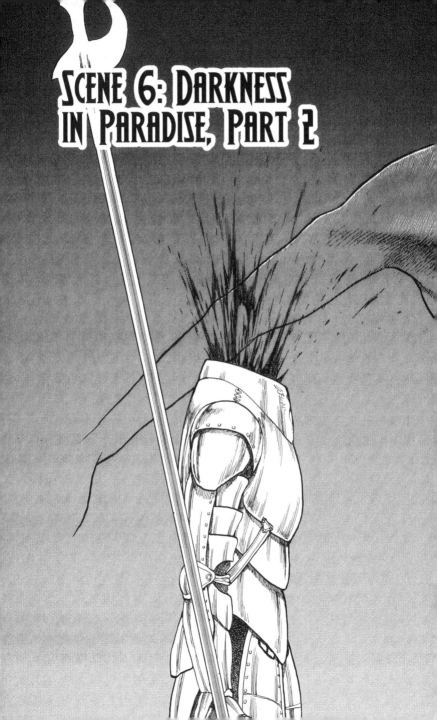

SCENE 6: DARKNESS IN PARADISE, PART 2

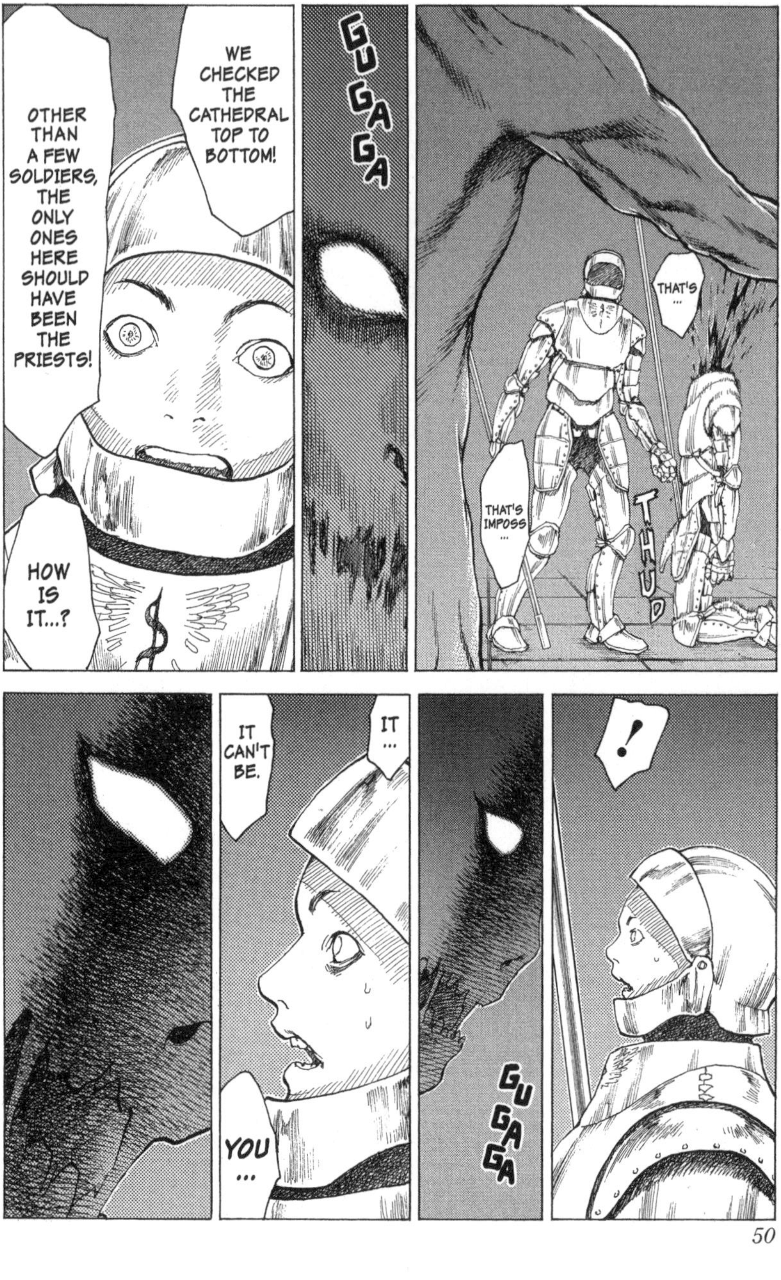
THAT'S ...
THAT'S IMPOSS ...
THUD
GUGAGA
WE CHECKED THE CATHEDRAL TOP TO BOTTOM!
OTHER THAN A FEW SOLDIERS, THE ONLY ONES HERE SHOULD HAVE BEEN THE PRIESTS!
HOW IS IT...?
!
GUGAGA
IT ...
IT CAN'T BE.
YOU ...

READ THIS WAY

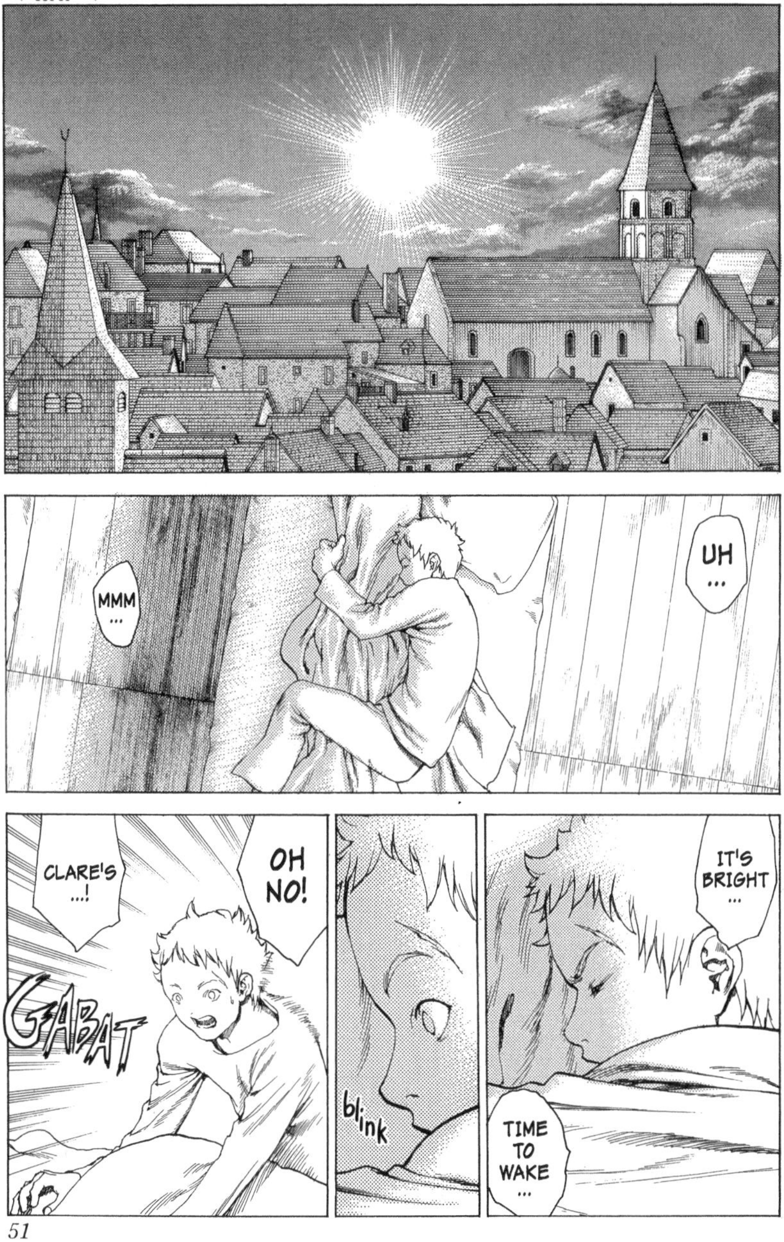
UH ...
MMM ...
IT'S BRIGHT ...
TIME TO WAKE ...
blink
OH NO!
CLARE'S ...!
GABAT

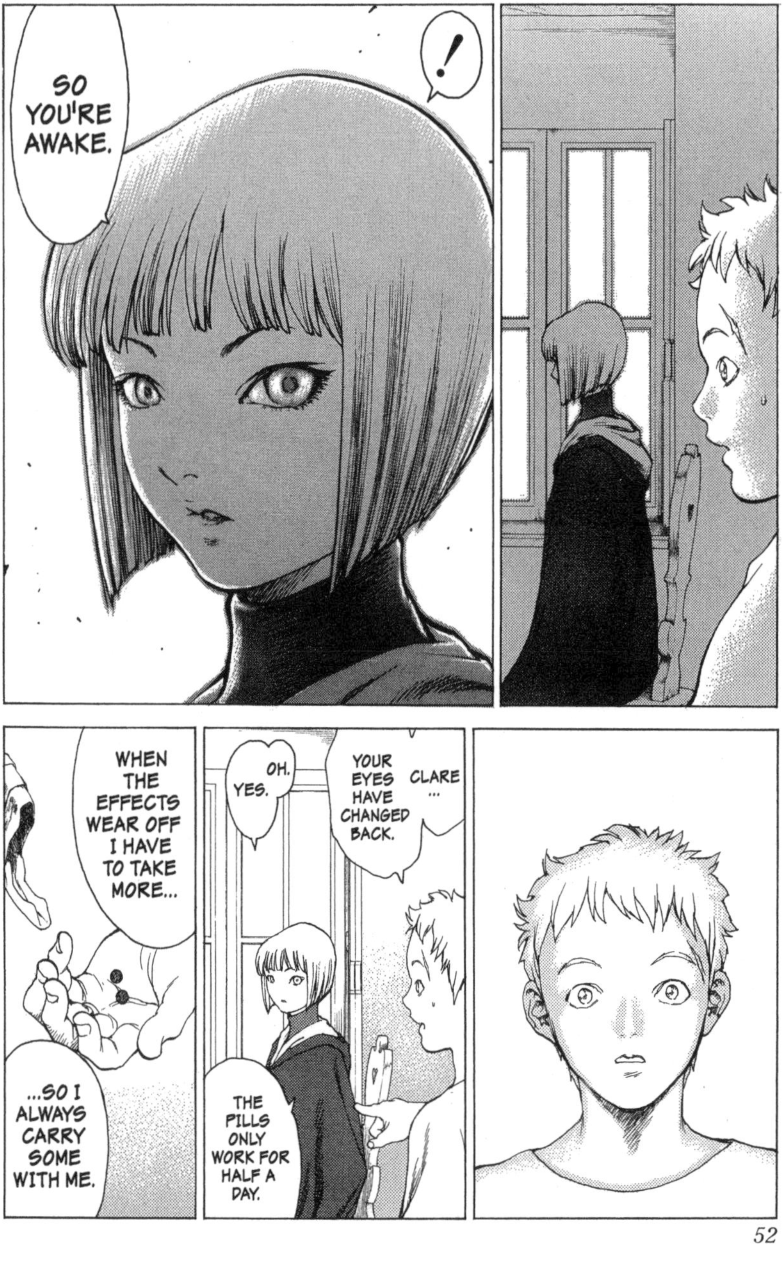
!
SO YOU'RE AWAKE.
CLARE ...
YOUR EYES HAVE CHANGED BACK.
OH. YES.
THE PILLS ONLY WORK FOR HALF A DAY.
WHEN THE EFFECTS WEAR OFF I HAVE TO TAKE MORE...
...SO I ALWAYS CARRY SOME WITH ME.

READ THIS WAY

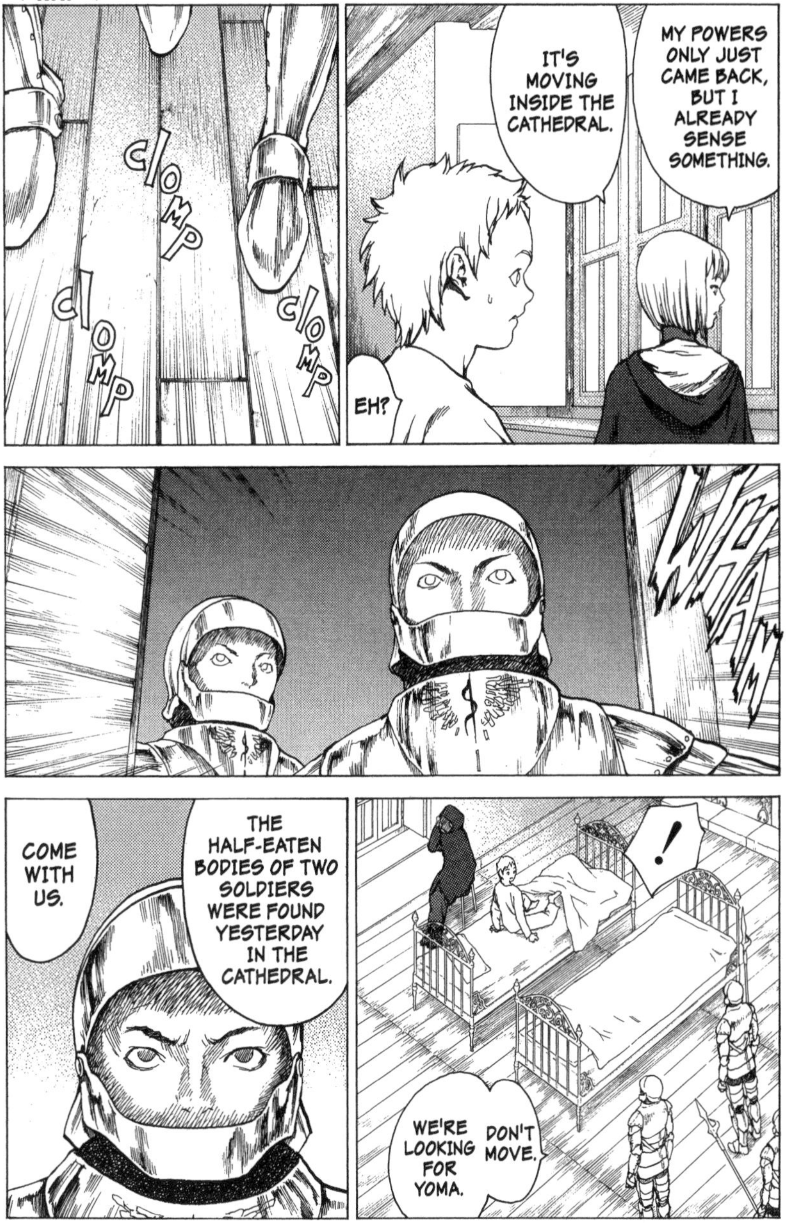
MY POWERS ONLY JUST CAME BACK, BUT I ALREADY SENSE SOMETHING.
IT'S MOVING INSIDE THE CATHEDRAL.
EH?
CLOMP
CLOMP
CLOMP
WHAM
!
DON'T MOVE.
WE'RE LOOKING FOR YOMA.
THE HALF-EATEN BODIES OF TWO SOLDIERS WERE FOUND YESTERDAY IN THE CATHEDRAL.
COME WITH US.

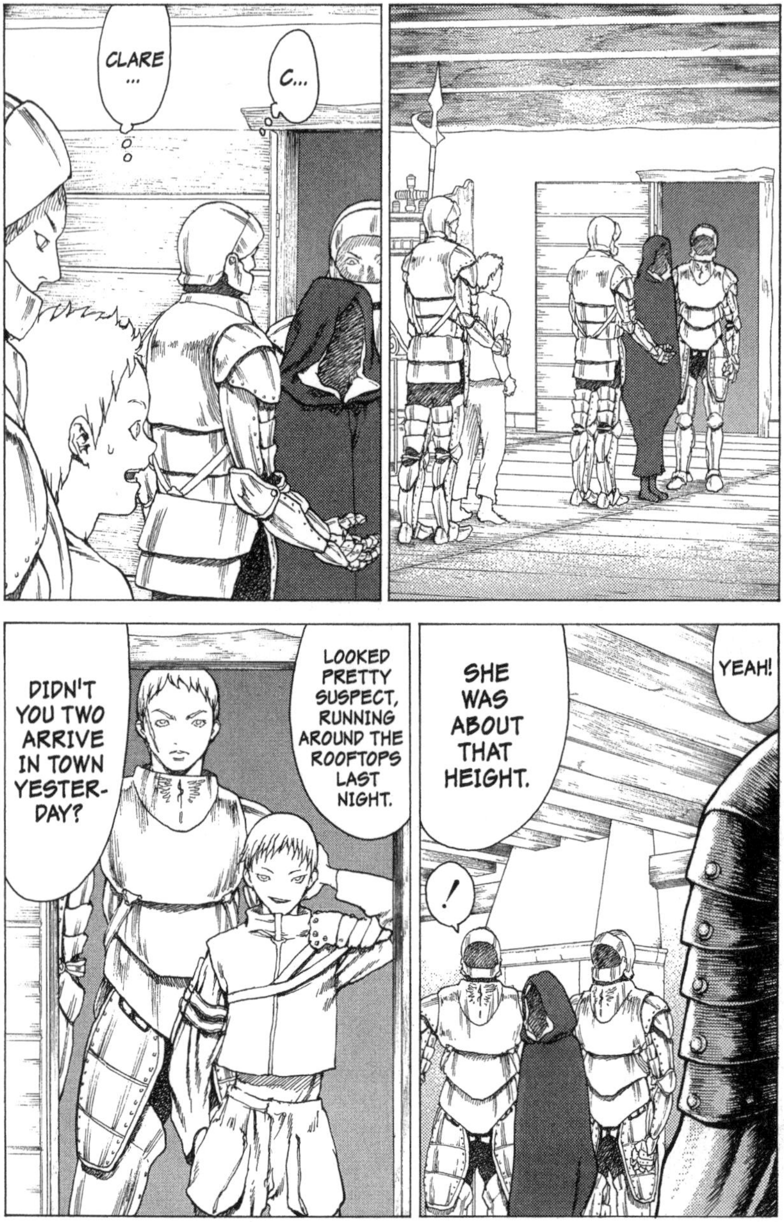
C...
CLARE ...
YEAH!
SHE WAS ABOUT THAT HEIGHT.
!
LOOKED PRETTY SUSPECT, RUNNING AROUND THE ROOFTOPS LAST NIGHT.
DIDN'T YOU TWO ARRIVE IN TOWN YESTER-DAY?

READ THIS WAY

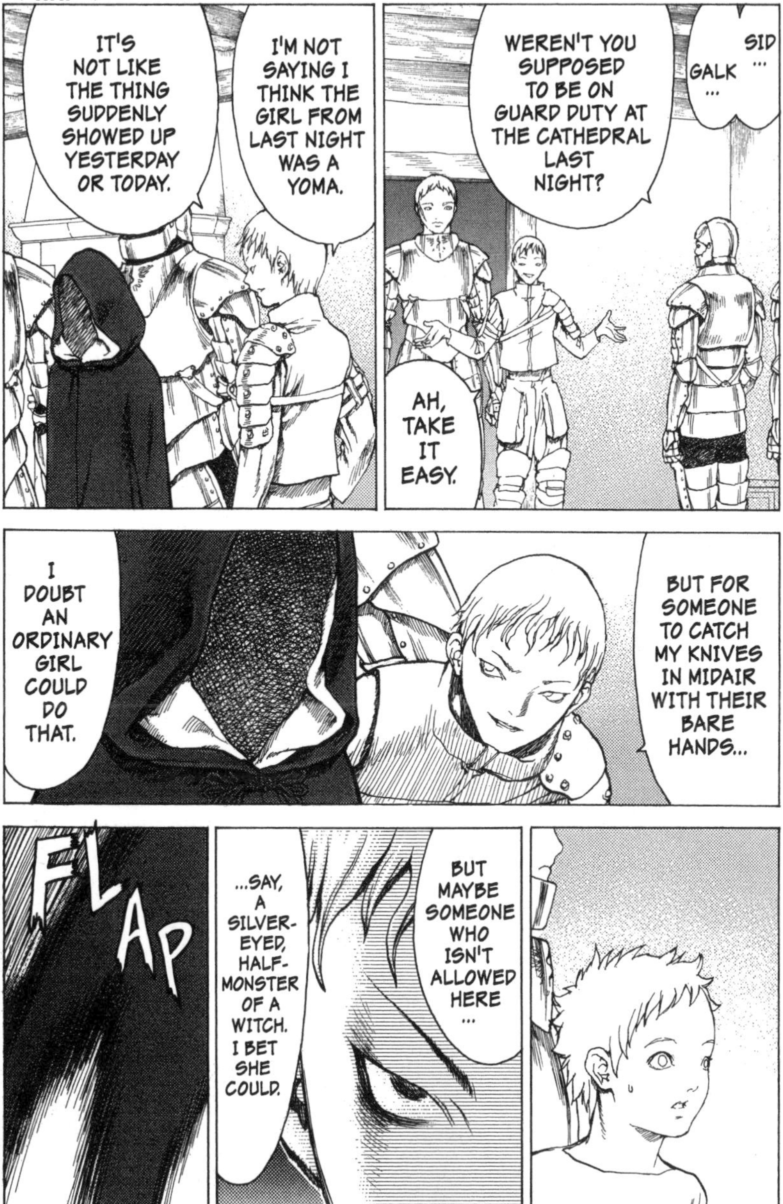
SID ...
GALK ...
WEREN'T YOU SUPPOSED TO BE ON GUARD DUTY AT THE CATHEDRAL LAST NIGHT?
AH, TAKE IT EASY.
I'M NOT SAYING I THINK THE GIRL FROM LAST NIGHT WAS A YOMA.
IT'S NOT LIKE THE THING SUDDENLY SHOWED UP YESTERDAY OR TODAY.
BUT FOR SOMEONE TO CATCH MY KNIVES IN MIDAIR WITH THEIR BARE HANDS...
I DOUBT AN ORDINARY GIRL COULD DO THAT.
BUT MAYBE SOMEONE WHO ISN'T ALLOWED HERE ...
...SAY, A SILVER-EYED, HALF-MONSTER OF A WITCH. I BET SHE COULD.
FLAP

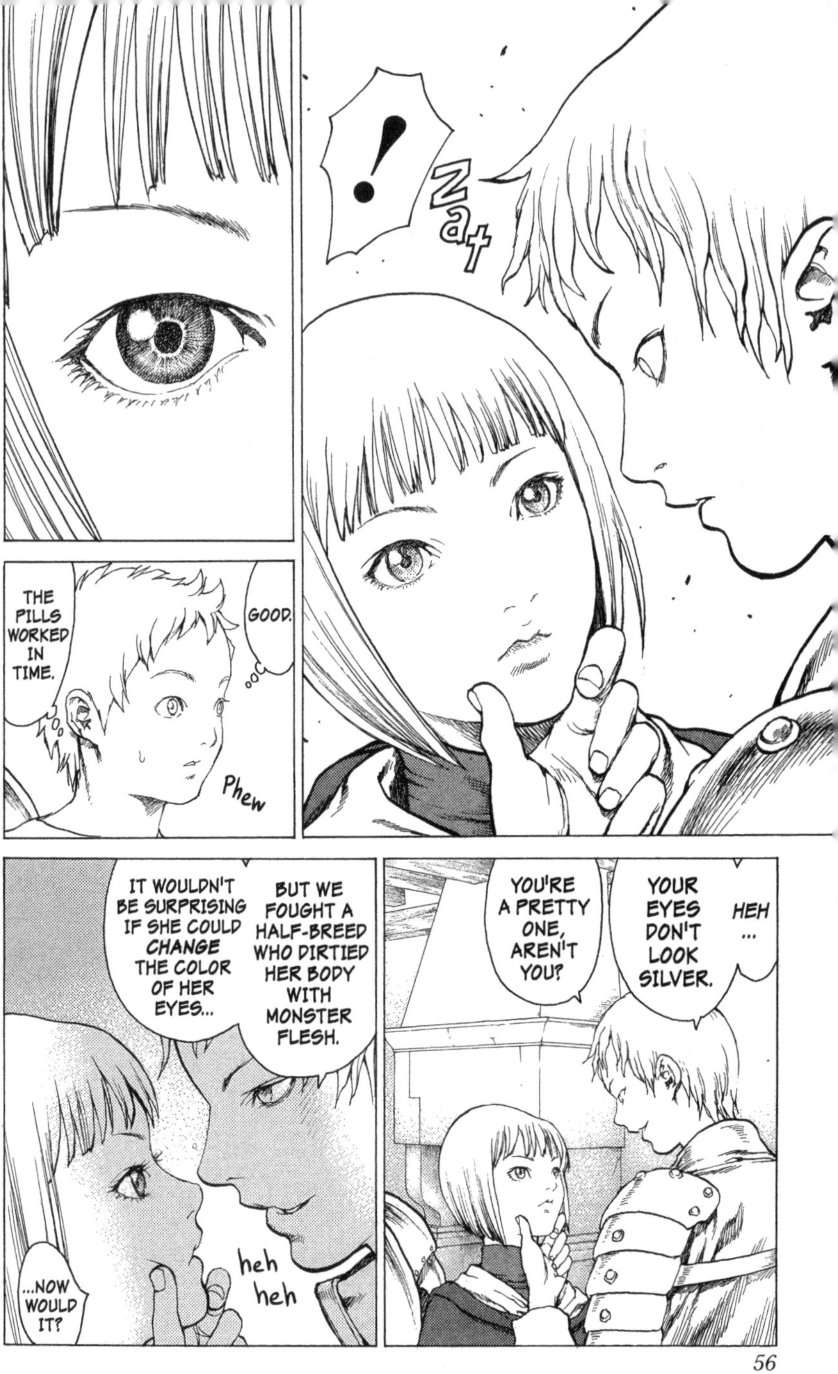
!
Zat
GOOD.
THE PILLS WORKED IN TIME.
Phew
HEH ...
YOUR EYES DON'T LOOK SILVER.
YOU'RE A PRETTY ONE, AREN'T YOU?
BUT WE FOUGHT A HALF-BREED WHO DIRTIED HER BODY WITH MONSTER FLESH.
IT WOULDN'T BE SURPRISING IF SHE COULD CHANGE THE COLOR OF HER EYES...
heh heh
...NOW WOULD IT?

READ THIS WAY

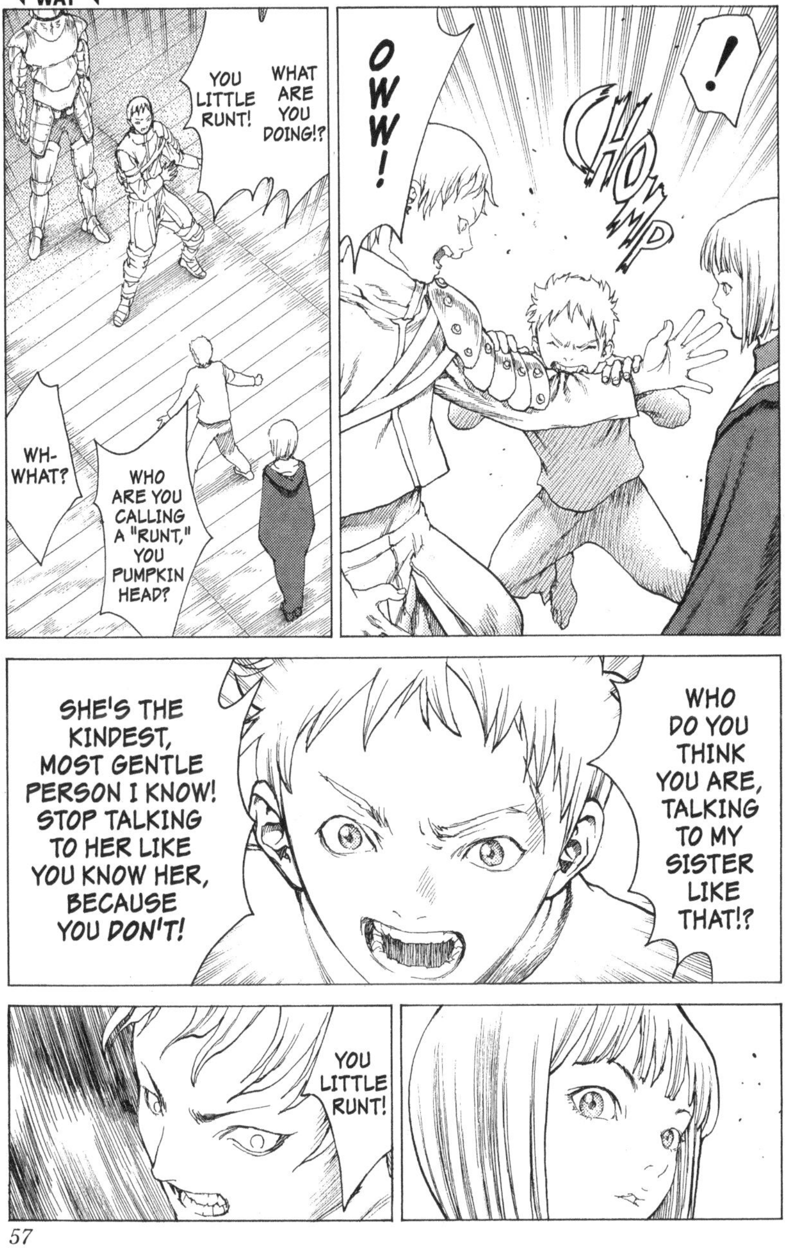
!
CHOMP
OWW!
WHAT ARE YOU DOING!?
YOU LITTLE RUNT!
WHO ARE YOU CALLING A "RUNT," YOU PUMPKIN HEAD?
WH-WHAT?
WHO DO YOU THINK YOU ARE, TALKING TO MY SISTER LIKE THAT!?
SHE'S THE KINDEST, MOST GENTLE PERSON I KNOW! STOP TALKING TO HER LIKE YOU KNOW HER, BECAUSE YOU DON'T!
YOU LITTLE RUNT!

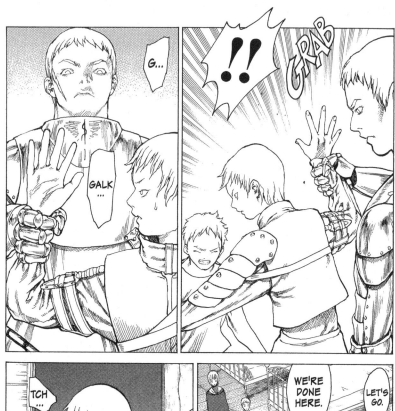

G...

GALK...

!!

GRAB

TCH...

WE'RE DONE HERE.

LET'S GO.

UH... BUT...

SLAM

CLOMP

READ THIS WAY

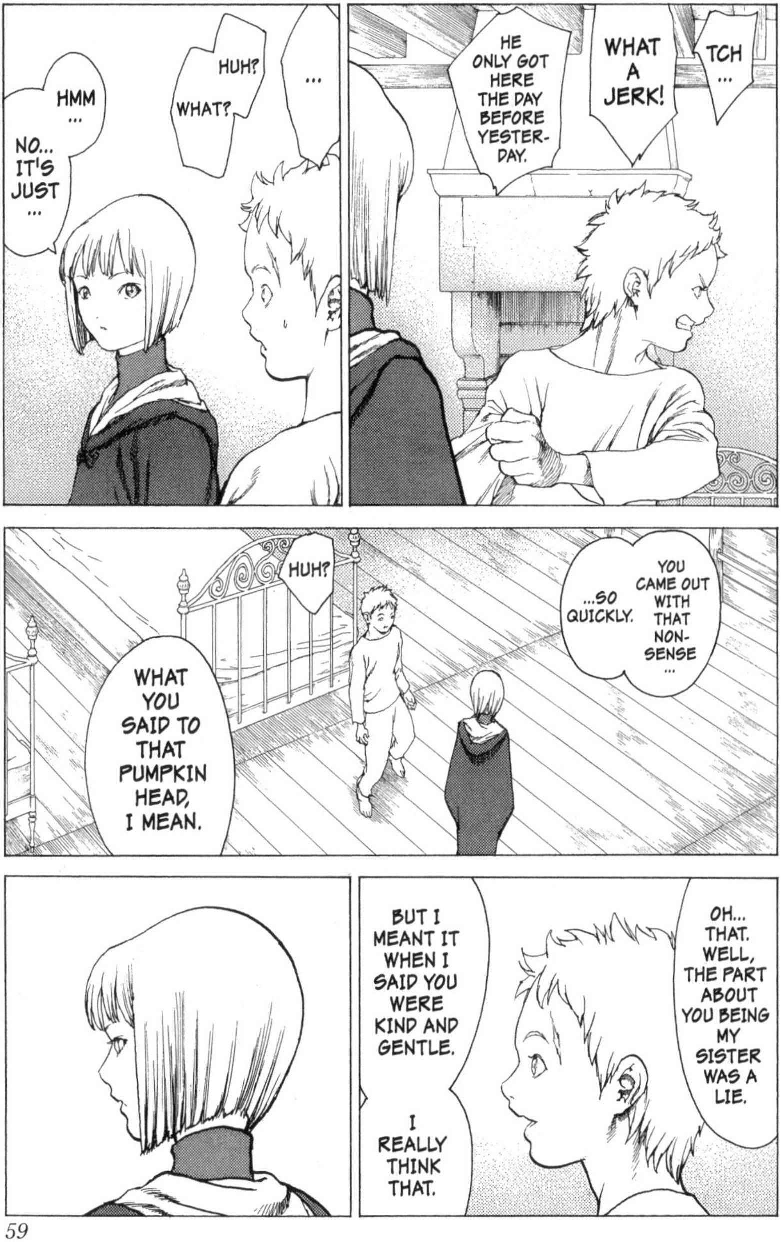
TCH ...
WHAT A JERK!
HE ONLY GOT HERE THE DAY BEFORE YESTER-DAY.
...
HUH? WHAT?
HMM ... NO... IT'S JUST ...
YOU CAME OUT WITH THAT NON-SENSE ... ...SO QUICKLY.
HUH?
WHAT YOU SAID TO THAT PUMPKIN HEAD, I MEAN.
OH... THAT. WELL, THE PART ABOUT YOU BEING MY SISTER WAS A LIE.
BUT I MEANT IT WHEN I SAID YOU WERE KIND AND GENTLE.
I REALLY THINK THAT.

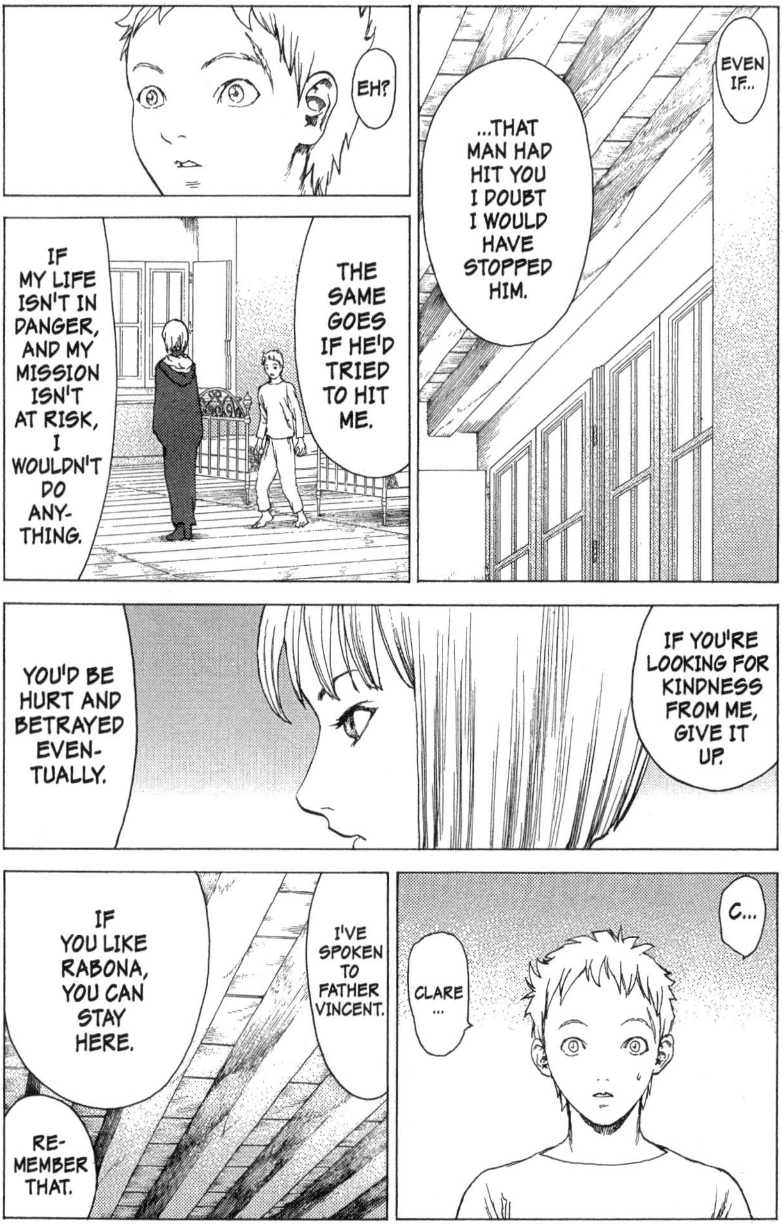
EVEN IF...
...THAT MAN HAD HIT YOU I DOUBT I WOULD HAVE STOPPED HIM.
EH?
THE SAME GOES IF HE'D TRIED TO HIT ME.
IF MY LIFE ISN'T IN DANGER, AND MY MISSION ISN'T AT RISK, I WOULDN'T DO ANY-THING.
IF YOU'RE LOOKING FOR KINDNESS FROM ME, GIVE IT UP.
YOU'D BE HURT AND BETRAYED EVEN-TUALLY.
C...
CLARE ...
I'VE SPOKEN TO FATHER VINCENT.
IF YOU LIKE RABONA, YOU CAN STAY HERE.
RE-MEMBER THAT.

READ THIS WAY

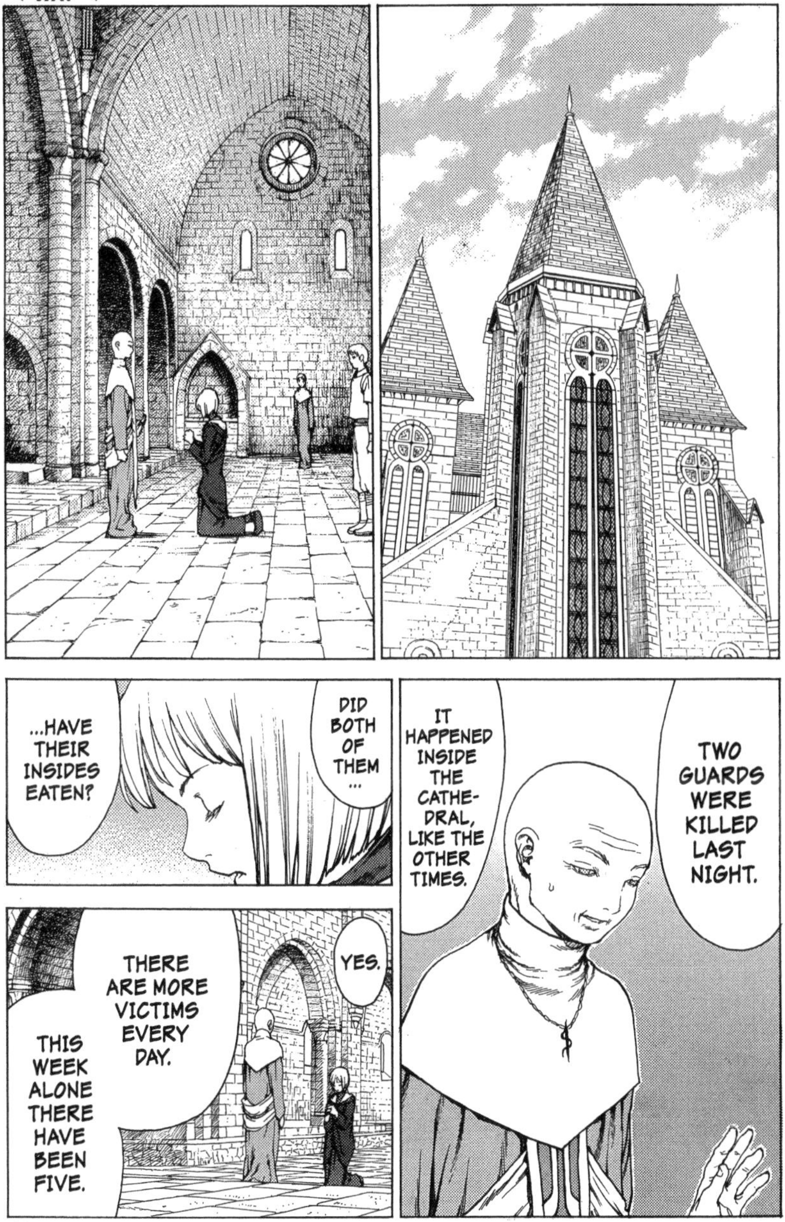
TWO GUARDS WERE KILLED LAST NIGHT.
IT HAPPENED INSIDE THE CATHEDRAL, LIKE THE OTHER TIMES.
DID BOTH OF THEM...
...HAVE THEIR INSIDES EATEN?
YES.
THERE ARE MORE VICTIMS EVERY DAY.
THIS WEEK ALONE THERE HAVE BEEN FIVE.

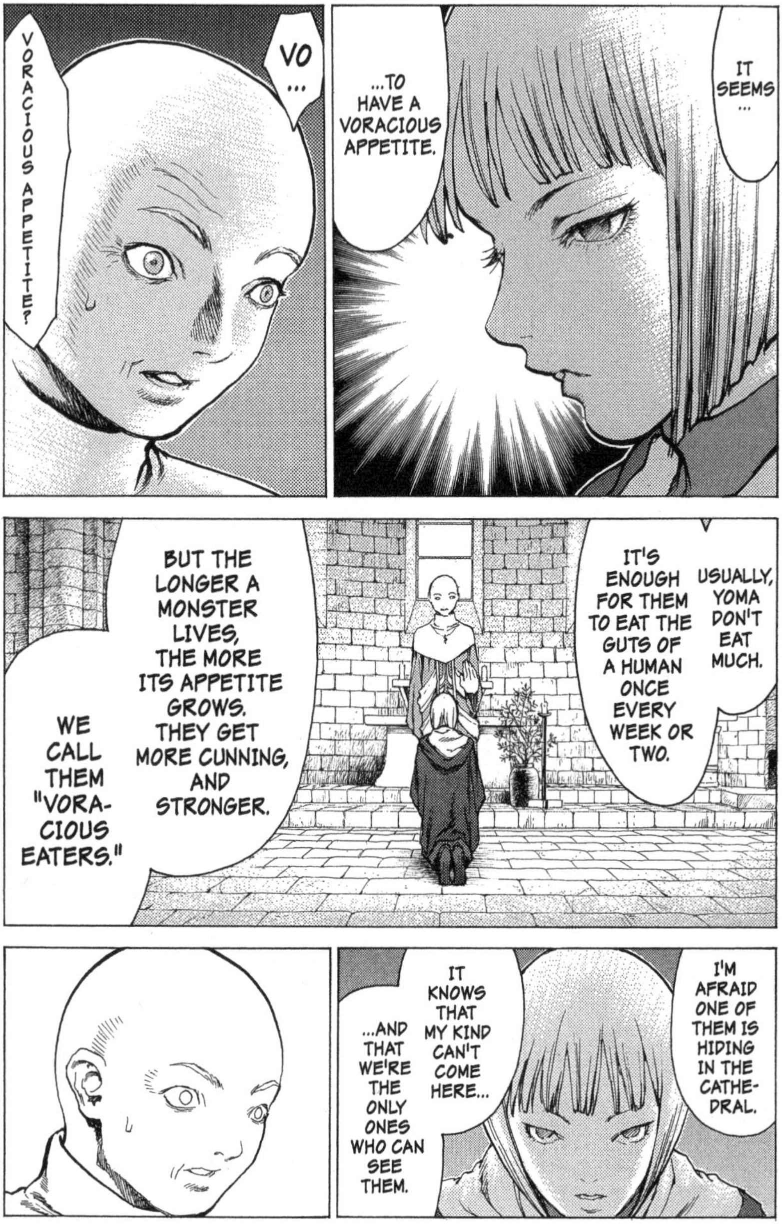
IT SEEMS...
...TO HAVE A VORACIOUS APPETITE.
VO...
VORACIOUS APPETITE?
USUALLY, YOMA DON'T EAT MUCH.
IT'S ENOUGH FOR THEM TO EAT THE GUTS OF A HUMAN ONCE EVERY WEEK OR TWO.
BUT THE LONGER A MONSTER LIVES, THE MORE ITS APPETITE GROWS. THEY GET MORE CUNNING, AND STRONGER.
WE CALL THEM "VORA-CIOUS EATERS."
I'M AFRAID ONE OF THEM IS HIDING IN THE CATHE-DRAL.
IT KNOWS THAT MY KIND CAN'T COME HERE...
...AND THAT WE'RE THE ONLY ONES WHO CAN SEE THEM.

READ THIS WAY

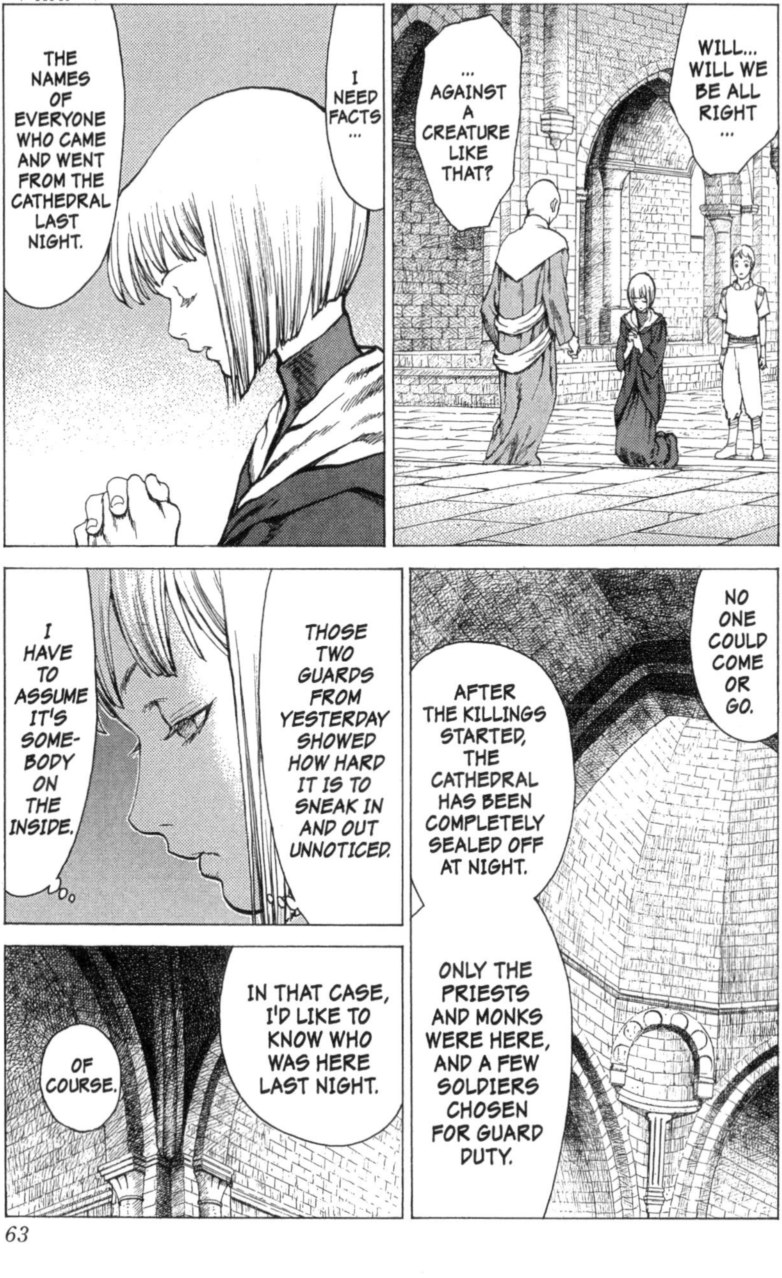

WILL... WILL WE BE ALL RIGHT ...
... AGAINST A CREATURE LIKE THAT?
I NEED FACTS ...
THE NAMES OF EVERYONE WHO CAME AND WENT FROM THE CATHEDRAL LAST NIGHT.
NO ONE COULD COME OR GO.
AFTER THE KILLINGS STARTED, THE CATHEDRAL HAS BEEN COMPLETELY SEALED OFF AT NIGHT.
ONLY THE PRIESTS AND MONKS WERE HERE, AND A FEW SOLDIERS CHOSEN FOR GUARD DUTY.
THOSE TWO GUARDS FROM YESTERDAY SHOWED HOW HARD IT IS TO SNEAK IN AND OUT UNNOTICED.
I HAVE TO ASSUME IT'S SOMEBODY ON THE INSIDE.
IN THAT CASE, I'D LIKE TO KNOW WHO WAS HERE LAST NIGHT.
OF COURSE.

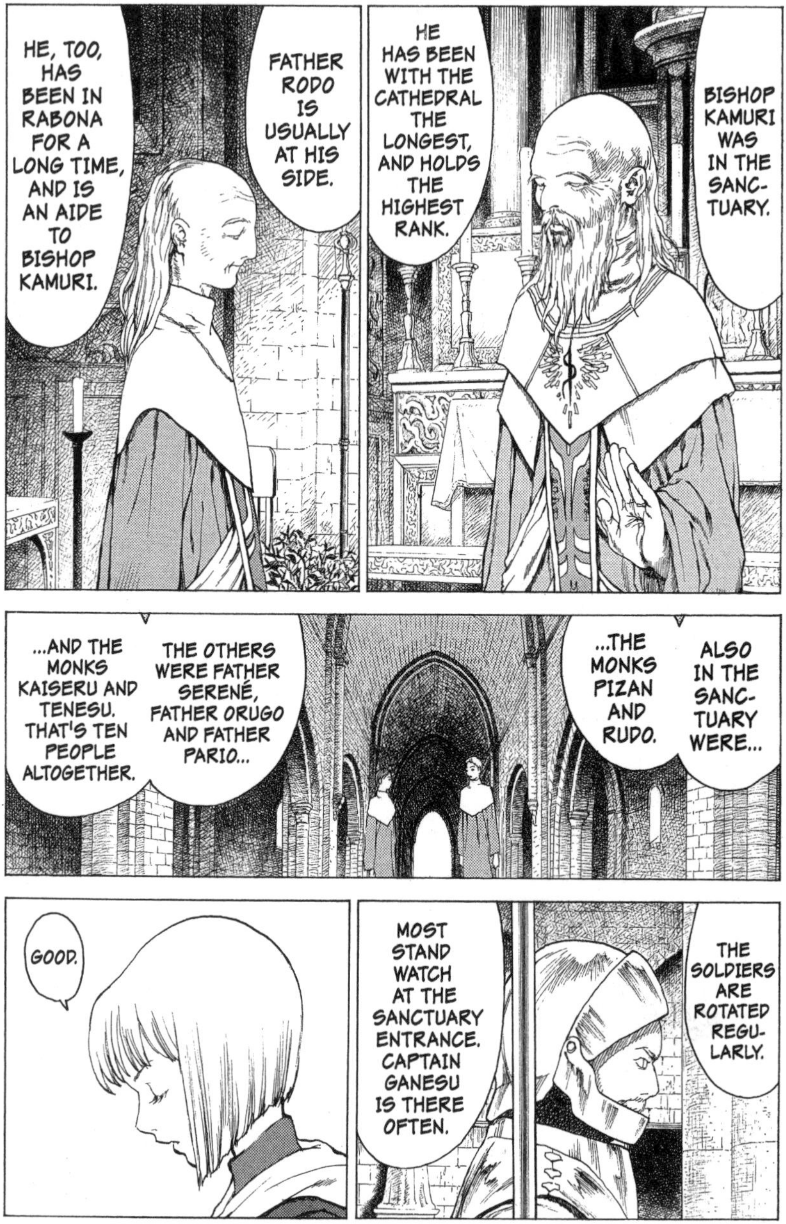
BISHOP KAMURI WAS IN THE SANCTUARY.
HE HAS BEEN WITH THE CATHEDRAL THE LONGEST, AND HOLDS THE HIGHEST RANK.
FATHER RODO IS USUALLY AT HIS SIDE.
HE, TOO, HAS BEEN IN RABONA FOR A LONG TIME, AND IS AN AIDE TO BISHOP KAMURI.
ALSO IN THE SANCTUARY WERE...
...THE MONKS PIZAN AND RUDO.
THE OTHERS WERE FATHER SERENÉ, FATHER ORUGO AND FATHER PARIO...
...AND THE MONKS KAISERU AND TENESU. THAT'S TEN PEOPLE ALTOGETHER.
THE SOLDIERS ARE ROTATED REGU-LARLY.
MOST STAND WATCH AT THE SANCTUARY ENTRANCE. CAPTAIN GANESU IS THERE OFTEN.
GOOD.

READ THIS WAY

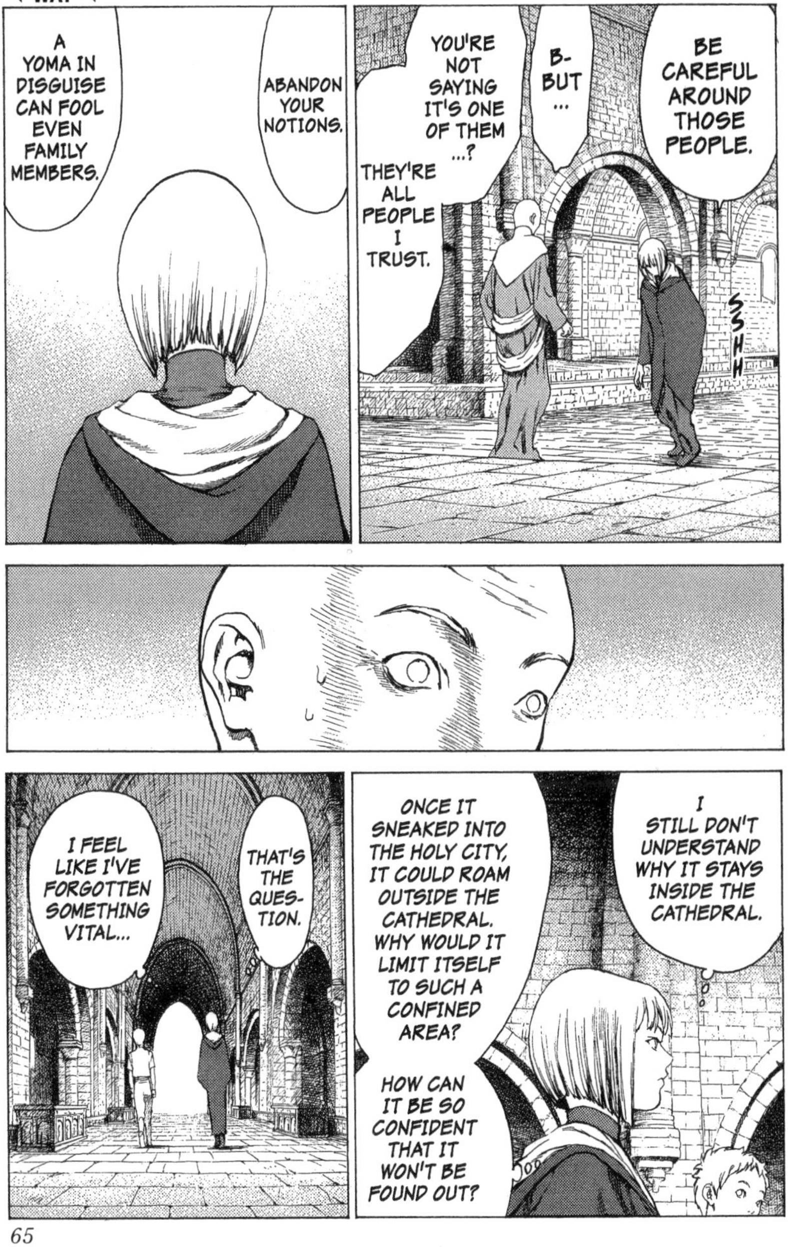

BE CAREFUL AROUND THOSE PEOPLE.
B-BUT ...
YOU'RE NOT SAYING IT'S ONE OF THEM ...?
THEY'RE ALL PEOPLE I TRUST.
SSHH
ABANDON YOUR NOTIONS.
A YOMA IN DISGUISE CAN FOOL EVEN FAMILY MEMBERS.
I STILL DON'T UNDERSTAND WHY IT STAYS INSIDE THE CATHEDRAL.
ONCE IT SNEAKED INTO THE HOLY CITY, IT COULD ROAM OUTSIDE THE CATHEDRAL. WHY WOULD IT LIMIT ITSELF TO SUCH A CONFINED AREA?
HOW CAN IT BE SO CONFIDENT THAT IT WON'T BE FOUND OUT?
THAT'S THE QUES-TION.
I FEEL LIKE I'VE FORGOTTEN SOMETHING VITAL...

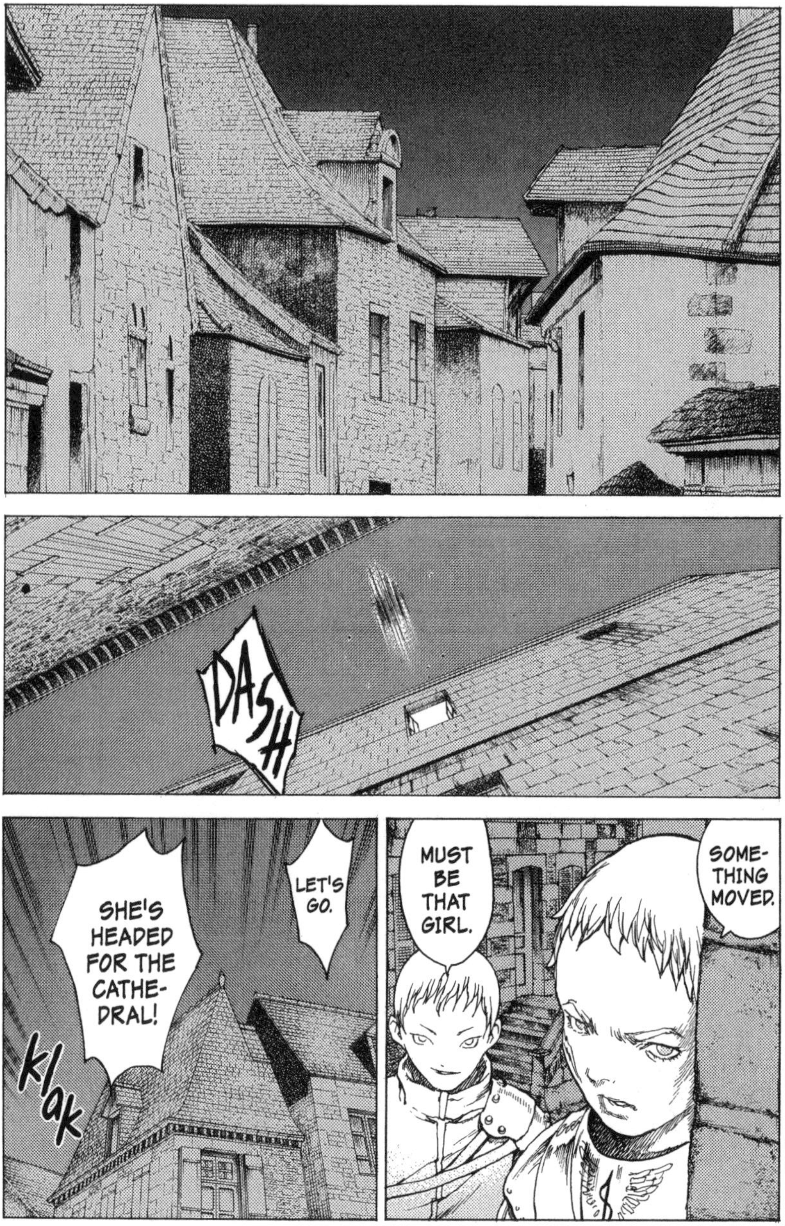
DASH
SOMETHING MOVED.
MUST BE THAT GIRL.
LET'S GO.
SHE'S HEADED FOR THE CATHEDRAL!
klak

READ THIS WAY

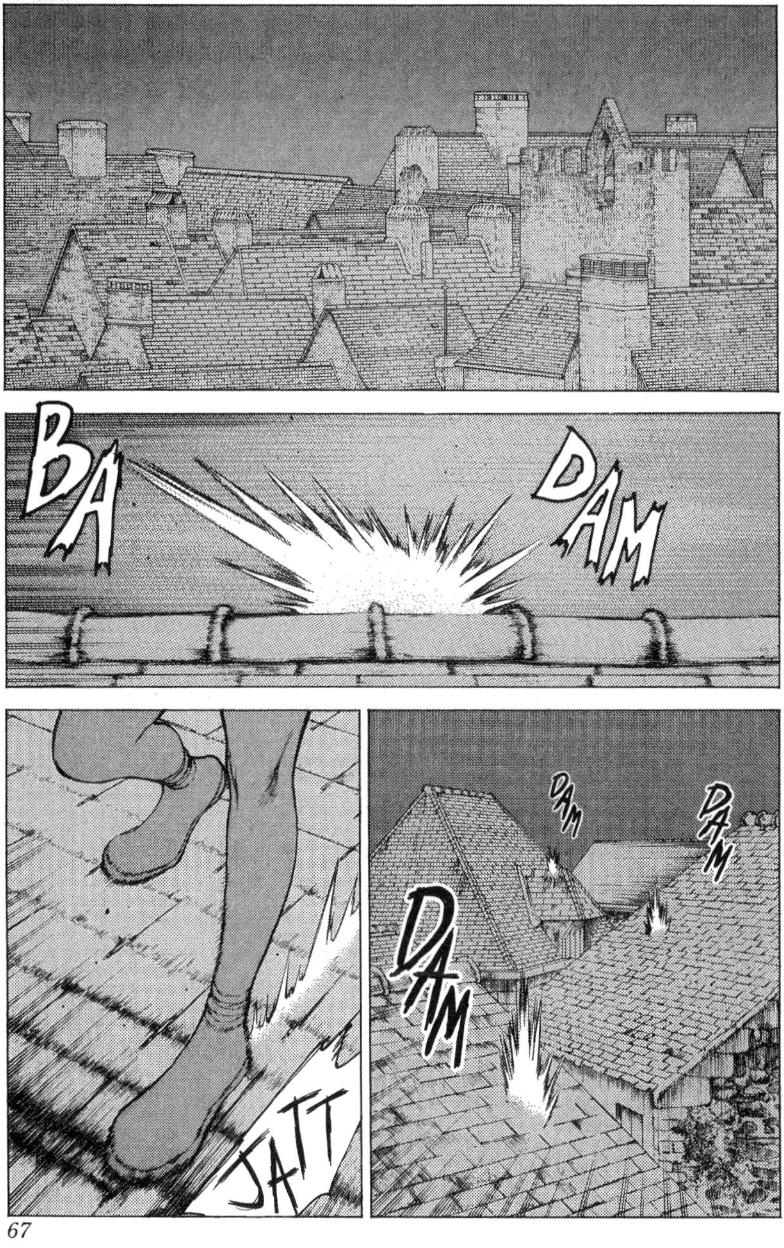
BA
DAM
DAM
DAM
DAM
JATT

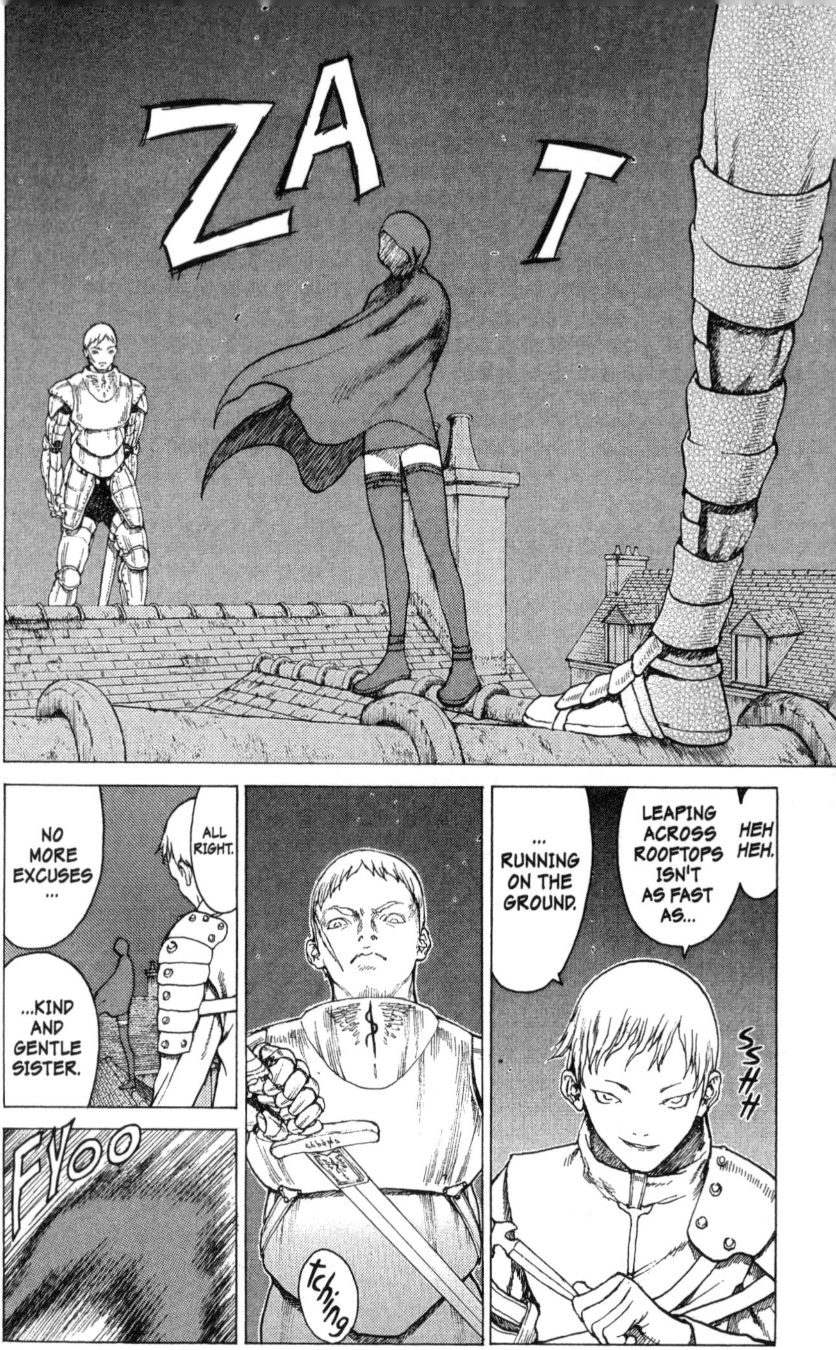
ZAT
HEH HEH.
LEAPING ACROSS ROOFTOPS ISN'T AS FAST AS...
...RUNNING ON THE GROUND.
SSHH
tching
ALL RIGHT.
NO MORE EXCUSES...
...KIND AND GENTLE SISTER.
FYOO

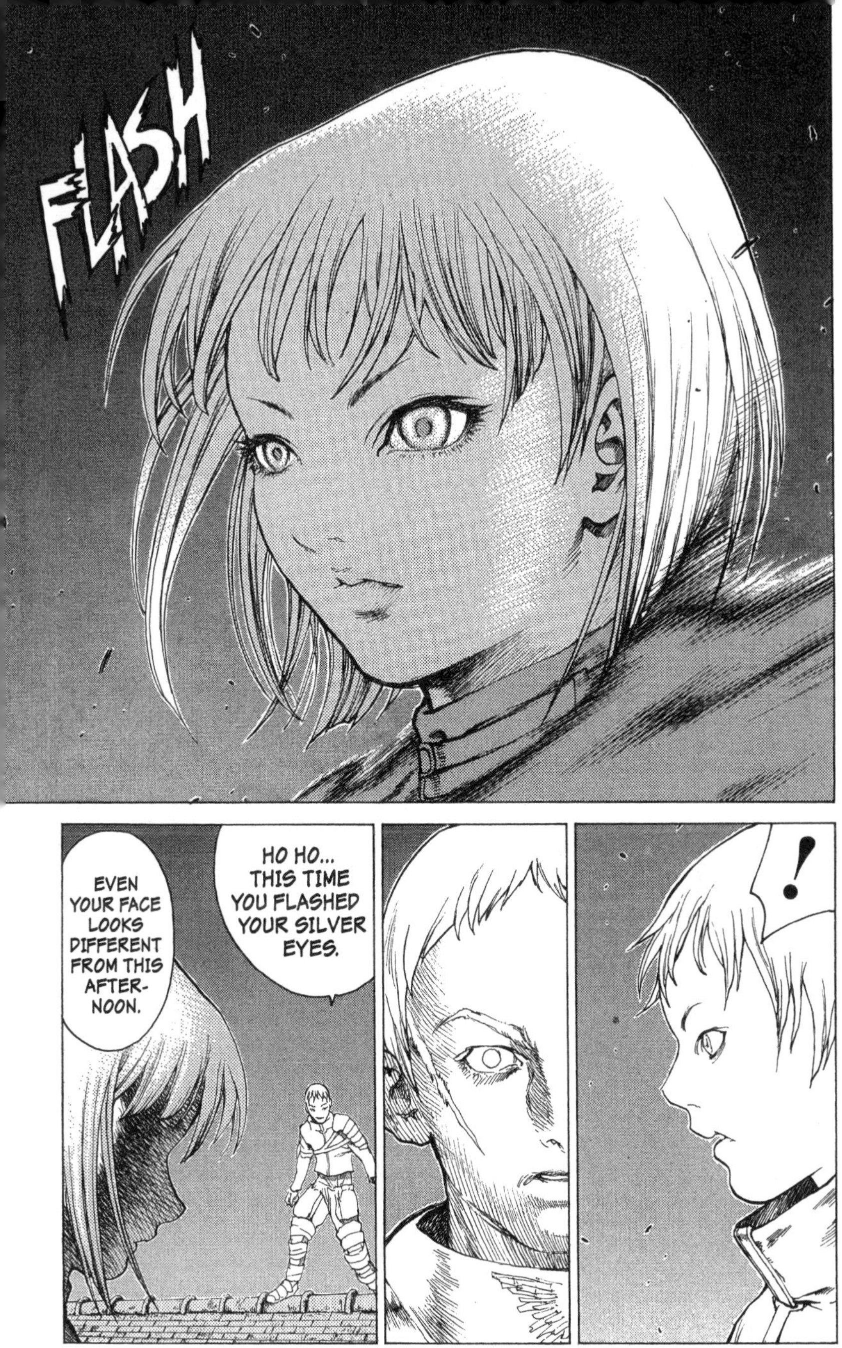
FLASH
!
HO HO... THIS TIME YOU FLASHED YOUR SILVER EYES.
EVEN YOUR FACE LOOKS DIFFERENT FROM THIS AFTER-NOON.

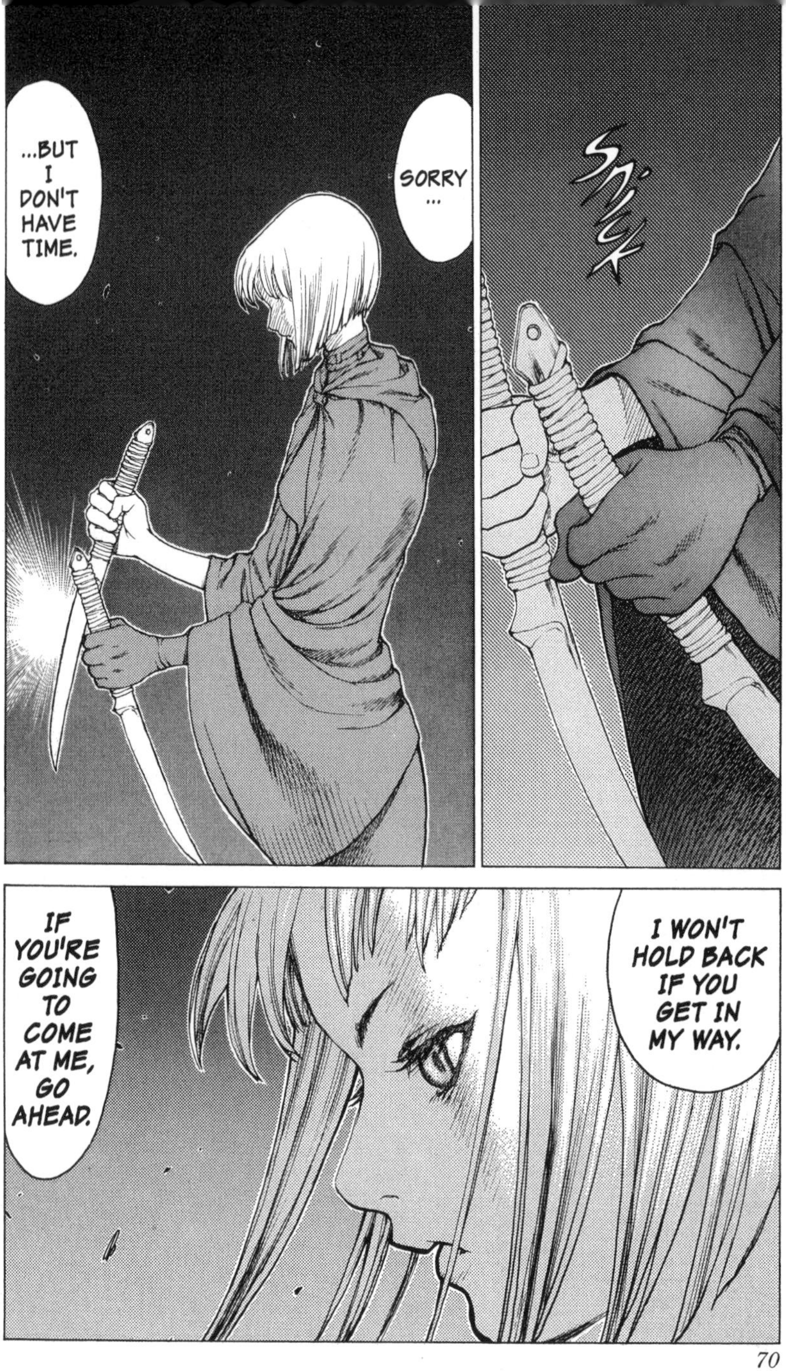
SNICK
SORRY...
...BUT I DON'T HAVE TIME.
I WON'T HOLD BACK IF YOU GET IN MY WAY.
IF YOU'RE GOING TO COME AT ME, GO AHEAD.

READ THIS WAY

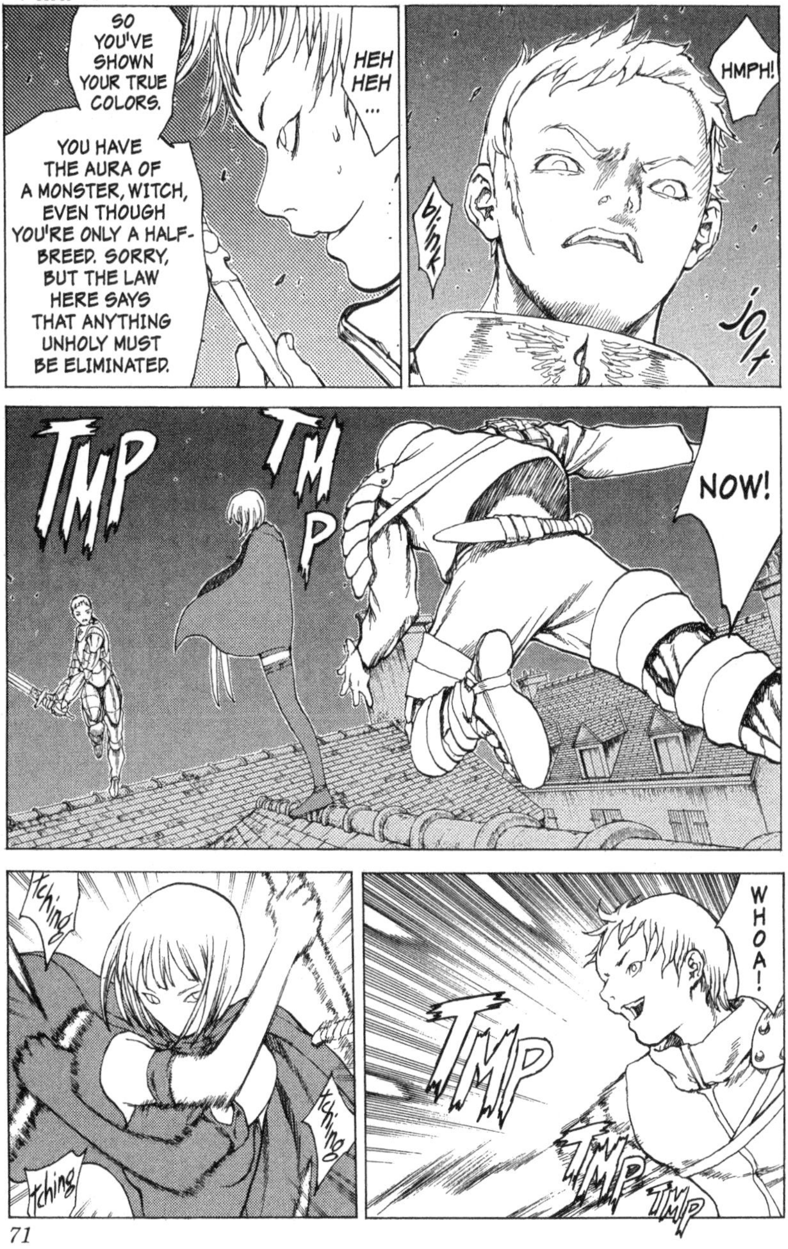
HMPH!
blink
jolt
SO YOU'VE SHOWN YOUR TRUE COLORS.
HEH HEH ...
YOU HAVE THE AURA OF A MONSTER, WITCH, EVEN THOUGH YOU'RE ONLY A HALF-BREED. SORRY, BUT THE LAW HERE SAYS THAT ANYTHING UNHOLY MUST BE ELIMINATED.
NOW!
TMP
TMP
WHOA!
TMP
TMP TMP
tching
tching
tching

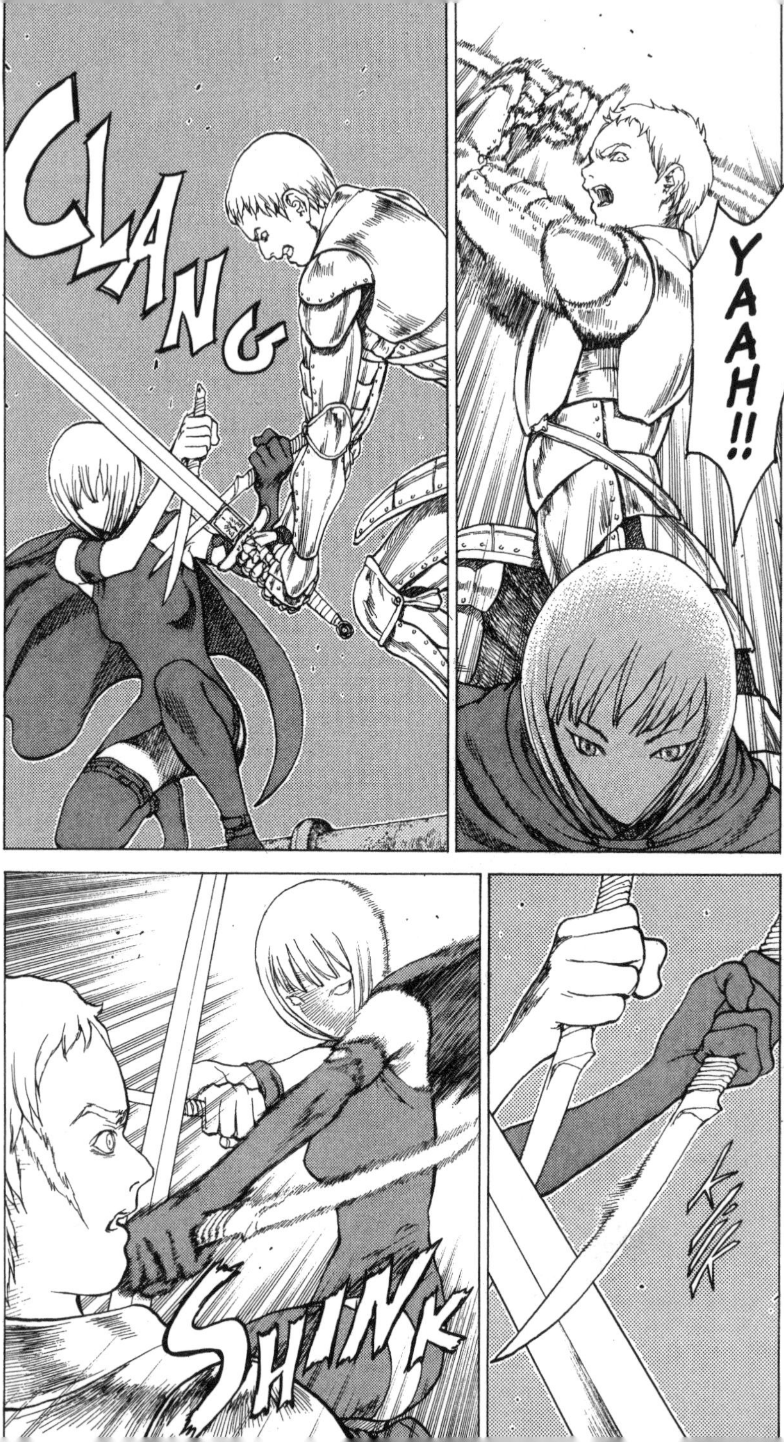
YAAH!!
CLANG
KRIK
SHINK

READ THIS WAY

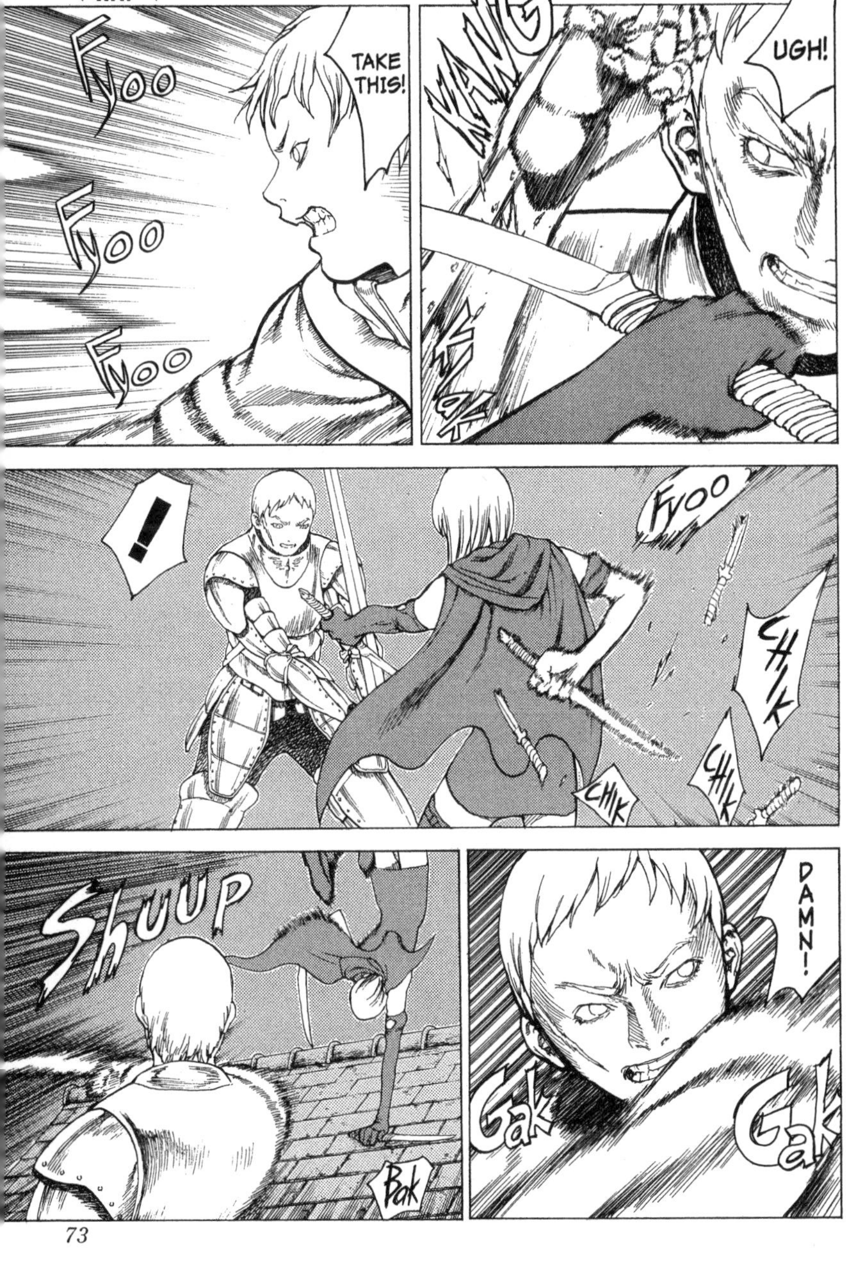
UGH!
WANG
Kwak
TAKE THIS!
Fyoo
Fyoo
Fyoo
Fyoo
CHIK
CHIK
CHIK
!
DAMN!
Gak
Gak
Shuup
Bak

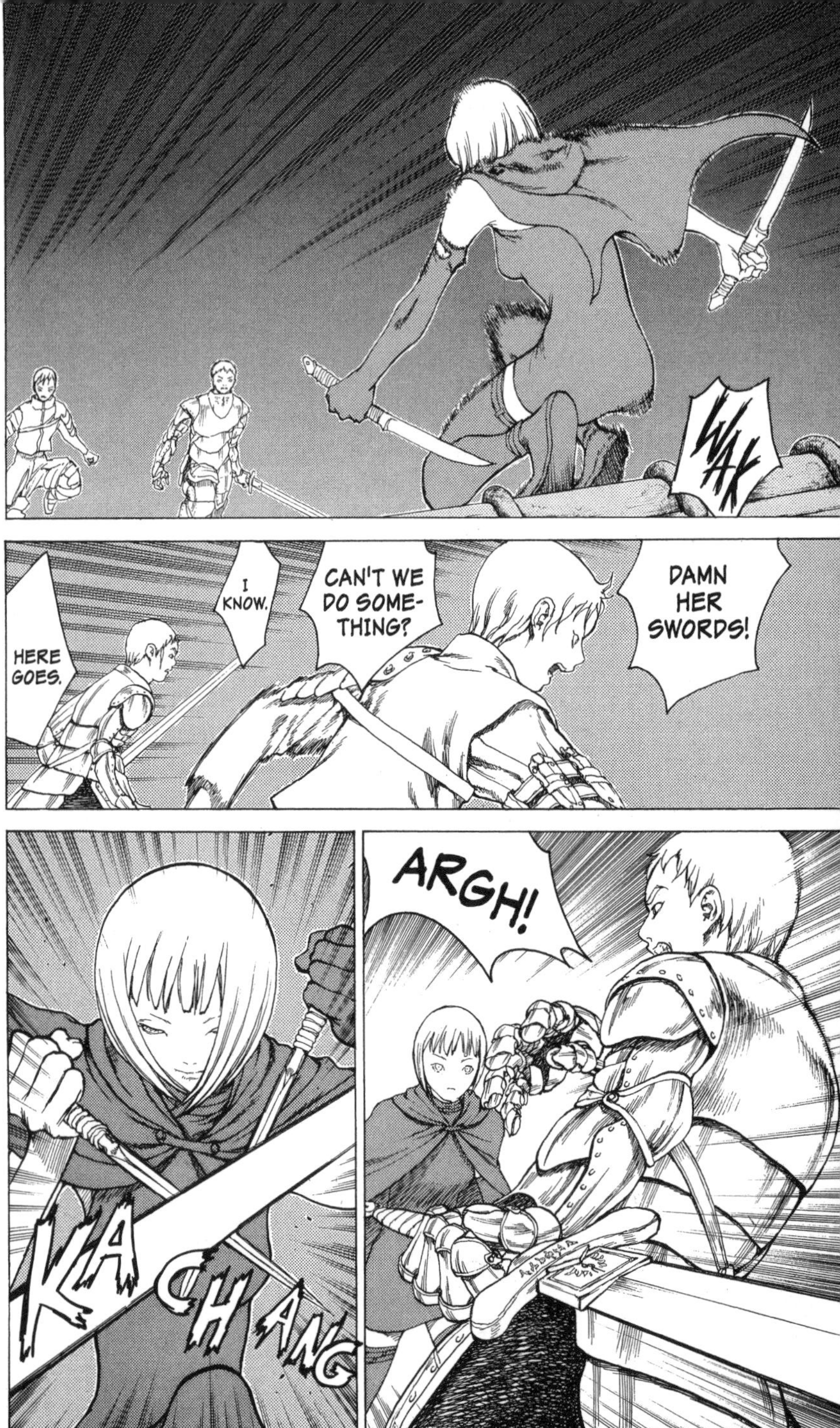
WAK
DAMN HER SWORDS!
CAN'T WE DO SOME-THING?
I KNOW.
HERE GOES.
ARGH!
KACHANG

READ THIS WAY

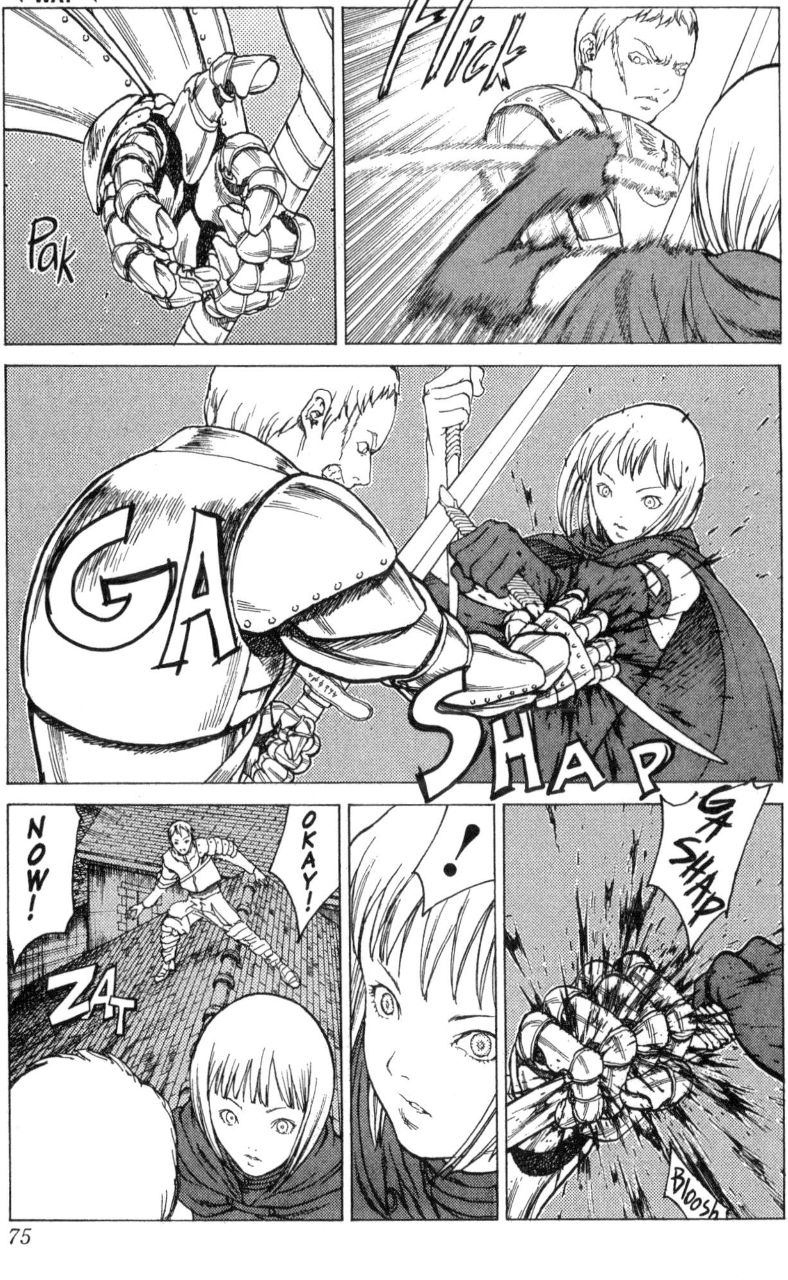

Flick
Pak
GA
SHAP
GA SHAP
Bloosh
!
OKAY!
NOW!
ZAT

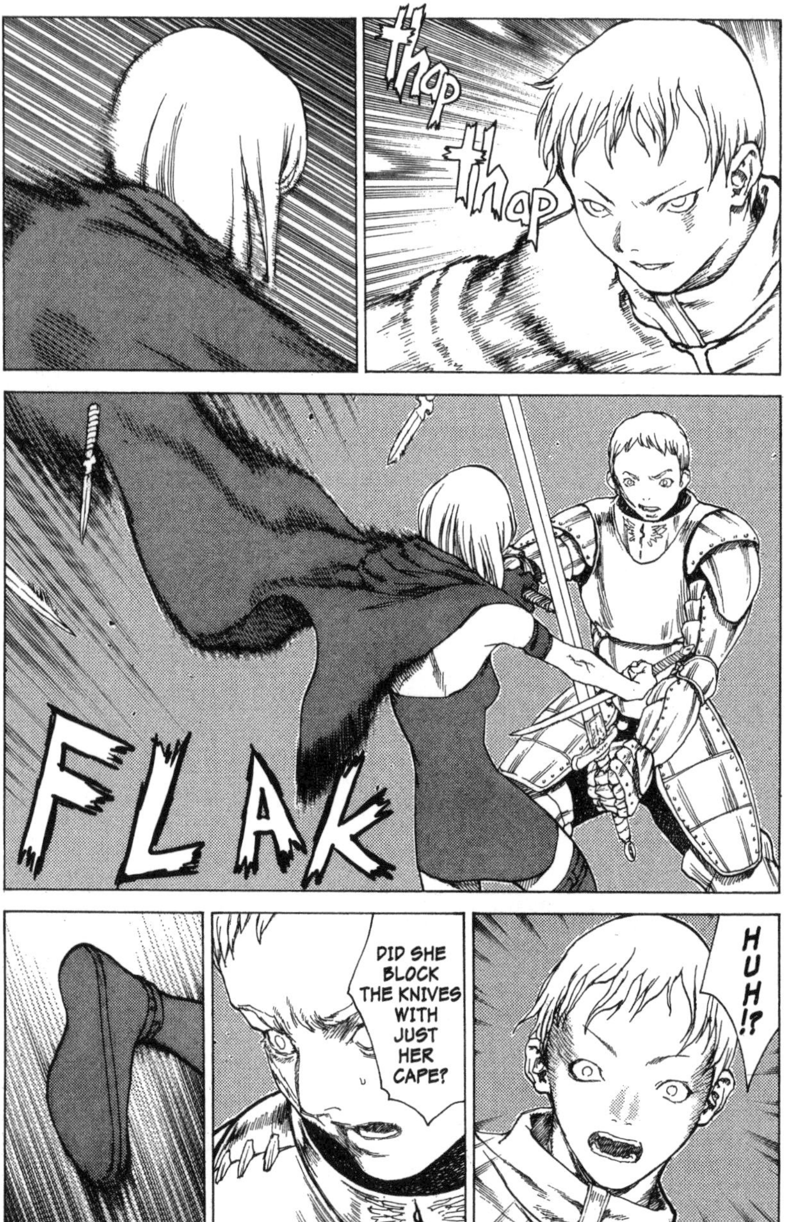
thap
thap
FLAK
HUH!?
DID SHE BLOCK THE KNIVES WITH JUST HER CAPE?

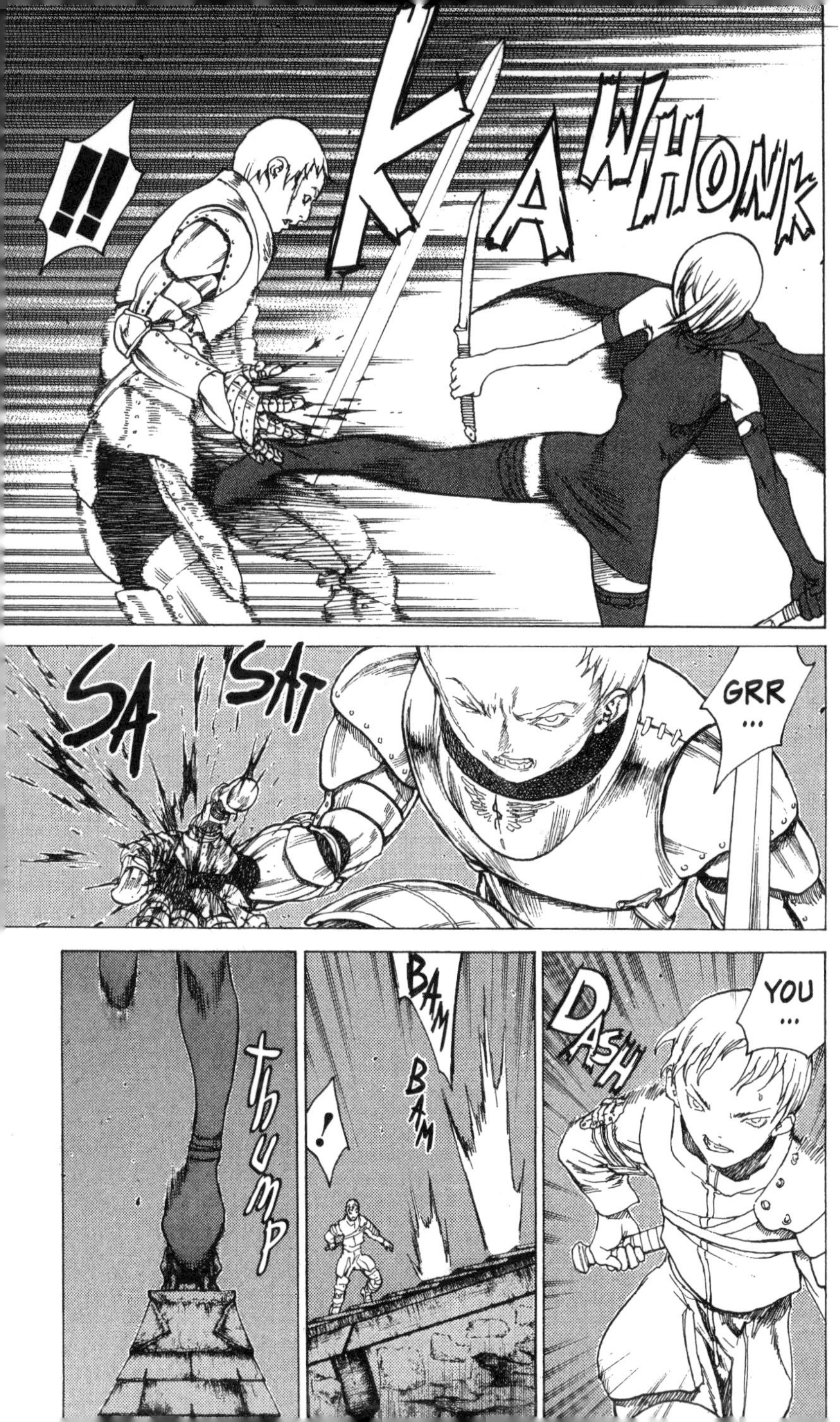
KA WHONK
!!
GRR ...
SA SAT
YOU ...
DASH
BAM BAM BAM
!
thump

Fyoo

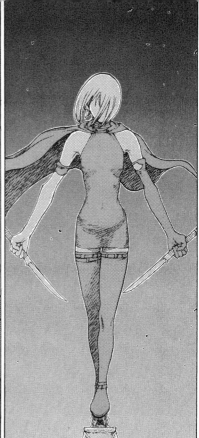

...A CLAY-MORE!

...A SILVER-EYED WITCH...

...
THAT'S...

SO
...

!

...

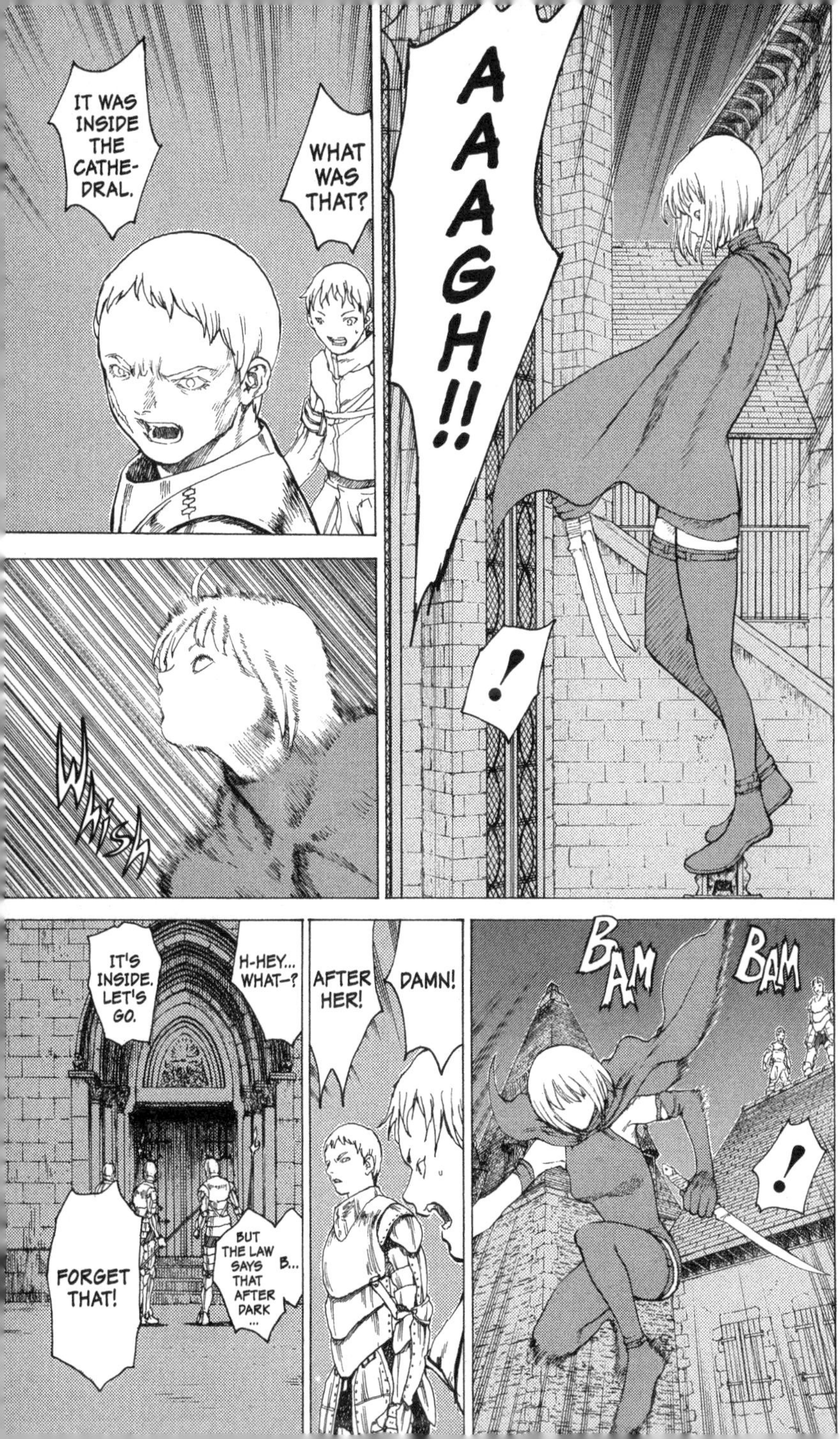

AAAAGH!!
!
WHAT WAS THAT?
IT WAS INSIDE THE CATHE-DRAL.
Whish
BAM
BAM
!
DAMN!
AFTER HER!
B...
H-HEY... WHAT—?
IT'S INSIDE. LET'S GO.
BUT THE LAW SAYS THAT AFTER DARK ...
FORGET THAT!

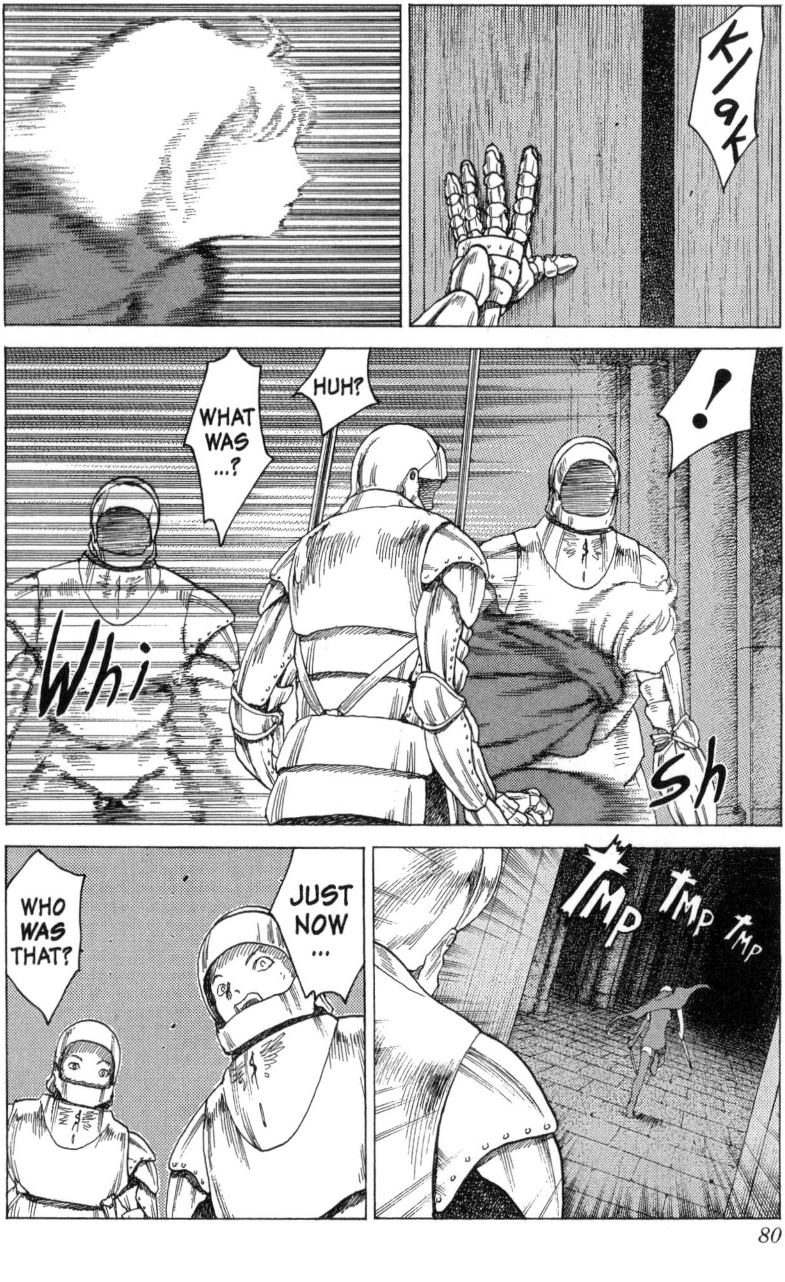
Klak
!
HUH?
WHAT WAS ...?
Sh
Whi
tmp tmp tmp
JUST NOW ...
WHO WAS THAT?

READ THIS WAY

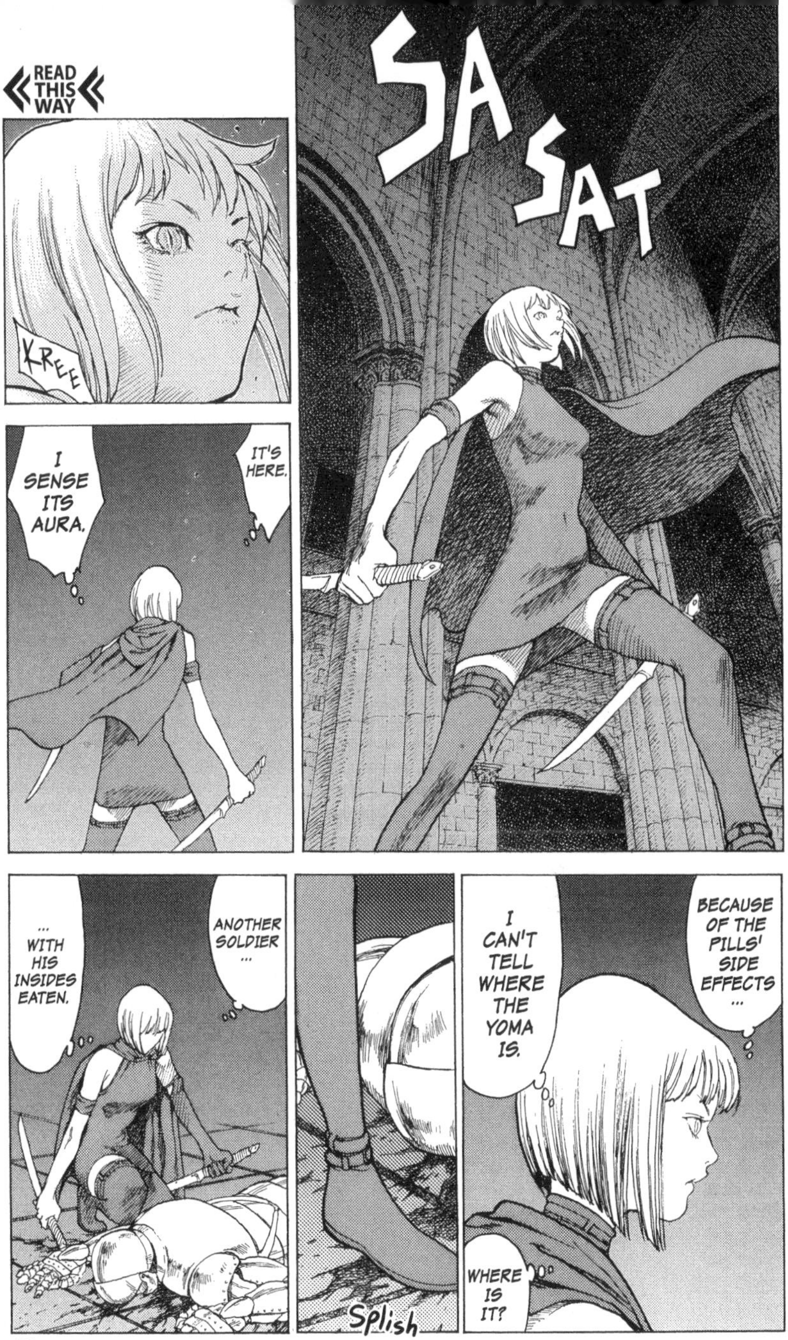

SA SAT
KREE
IT'S HERE.
I SENSE ITS AURA.
BECAUSE OF THE PILLS' SIDE EFFECTS ...
I CAN'T TELL WHERE THE YOMA IS.
WHERE IS IT?
Splish
ANOTHER SOLDIER ...
... WITH HIS INSIDES EATEN.

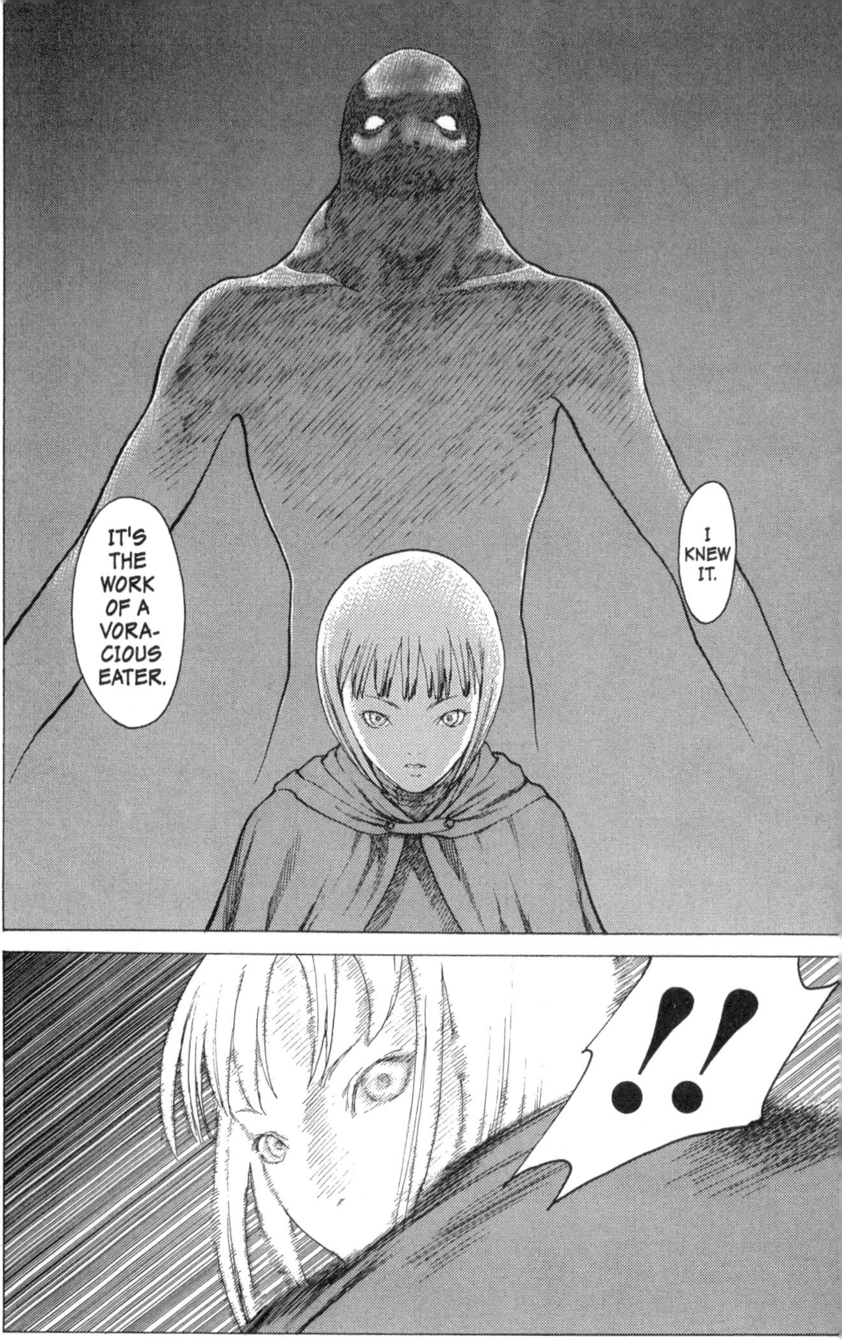
I KNEW IT.
IT'S THE WORK OF A VORACIOUS EATER.
!!

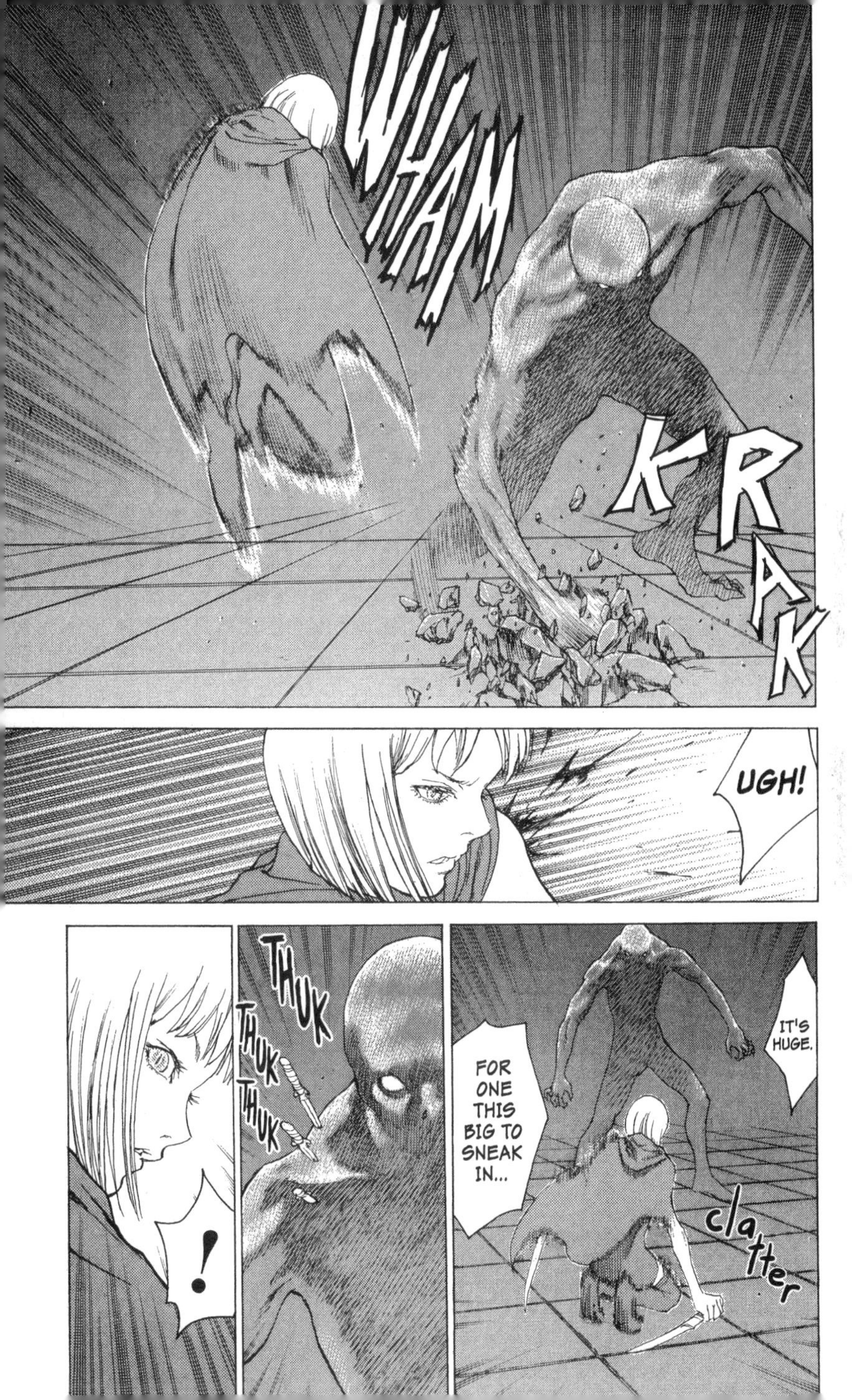
WHAM
KRAK
UGH!
IT'S HUGE.
FOR ONE THIS BIG TO SNEAK IN...
clatter
THUK
THUK
THUK
!

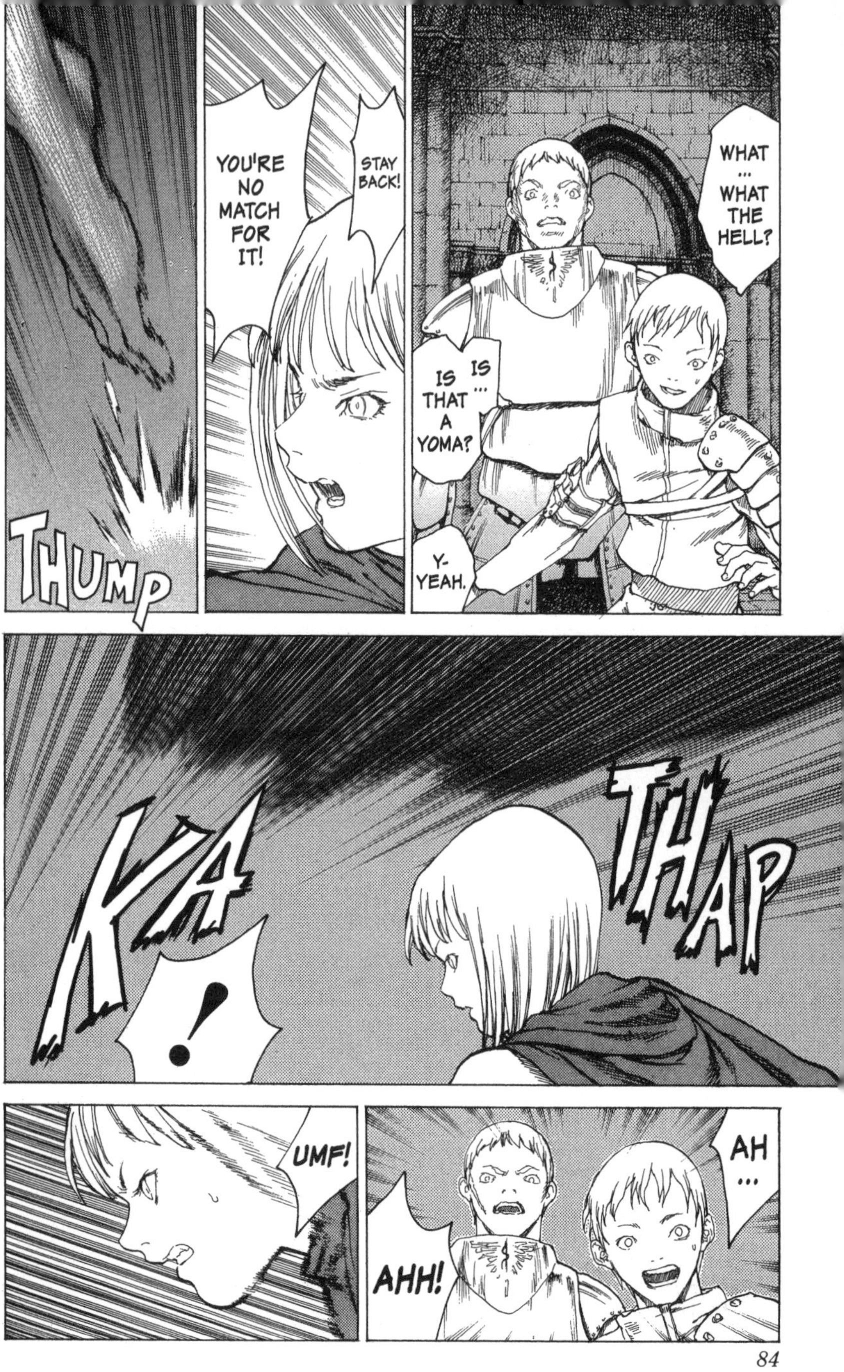
WHAT ... WHAT THE HELL?
IS ... IS THAT A YOMA?
Y-YEAH.
STAY BACK!
YOU'RE NO MATCH FOR IT!
THUMP
KA
THAP
!
AH ...
AHH!
UMF!

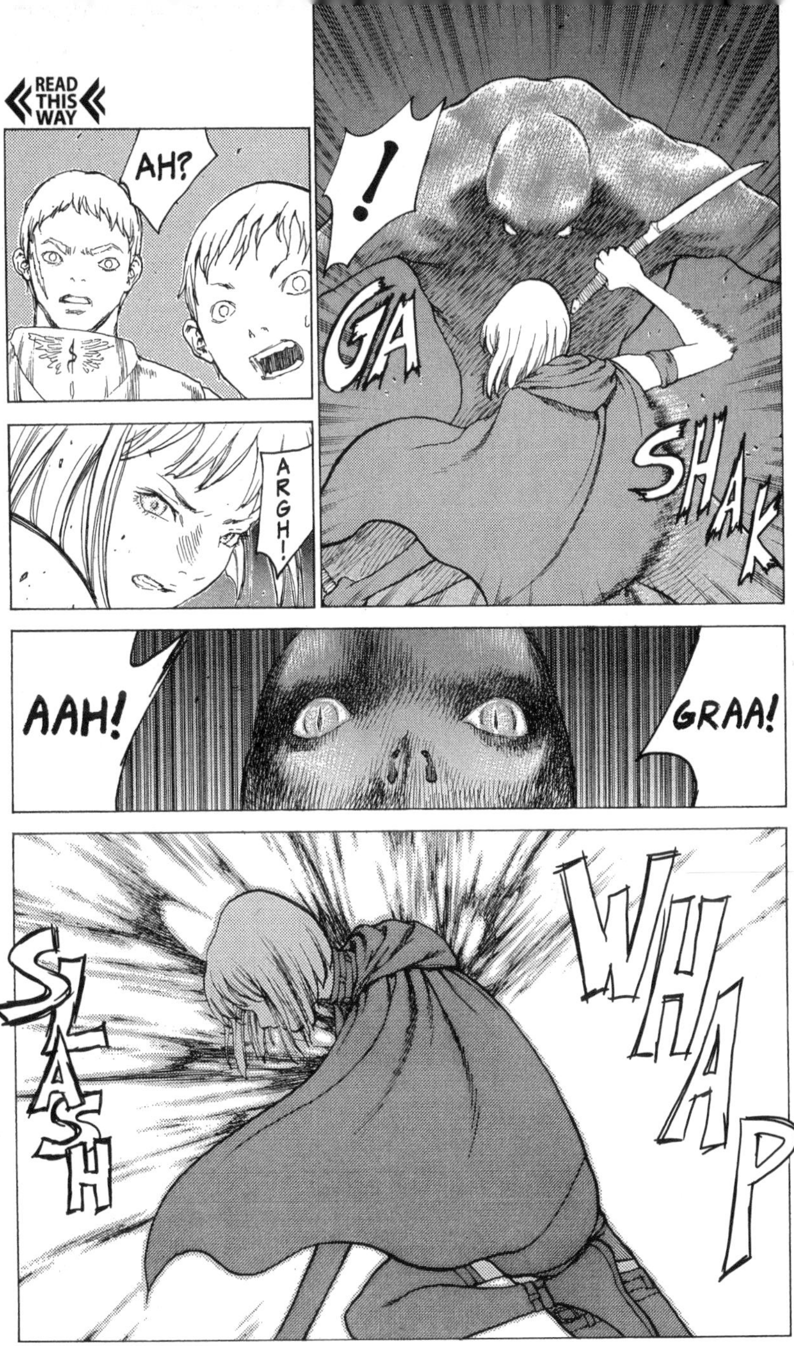
READ THIS WAY
!
GA
SHAK
AH?
ARGH!
GRAA!
AAH!
WHAP
SLASH

クレイモア
Claymore™

Scene 7: Darkness in Paradise, Part 3

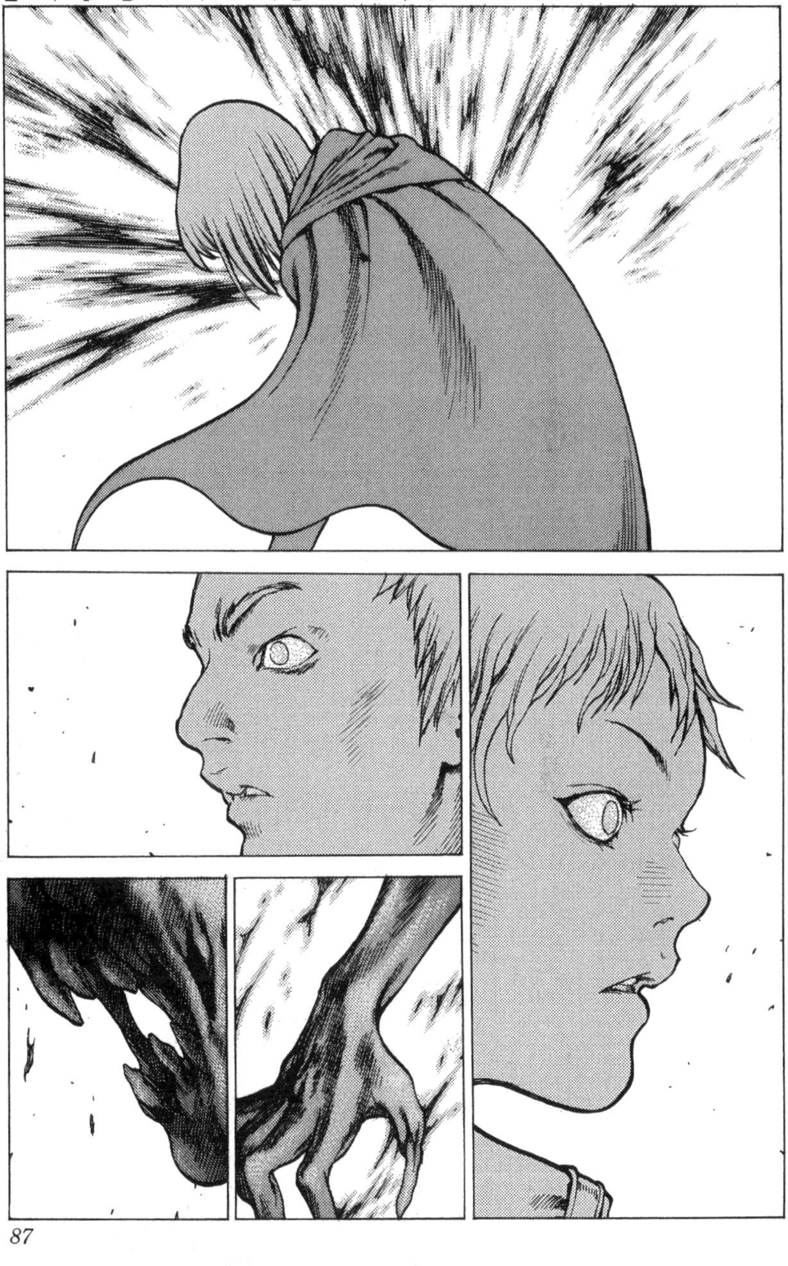

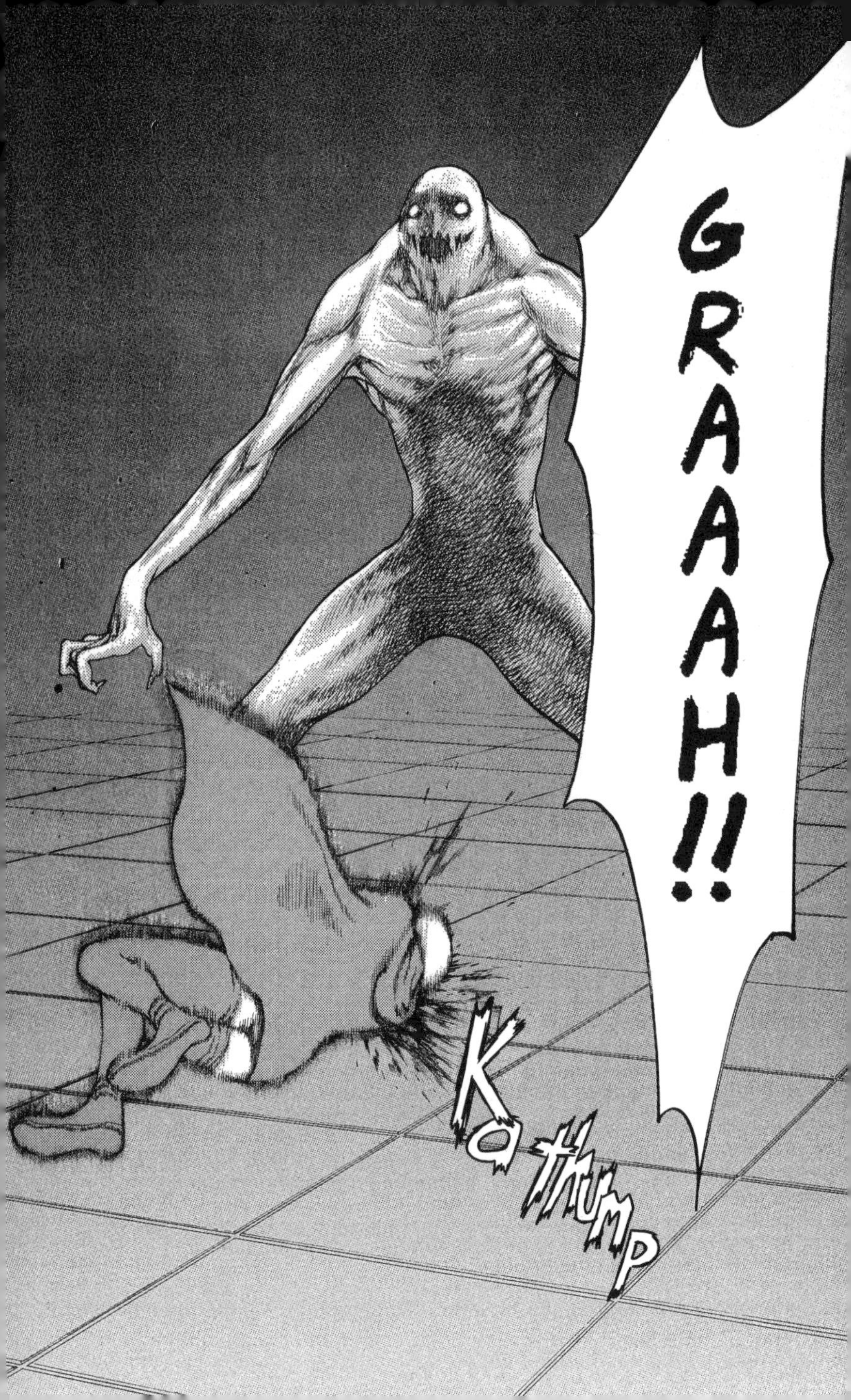
GRAAAH!!
Ka thump

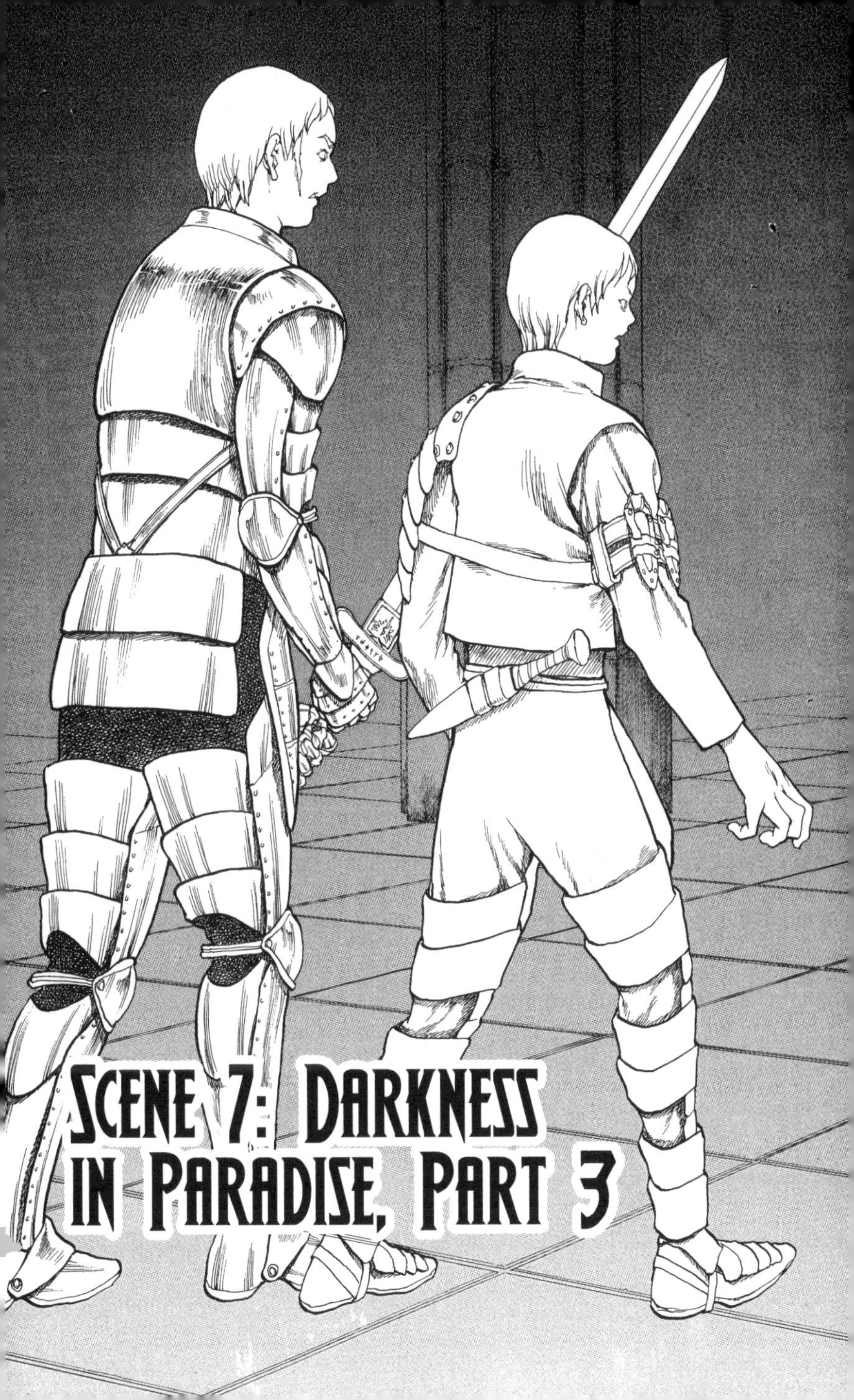
Scene 7: Darkness in Paradise, Part 3

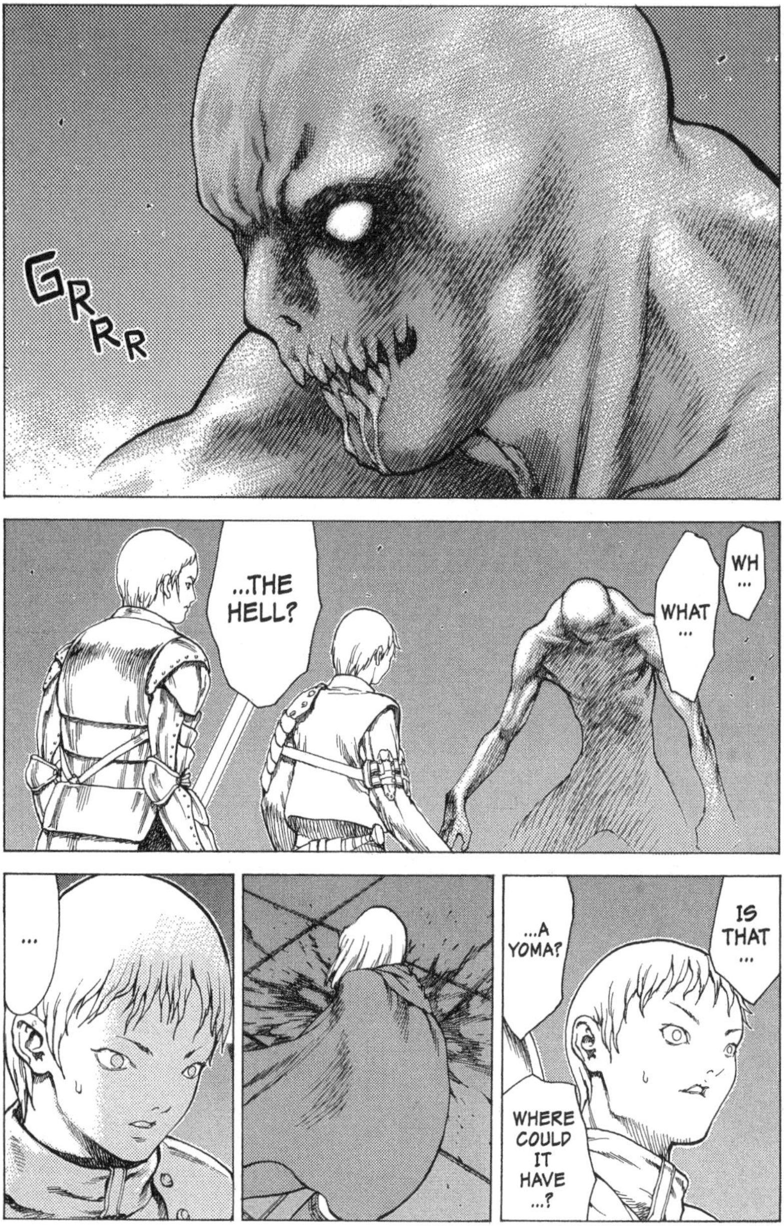
GRRR
WH ...
WHAT ...
...THE HELL?
IS THAT ...
...A YOMA?
WHERE COULD IT HAVE ...?
...

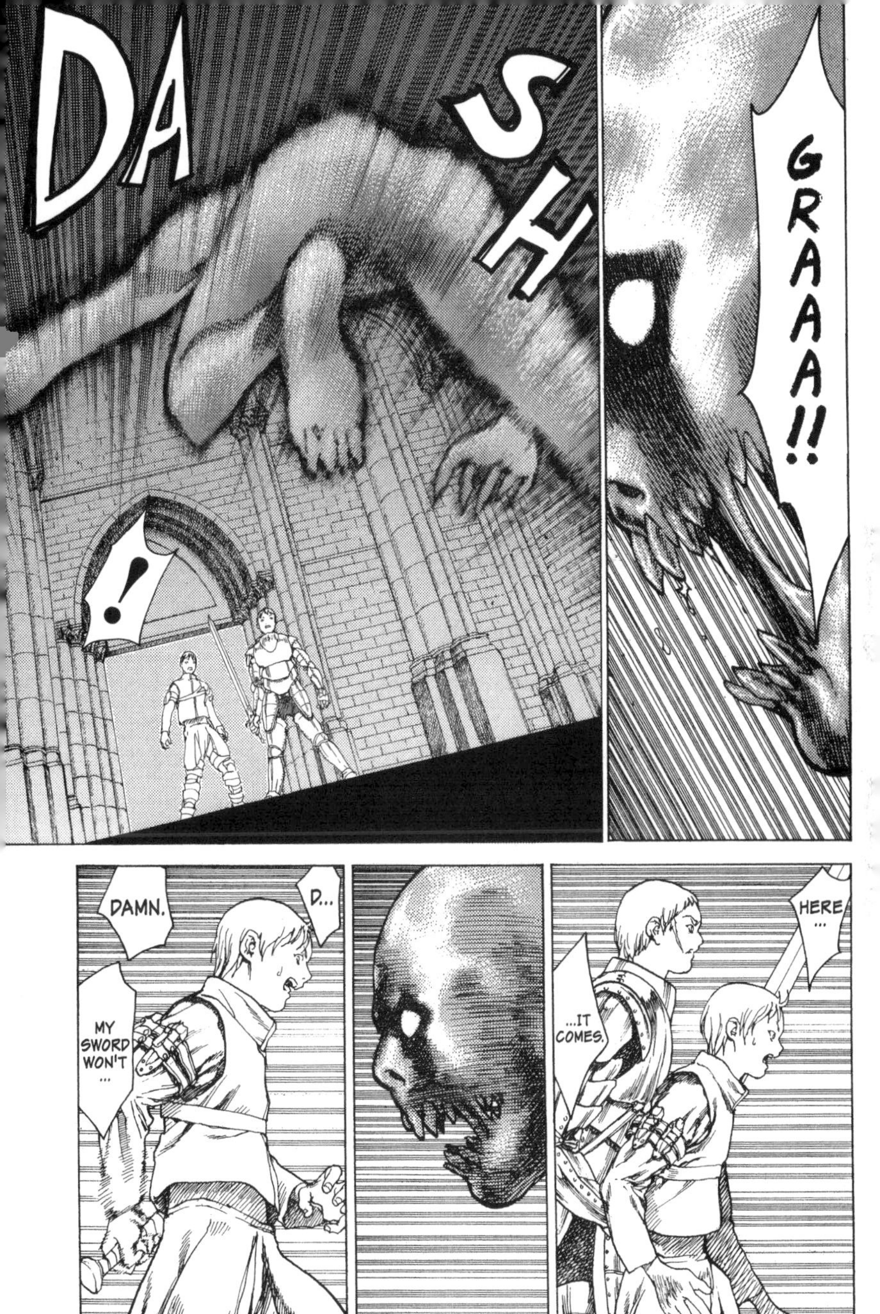
GRAAAA!!
DASH
!
HERE...
...IT COMES.
D...
DAMN.
MY SWORD WON'T ...

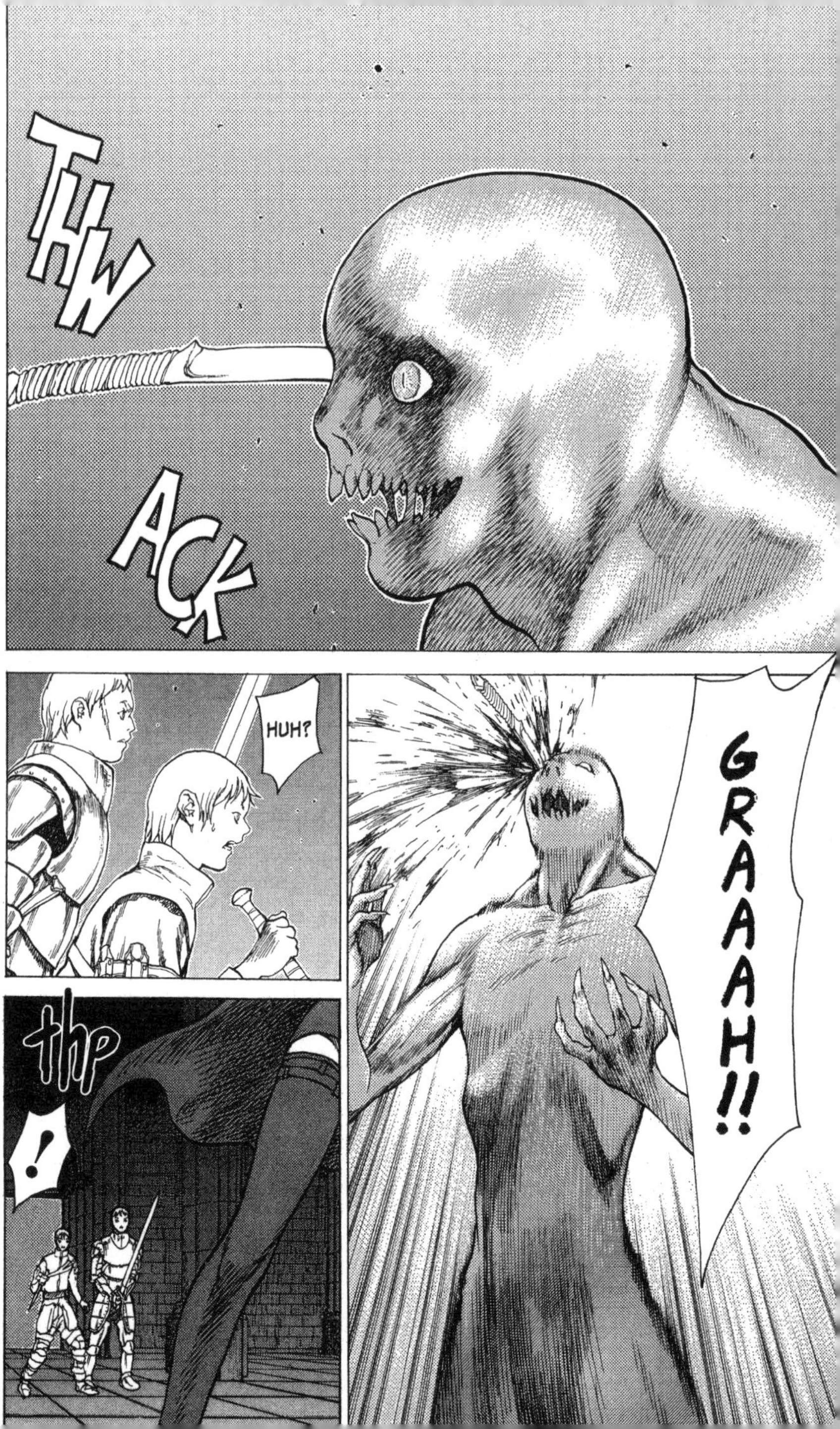
THWACK
GRAAAAH!!
HUH?
thp
!

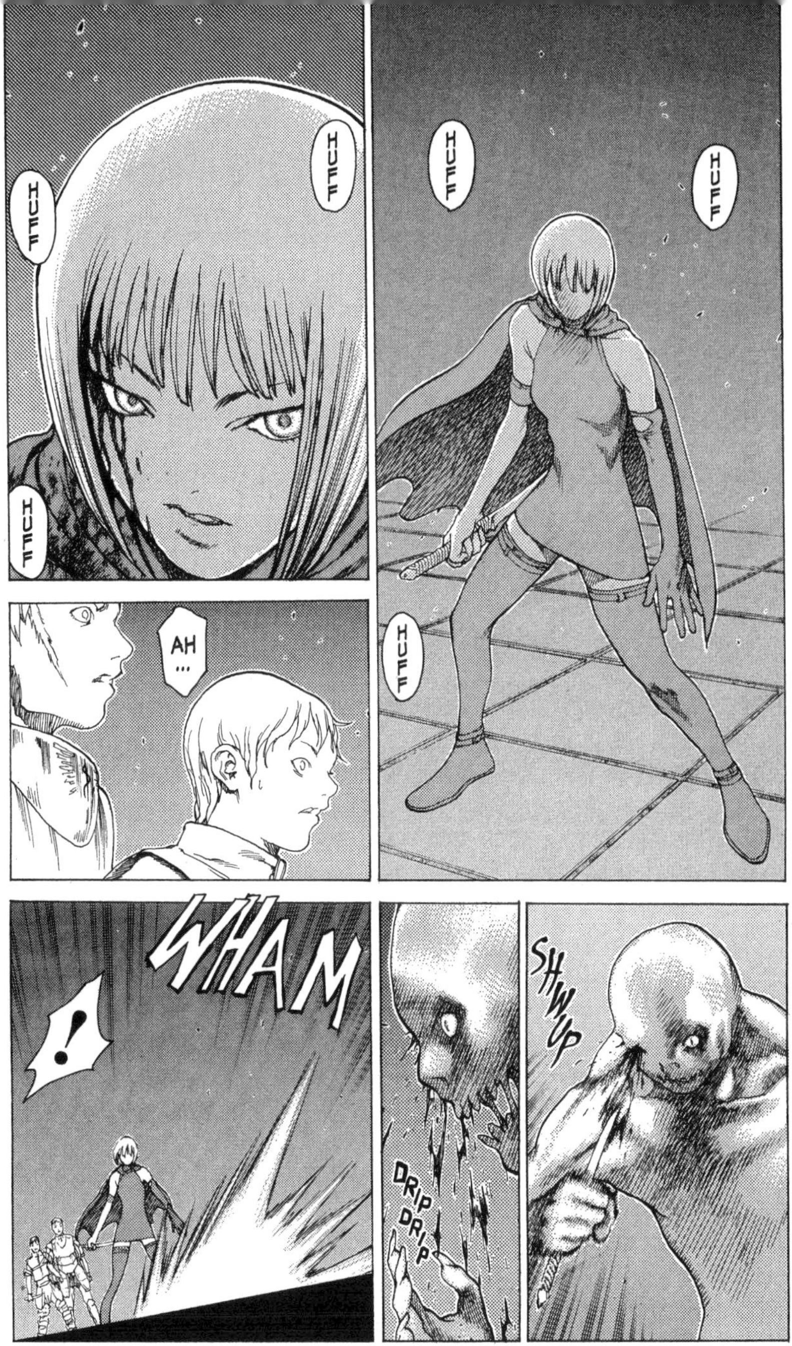
HUFF
HUFF
HUFF
HUFF
HUFF
HUFF
AH ...
SHWUP
DRIP DRIP DRIP
WHAM
!

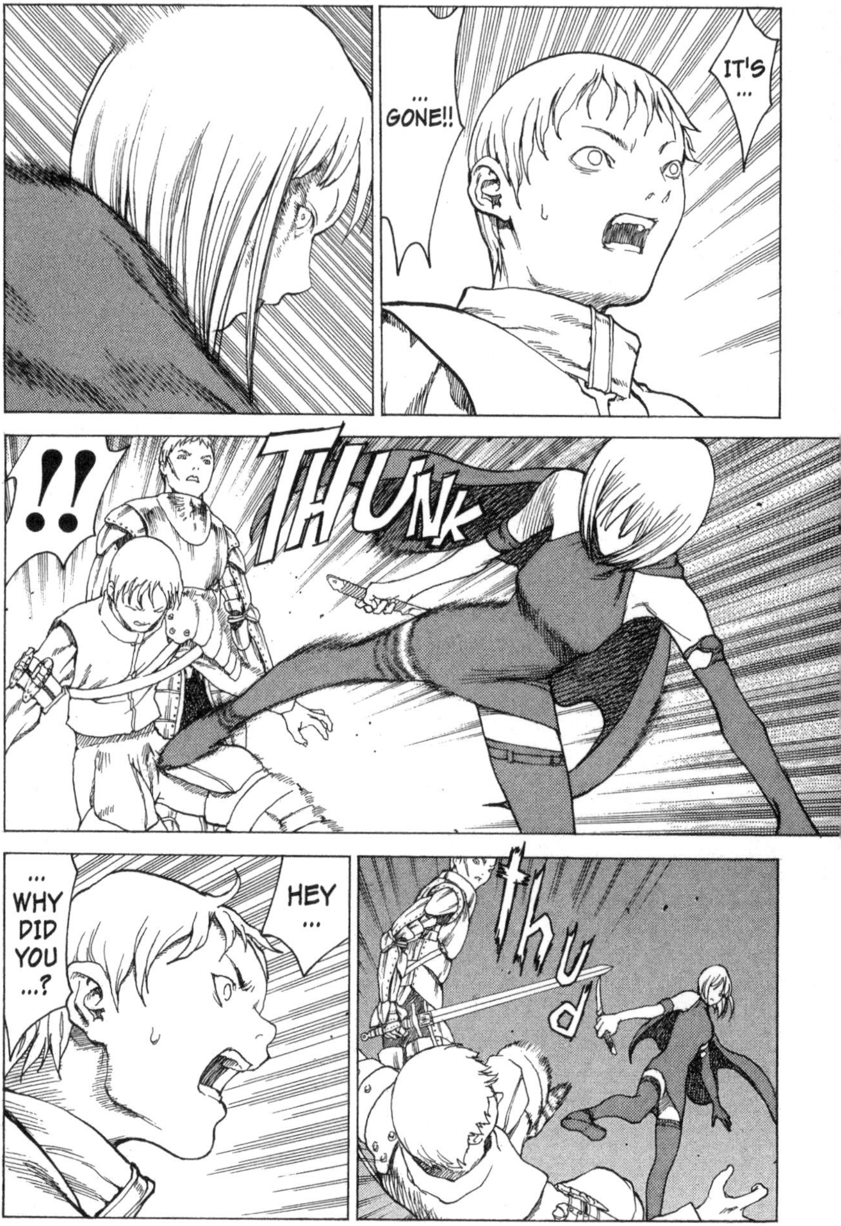
IT'S ...
... GONE!!
!!
THUNK
thud
HEY ...
... WHY DID YOU ...?

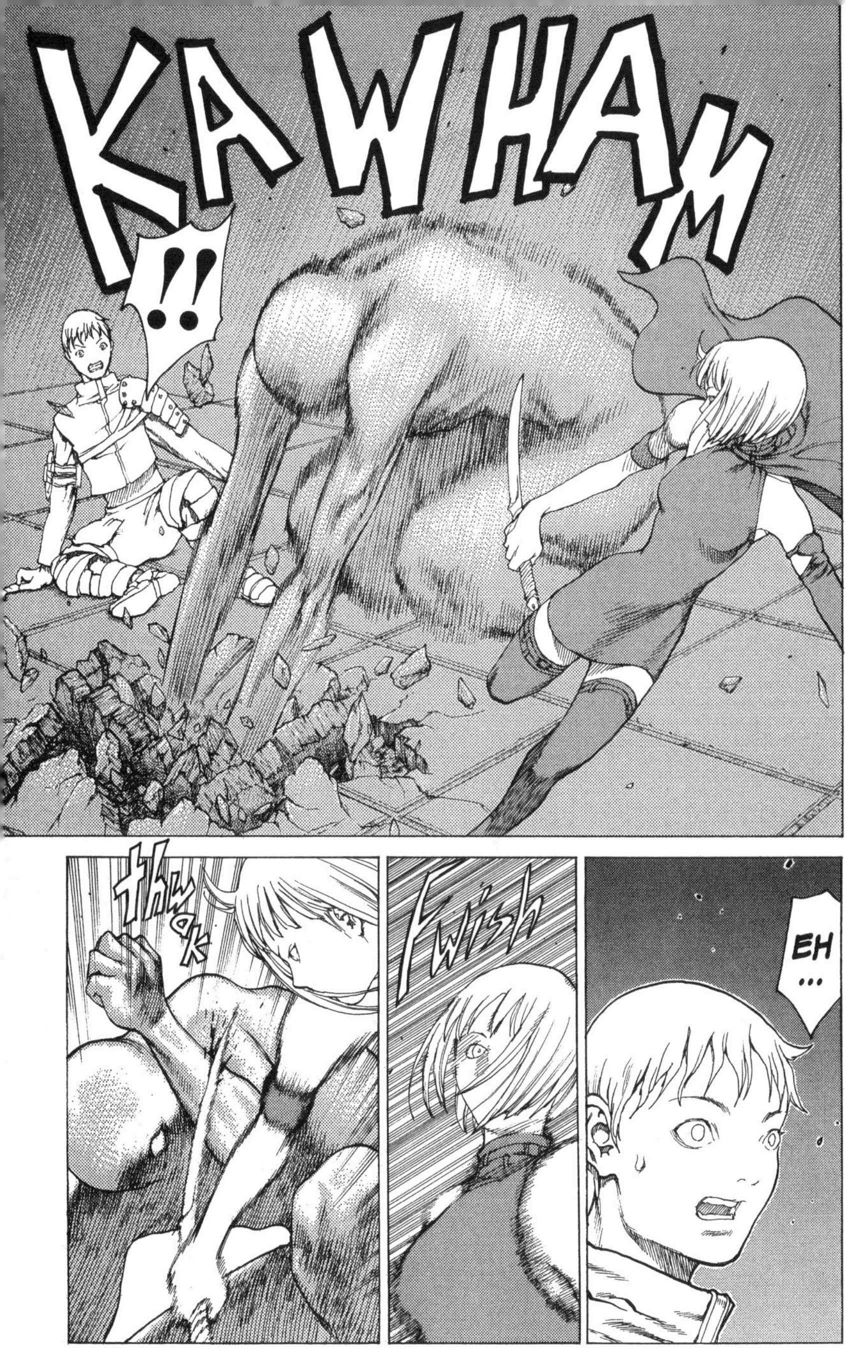
KAWHAM
!!
EH ...
fwish
thwak

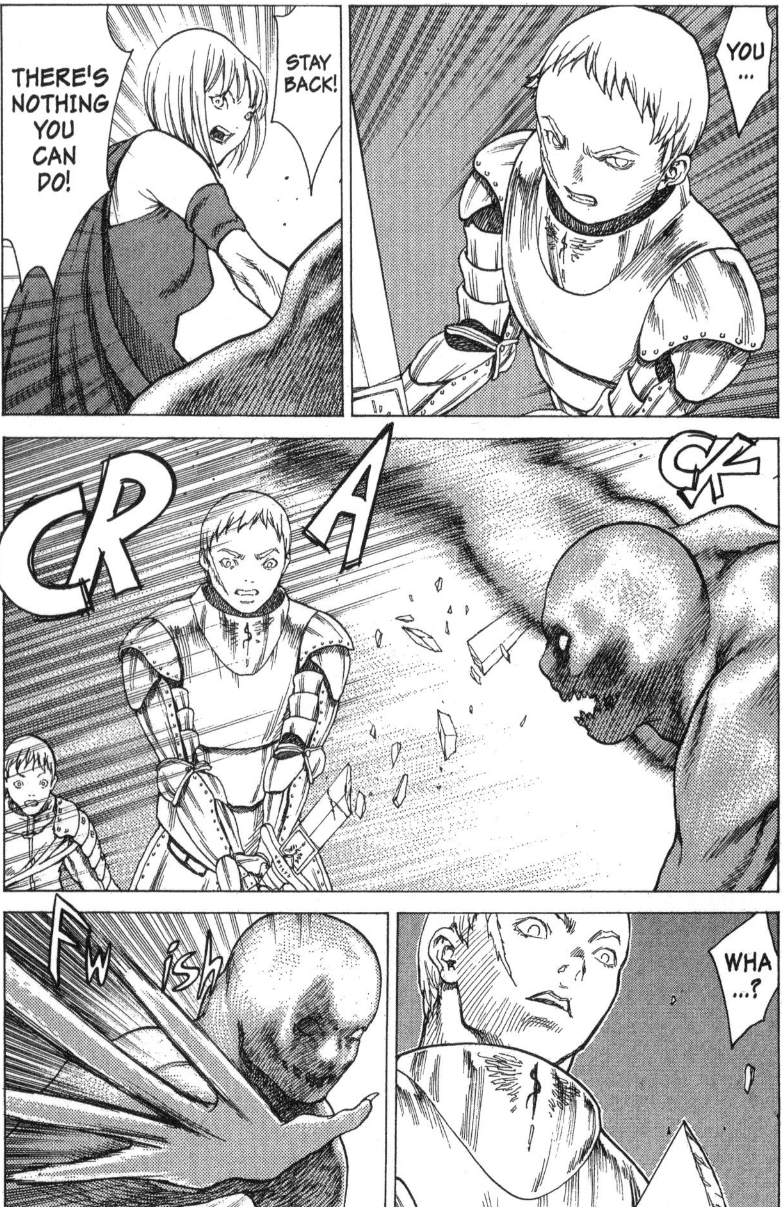
YOU ...
STAY BACK!
THERE'S NOTHING YOU CAN DO!
CR A CK
WHA ...?
Fw ish

READ THIS WAY

FWISH
!!!
THUNK
RUN!
GET OUT OF THE WAY!

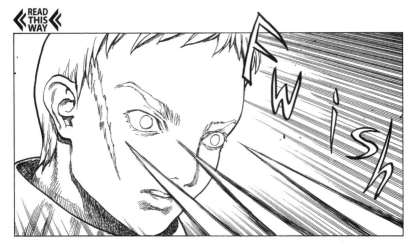

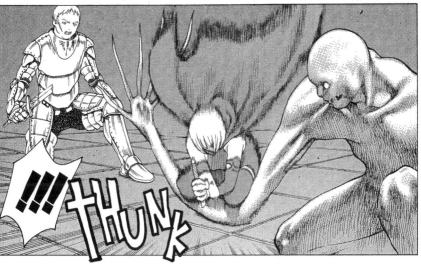

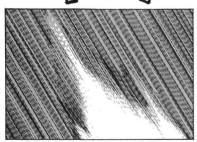

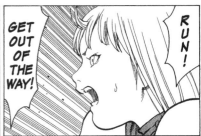

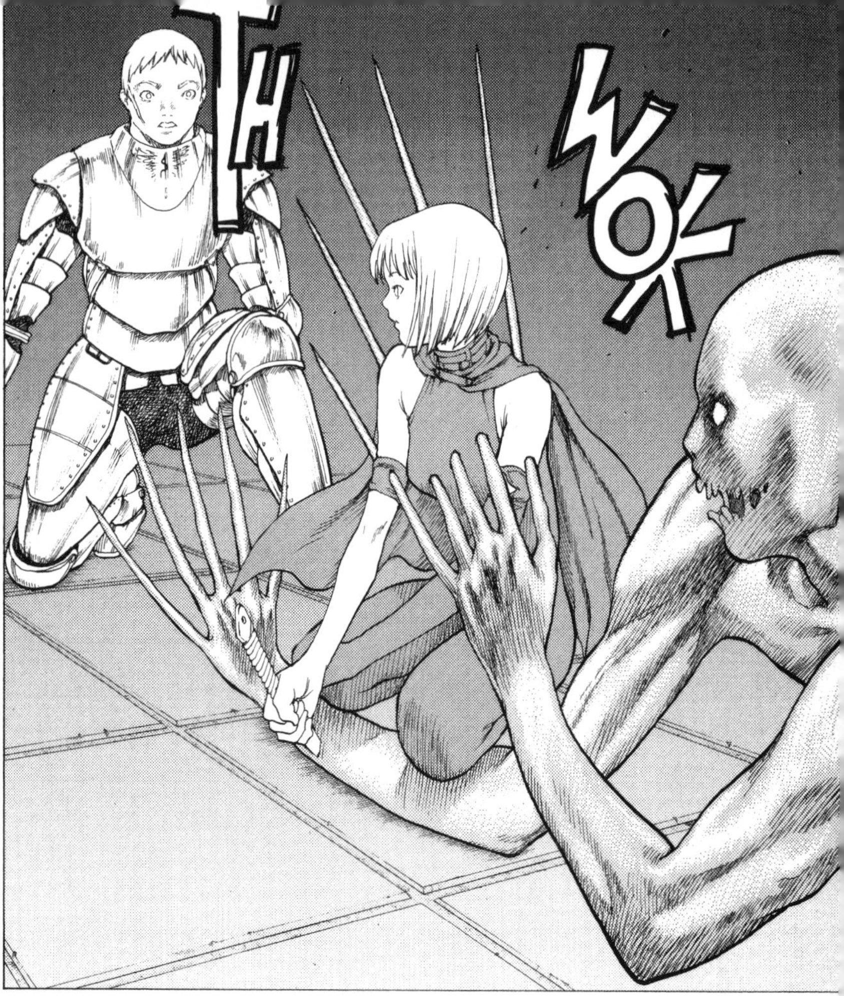
THWOK
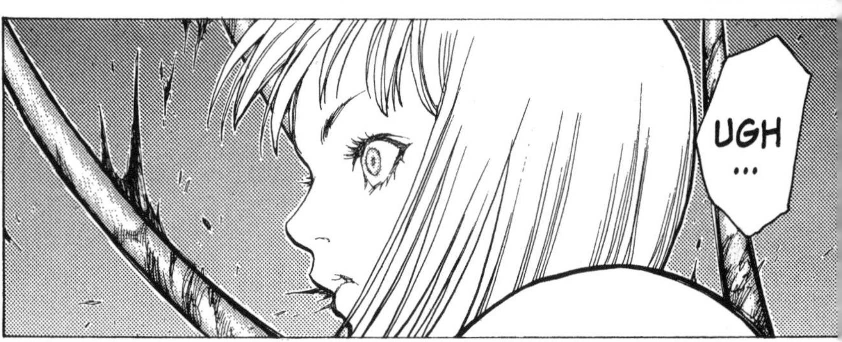
UGH ...

READ THIS WAY

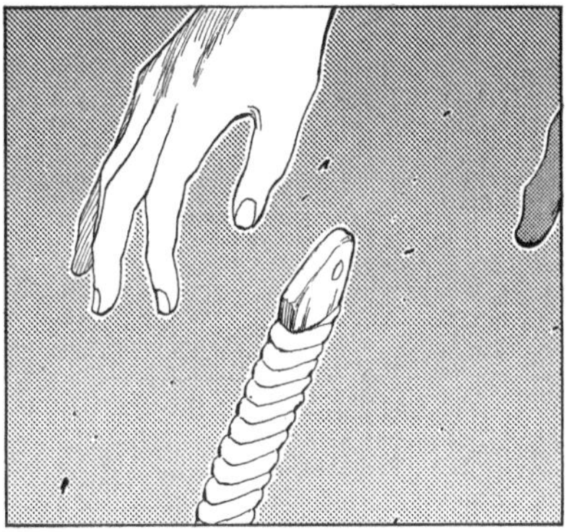

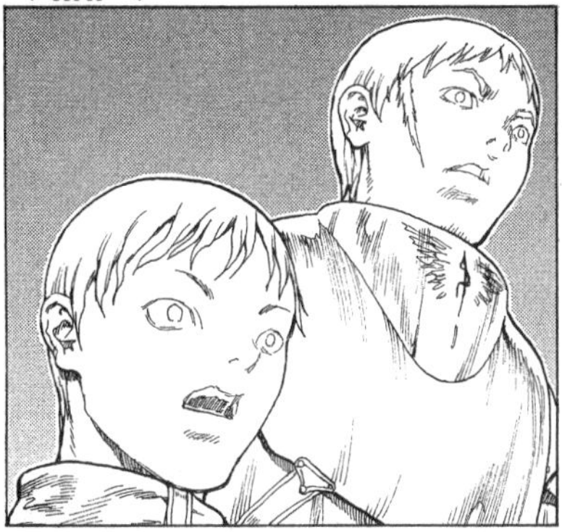

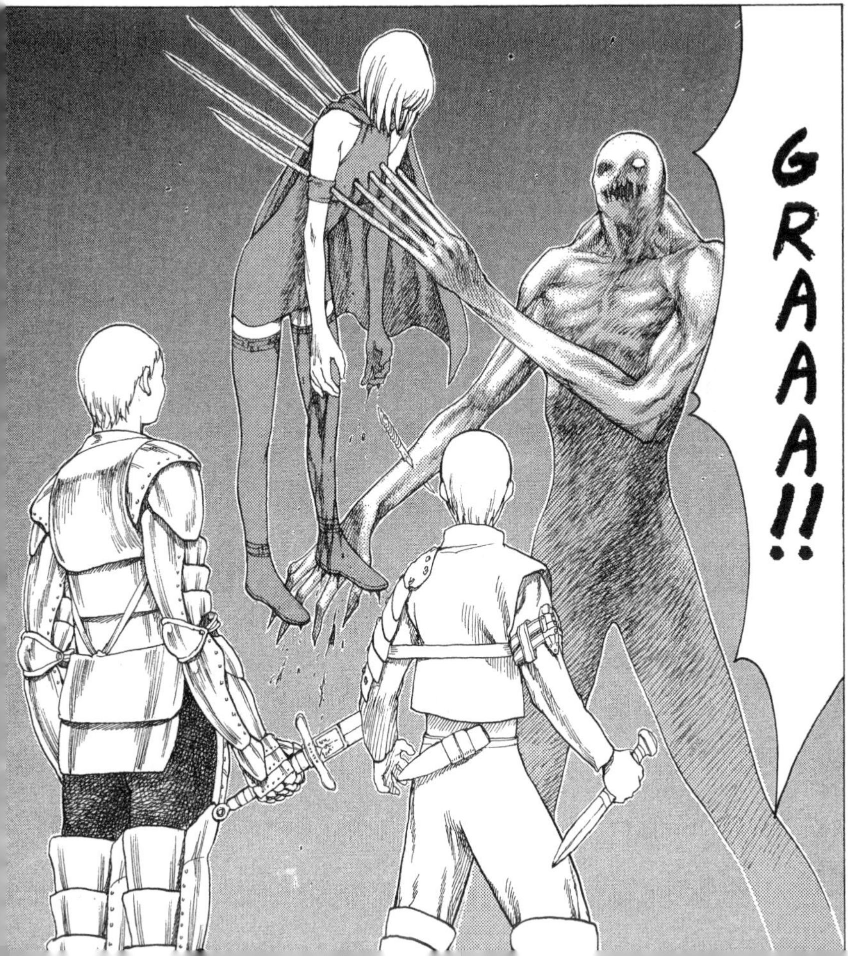
GRAAAA!!

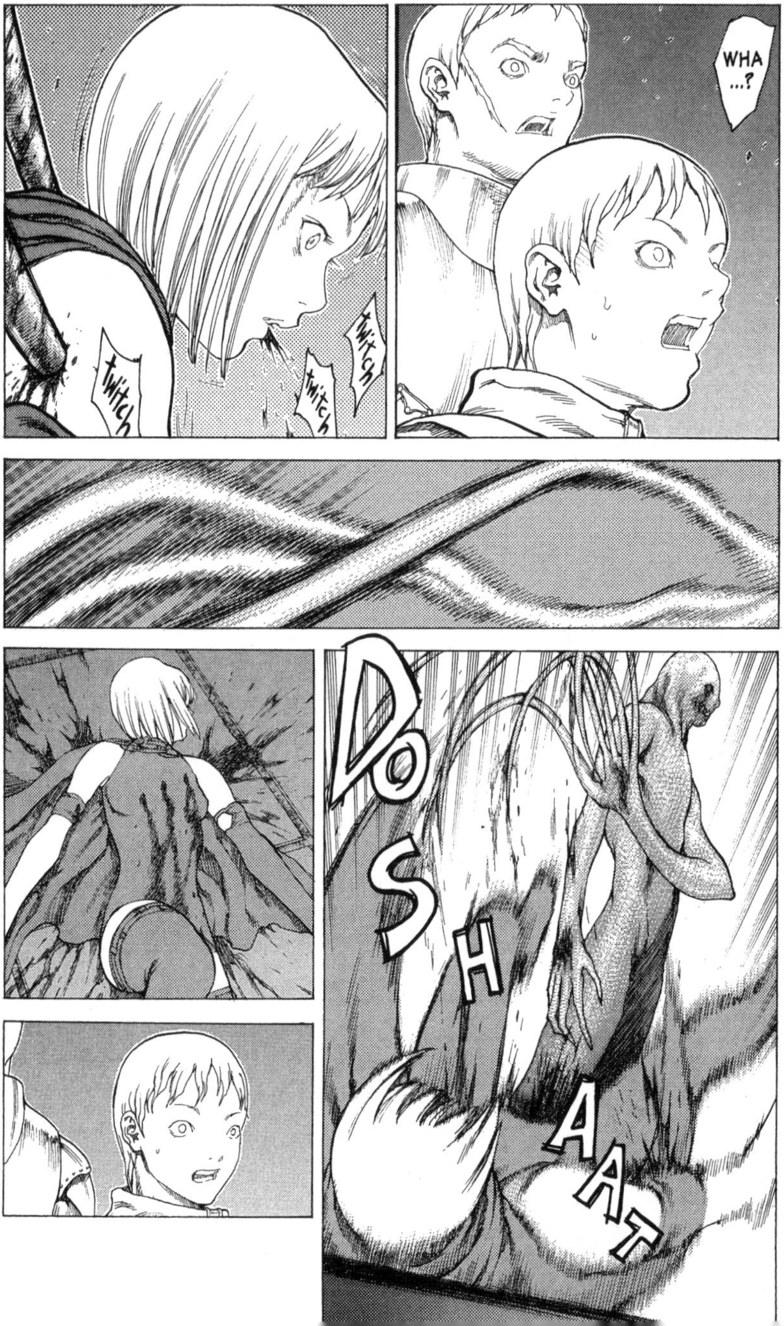
WHA ...?
twitch
twitch
twitch
DOSHAAT

READ THIS WAY

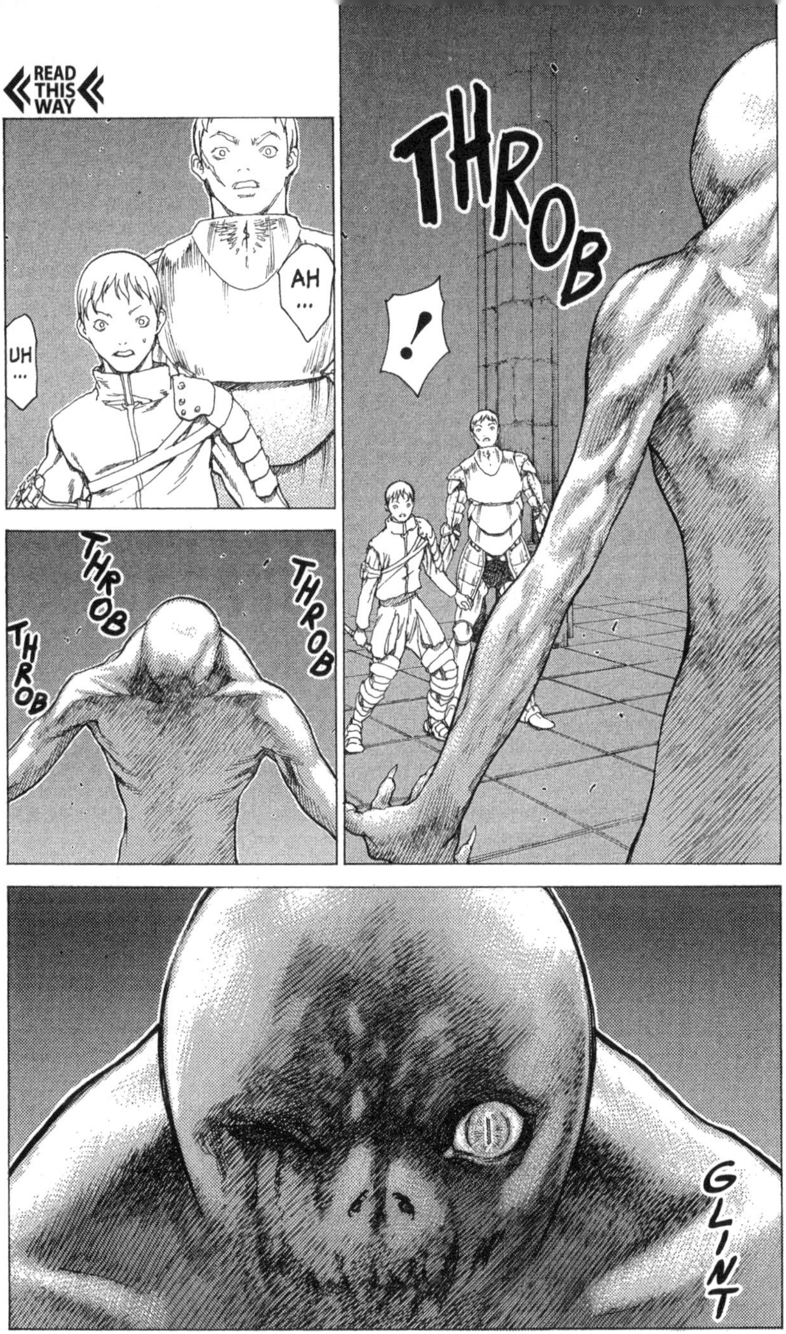
THROB
!
AH ...
UH ...
THROB
THROB
THROB
GLINT

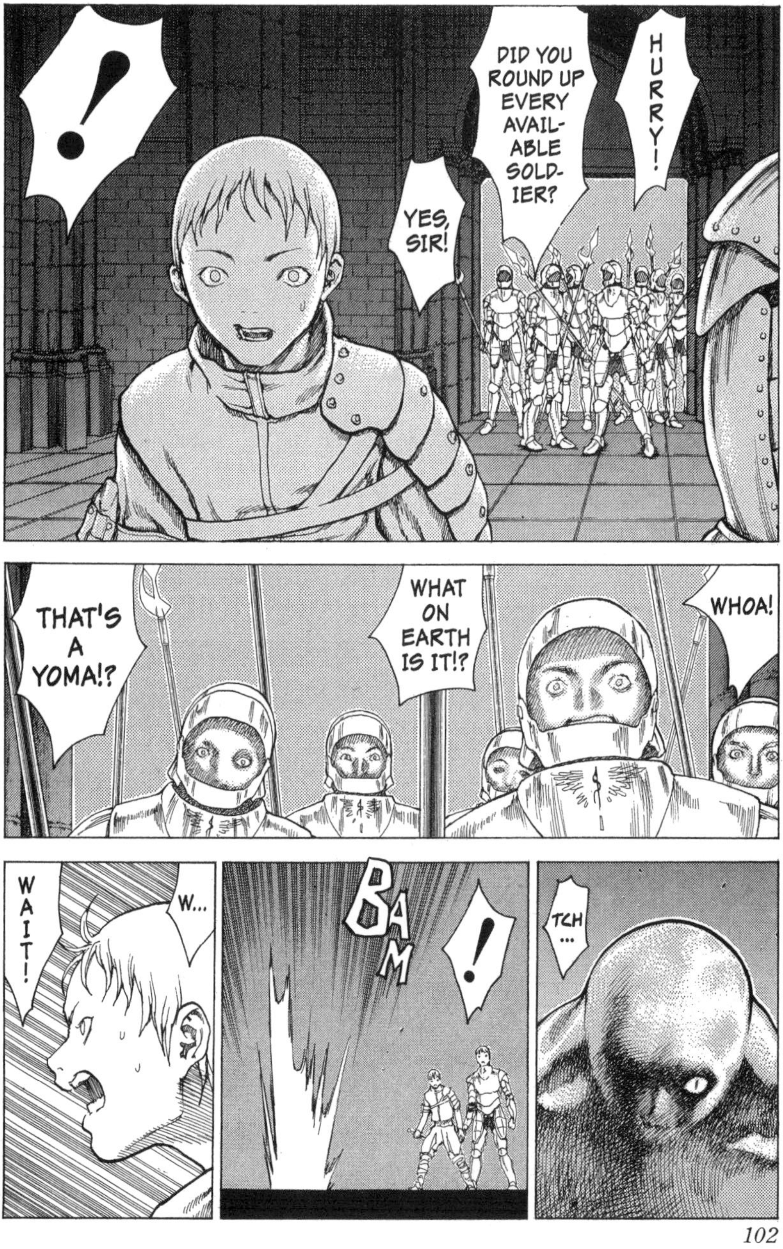
HURRY!
DID YOU ROUND UP EVERY AVAIL-ABLE SOLD-IER?
YES, SIR!
!
WHOA!
WHAT ON EARTH IS IT!?
THAT'S A YOMA!?
TCH ...
!
BAM
W...
WAIT!

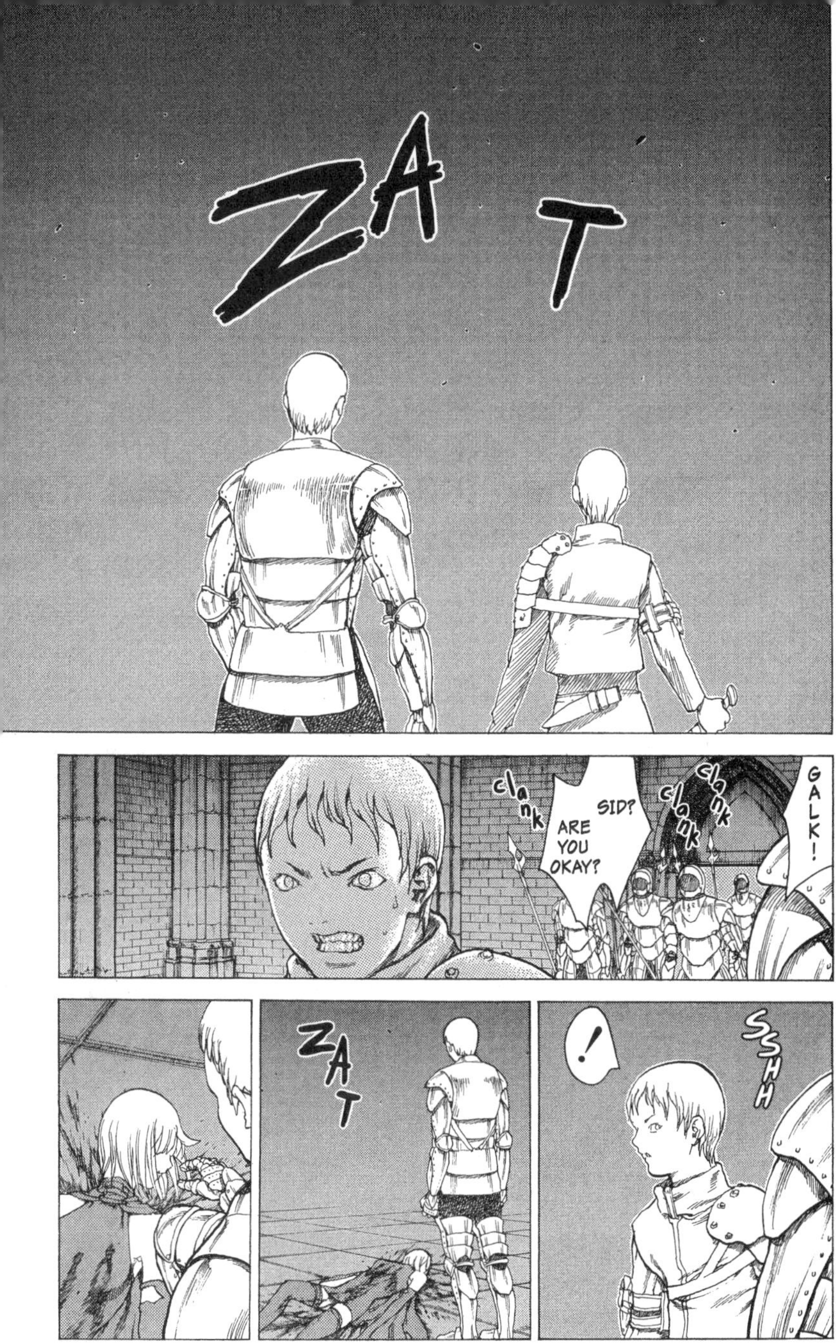
ZAT
GALK!
clank
clank
SID? ARE YOU OKAY?
clank
SSHH
!
ZAT

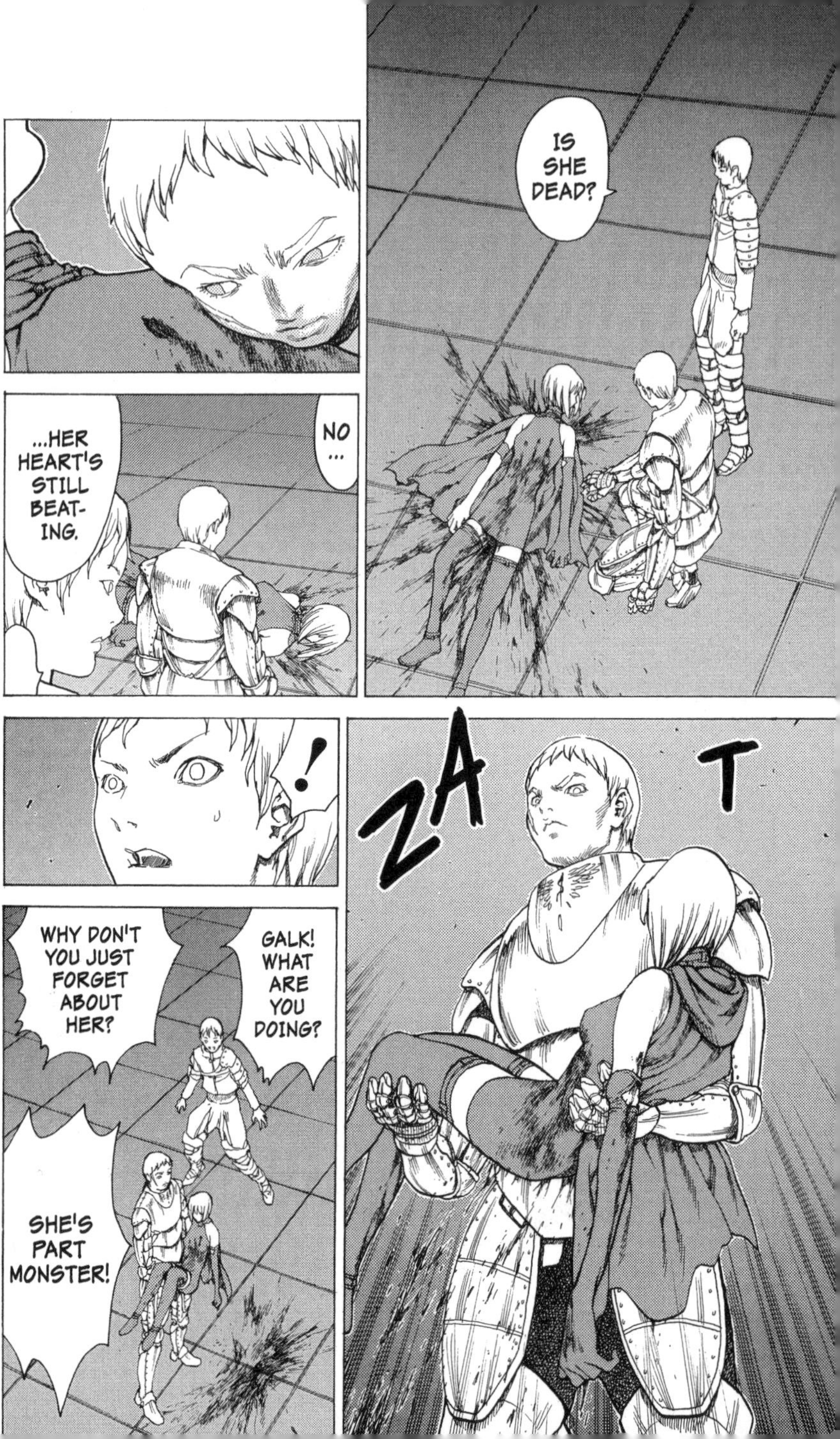
IS SHE DEAD?
NO ...
...HER HEART'S STILL BEAT-ING.
ZAT
!
GALK! WHAT ARE YOU DOING?
WHY DON'T YOU JUST FORGET ABOUT HER?
SHE'S PART MONSTER!

I OWE HER...

SHE SAVED MY LIFE.

...EVEN IF SHE IS PART MONSTER.

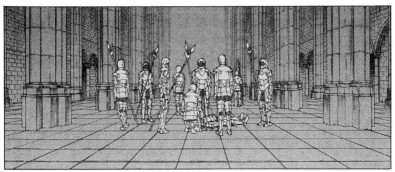

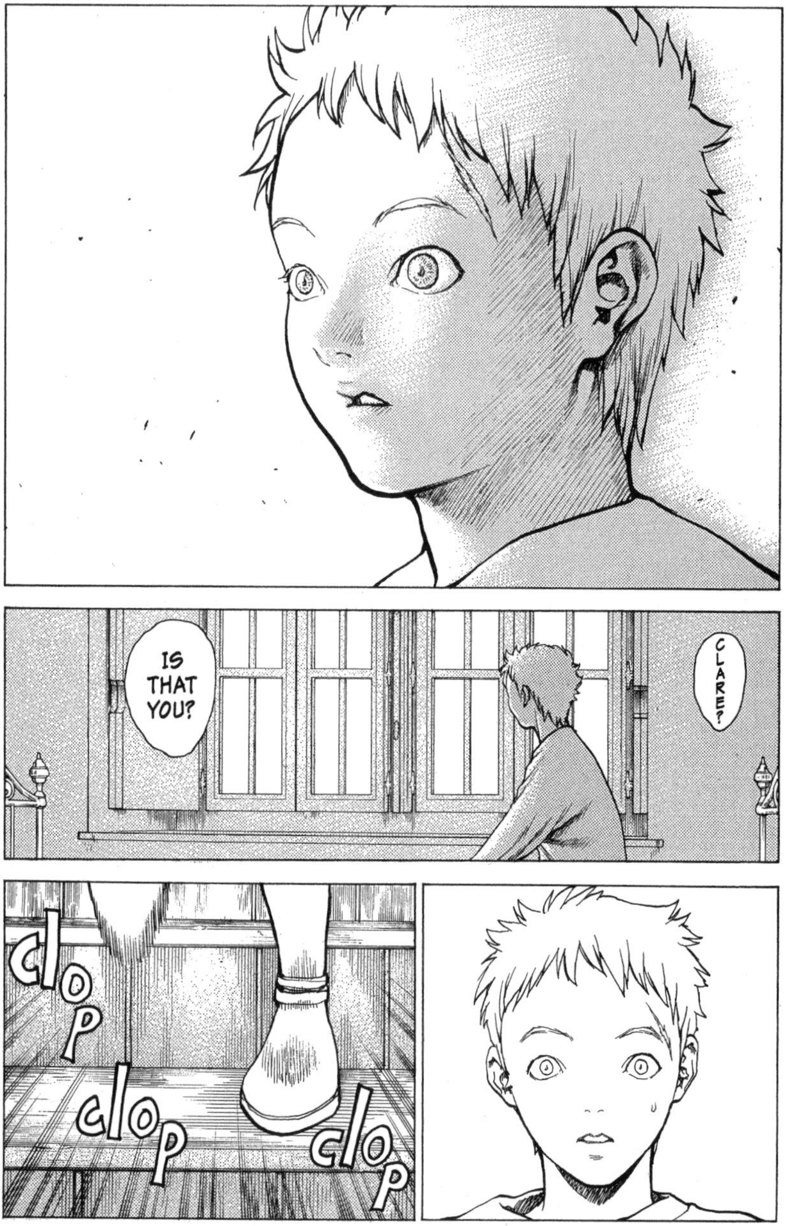
CLARE?
IS THAT YOU?
clop
clop
clop

READ THIS WAY

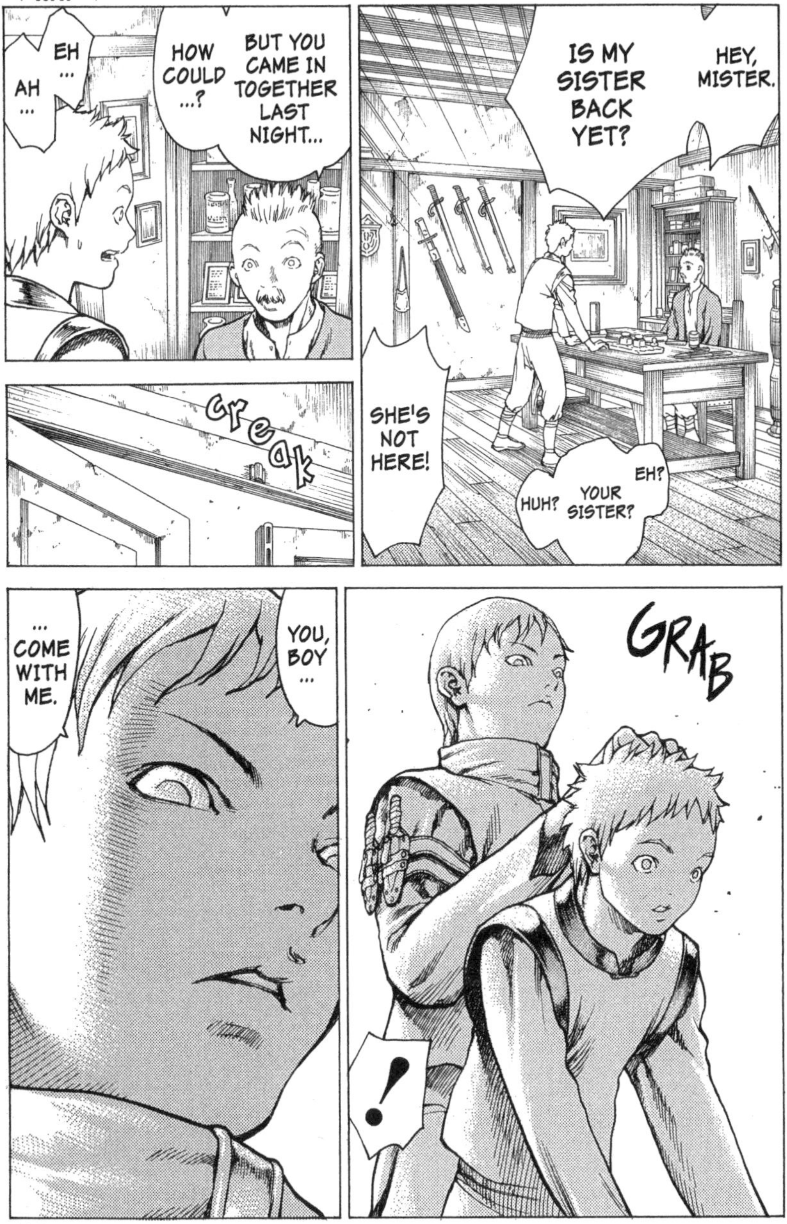
HEY, MISTER.
IS MY SISTER BACK YET?
EH?
YOUR SISTER?
HUH?
SHE'S NOT HERE!
BUT YOU CAME IN TOGETHER LAST NIGHT...
HOW COULD ...?
EH ...
AH ...
creak
GRAB
!
YOU, BOY ...
... COME WITH ME.

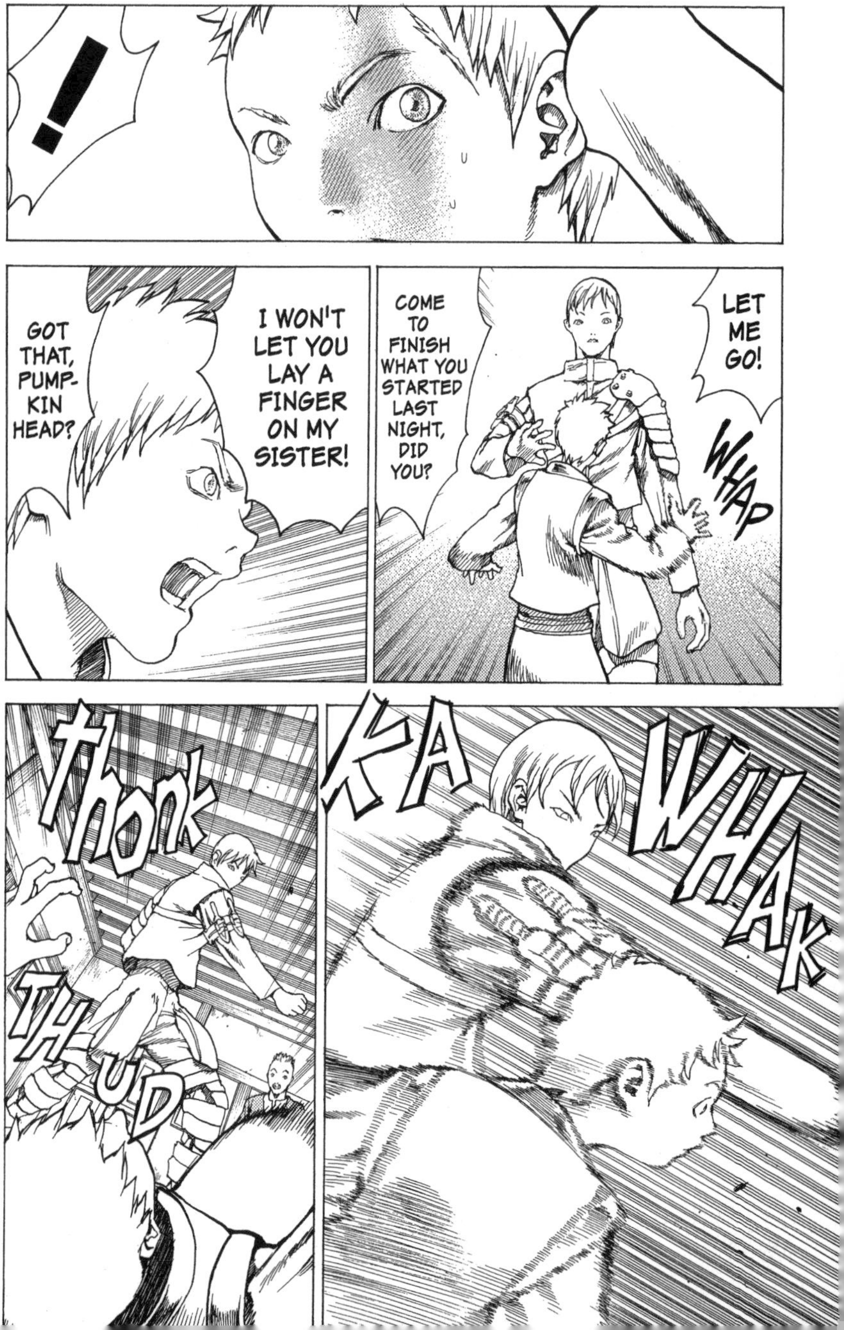
!
LET ME GO!
WHAP
COME TO FINISH WHAT YOU STARTED LAST NIGHT, DID YOU?
I WON'T LET YOU LAY A FINGER ON MY SISTER!
GOT THAT, PUMP-KIN HEAD?
KA WHAK
thonk
THUD

READ THIS WAY

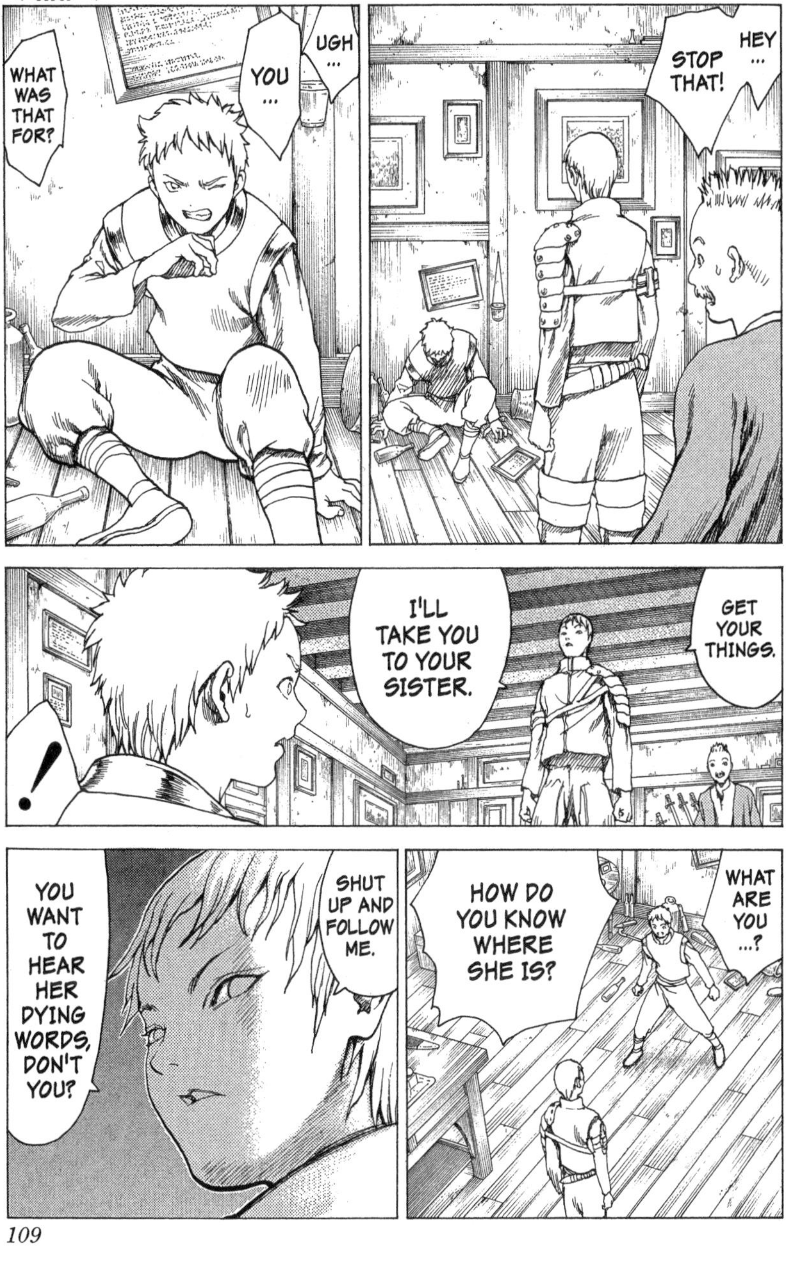

HEY ...
STOP THAT!
UGH ...
YOU ...
WHAT WAS THAT FOR?
GET YOUR THINGS.
I'LL TAKE YOU TO YOUR SISTER.
!
WHAT ARE YOU ...?
HOW DO YOU KNOW WHERE SHE IS?
SHUT UP AND FOLLOW ME.
YOU WANT TO HEAR HER DYING WORDS, DON'T YOU?

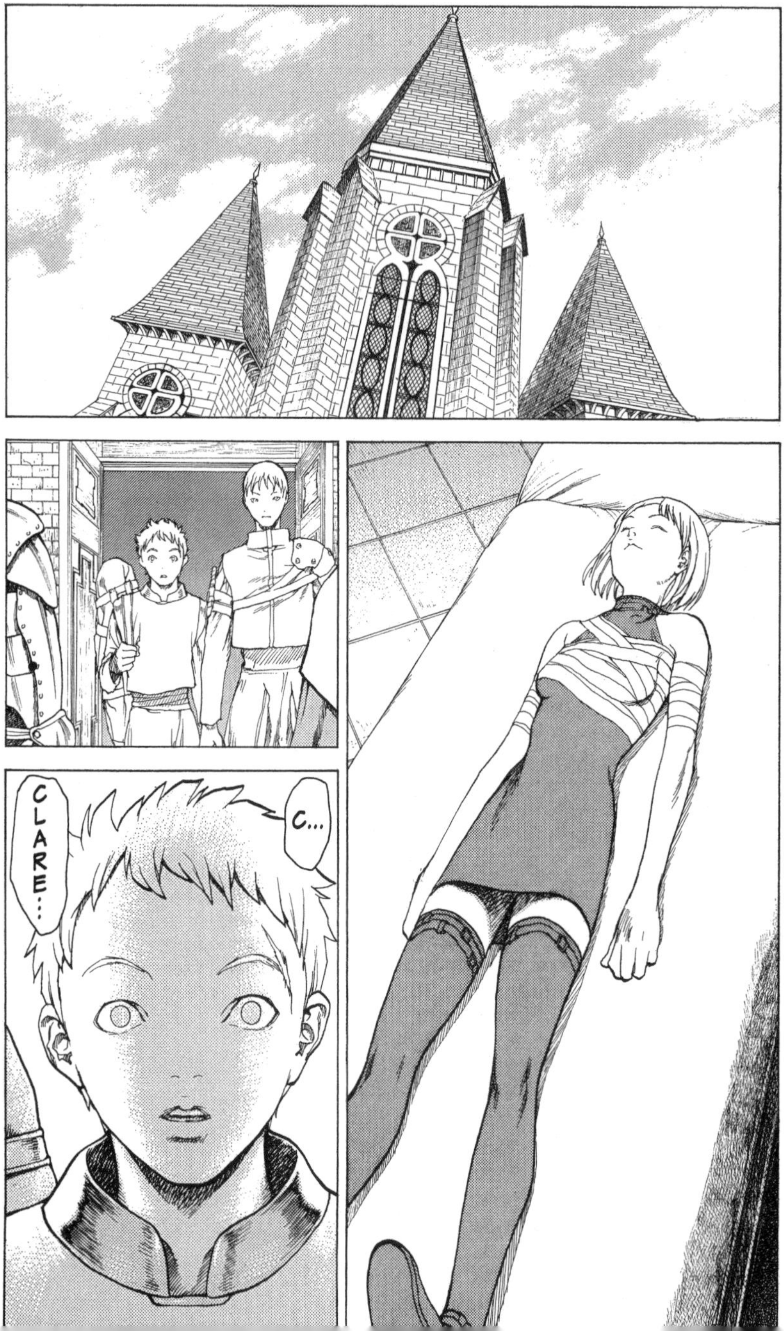
C...
CLARE...

READ THIS WAY

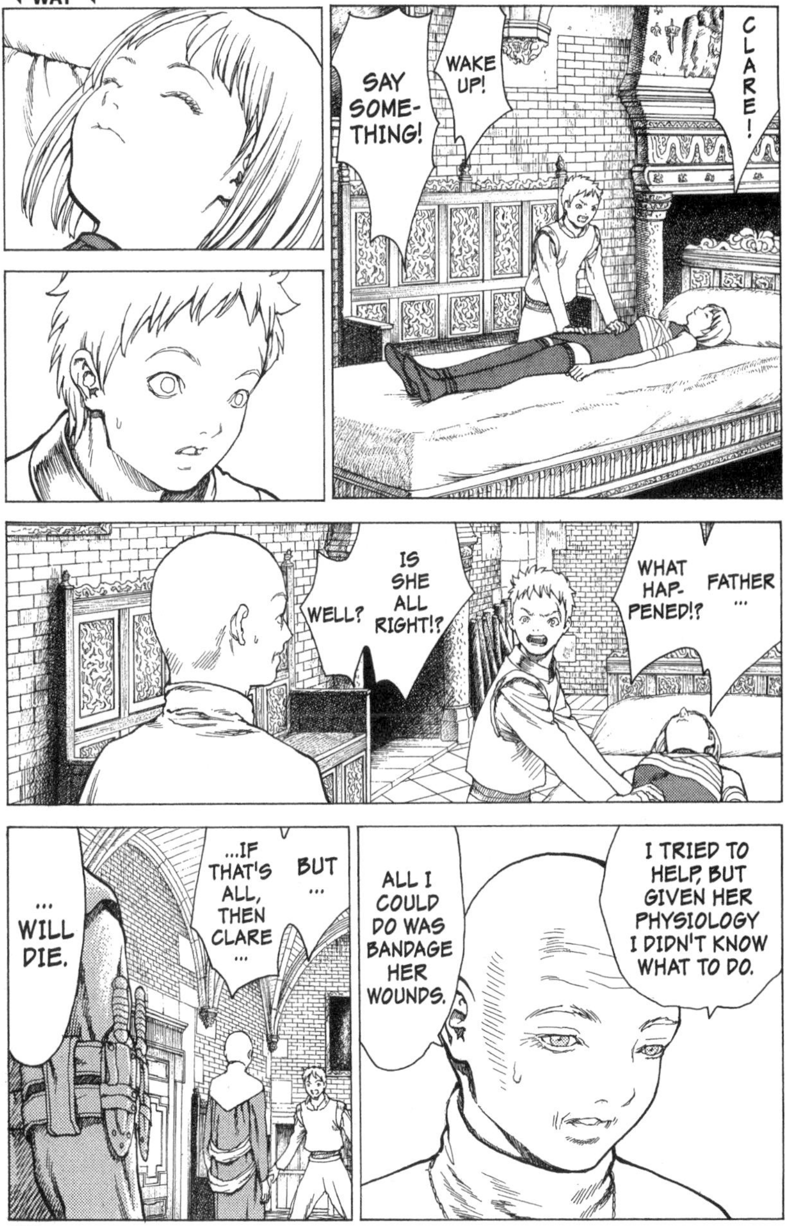

CLARE!
WAKE UP!
SAY SOMETHING!
FATHER...
WHAT HAPPENED!?
IS SHE ALL RIGHT!?
WELL?
I TRIED TO HELP, BUT GIVEN HER PHYSIOLOGY I DIDN'T KNOW WHAT TO DO.
ALL I COULD DO WAS BANDAGE HER WOUNDS.
BUT...
...IF THAT'S ALL, THEN CLARE...
...WILL DIE.

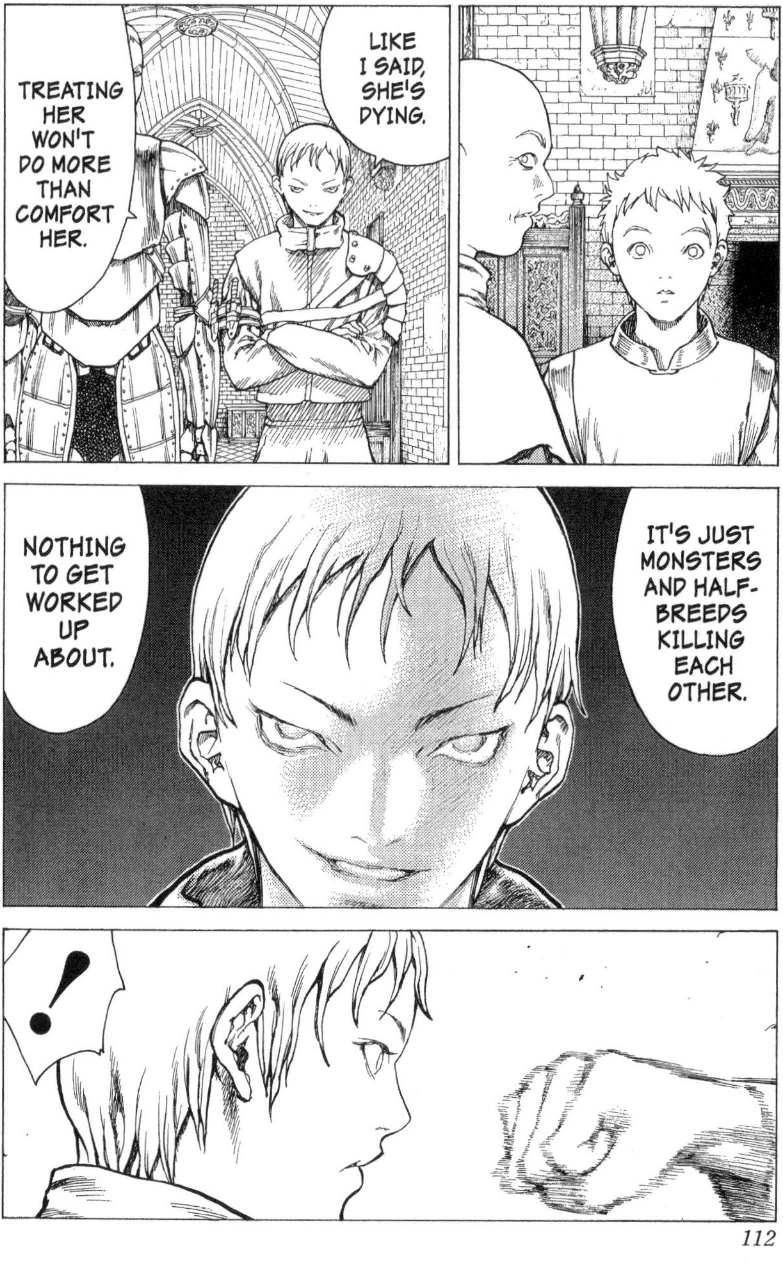
LIKE I SAID, SHE'S DYING.
TREATING HER WON'T DO MORE THAN COMFORT HER.
IT'S JUST MONSTERS AND HALF-BREEDS KILLING EACH OTHER.
NOTHING TO GET WORKED UP ABOUT.
!

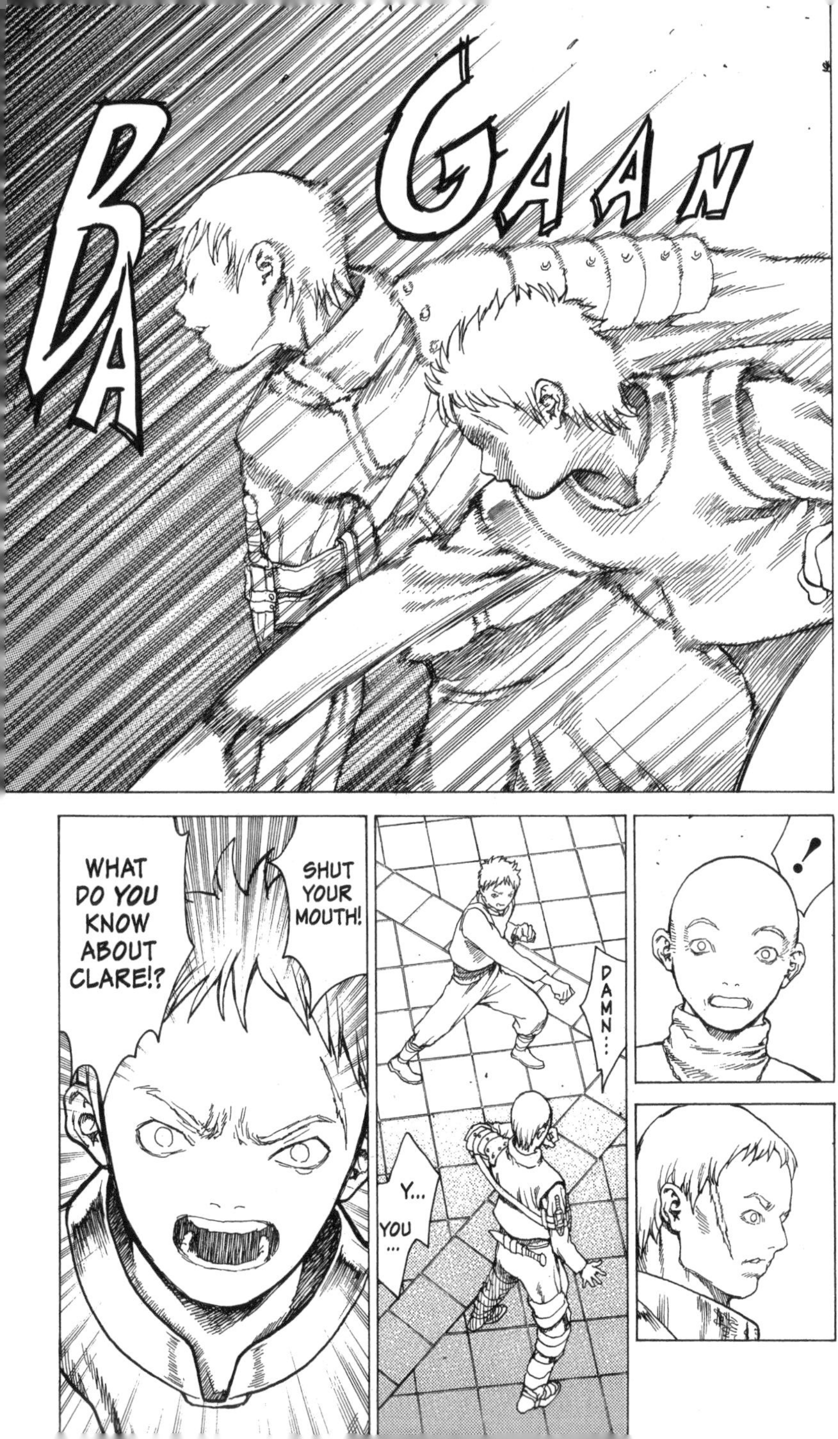
BA
GAAN
!
DAMN...
Y...
YOU...
SHUT YOUR MOUTH!
WHAT DO YOU KNOW ABOUT CLARE!?

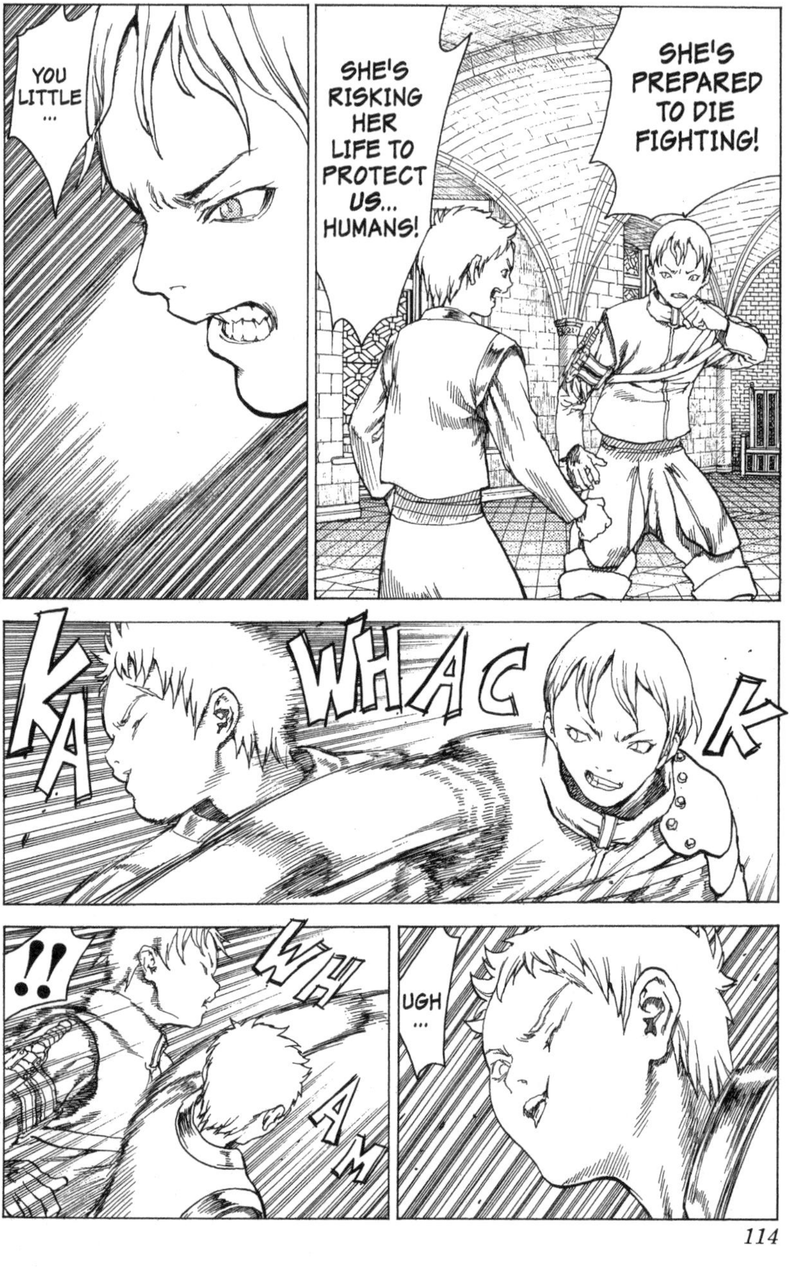
SHE'S PREPARED TO DIE FIGHTING!
SHE'S RISKING HER LIFE TO PROTECT US... HUMANS!
YOU LITTLE ...
KA WHACK
UGH ...
!!
WHAM

READ THIS WAY

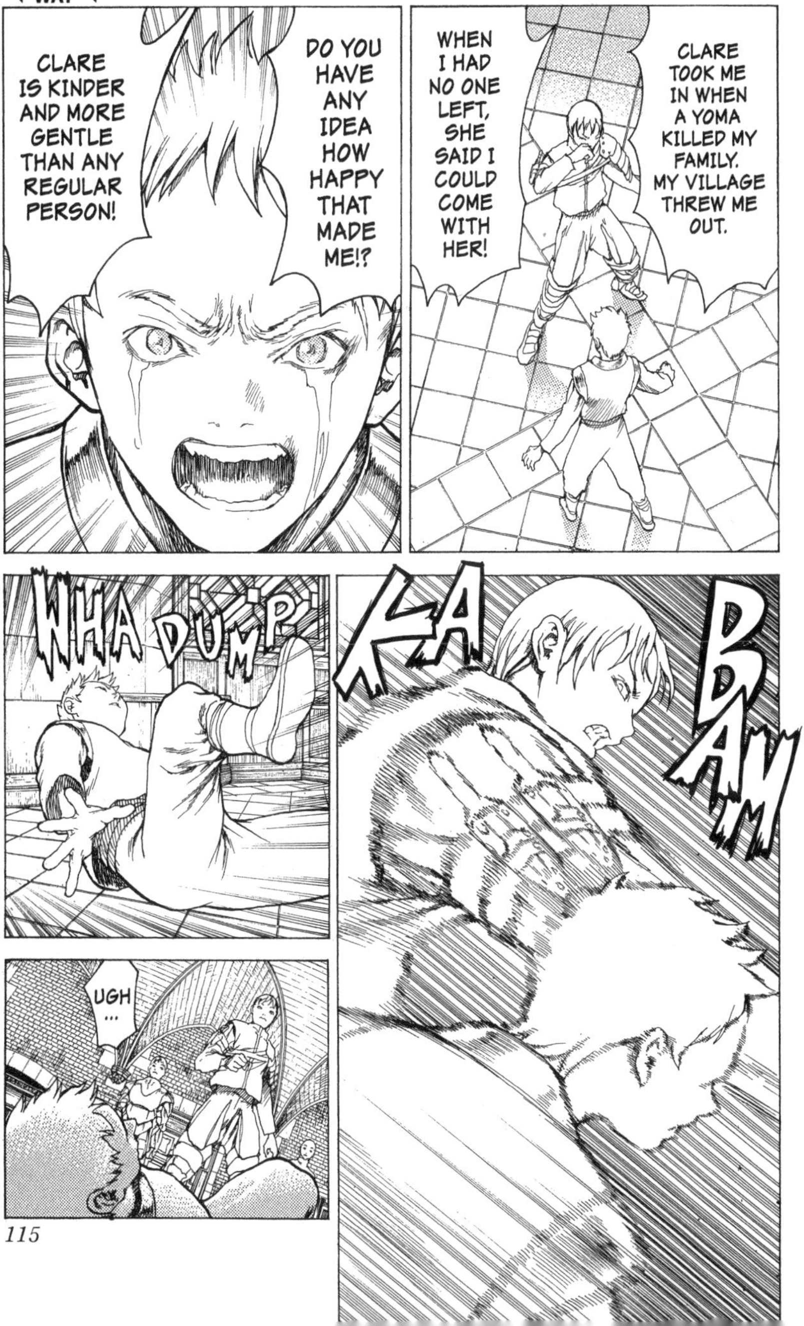
CLARE TOOK ME IN WHEN A YOMA KILLED MY FAMILY. MY VILLAGE THREW ME OUT.
WHEN I HAD NO ONE LEFT, SHE SAID I COULD COME WITH HER!
DO YOU HAVE ANY IDEA HOW HAPPY THAT MADE ME!?
CLARE IS KINDER AND MORE GENTLE THAN ANY REGULAR PERSON!
KA BAM
WHA DUMP
UGH ...

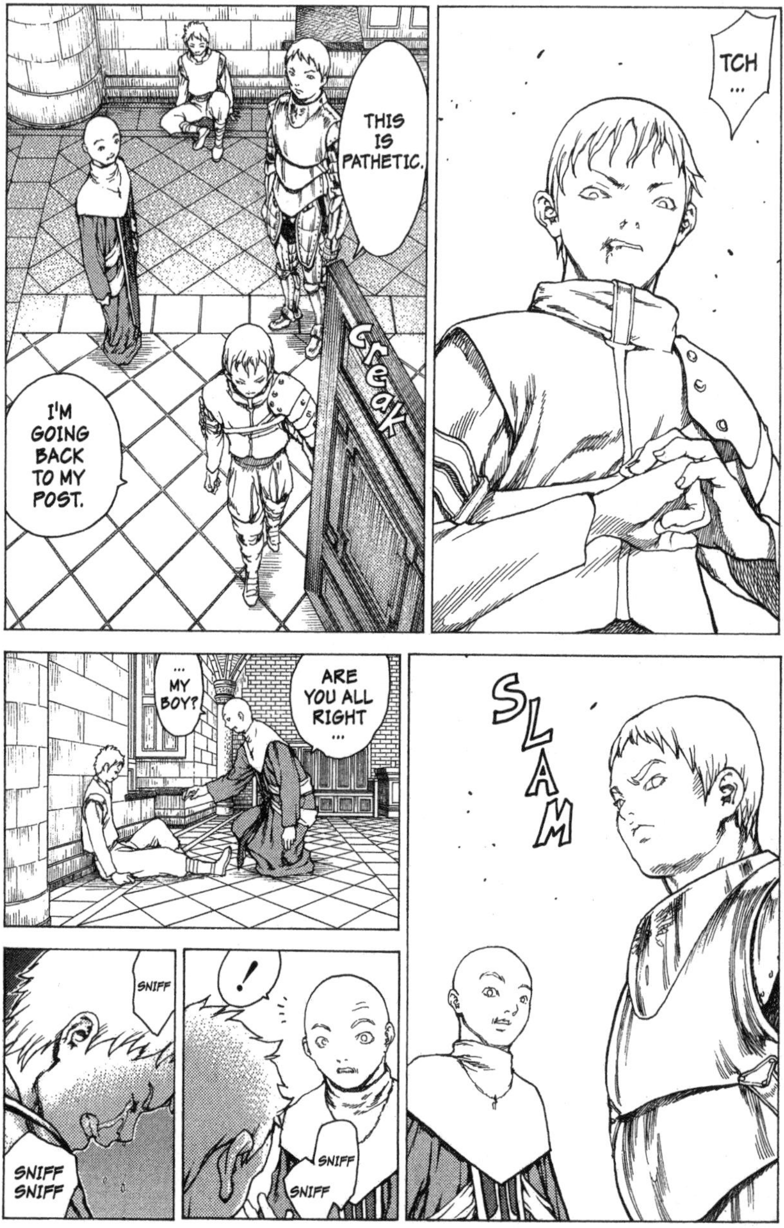
TCH ...
THIS IS PATHETIC.
creak
I'M GOING BACK TO MY POST.
SLAM
ARE YOU ALL RIGHT ...
... MY BOY?
!
SNIFF
SNIFF
SNIFF
SNIFF SNIFF

READ THIS WAY

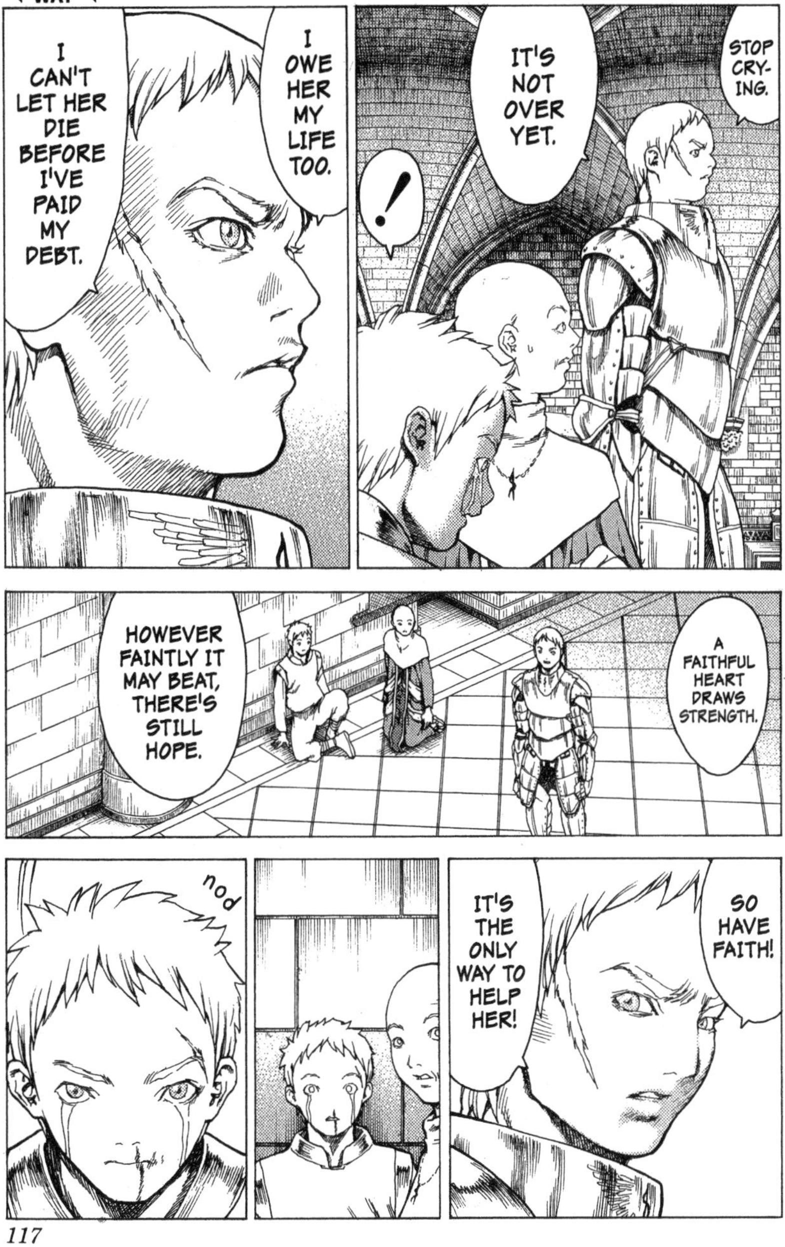
STOP CRY-ING.
IT'S NOT OVER YET.
!
I OWE HER MY LIFE TOO.
I CAN'T LET HER DIE BEFORE I'VE PAID MY DEBT.
A FAITHFUL HEART DRAWS STRENGTH.
HOWEVER FAINTLY IT MAY BEAT, THERE'S STILL HOPE.
SO HAVE FAITH!
IT'S THE ONLY WAY TO HELP HER!
nod

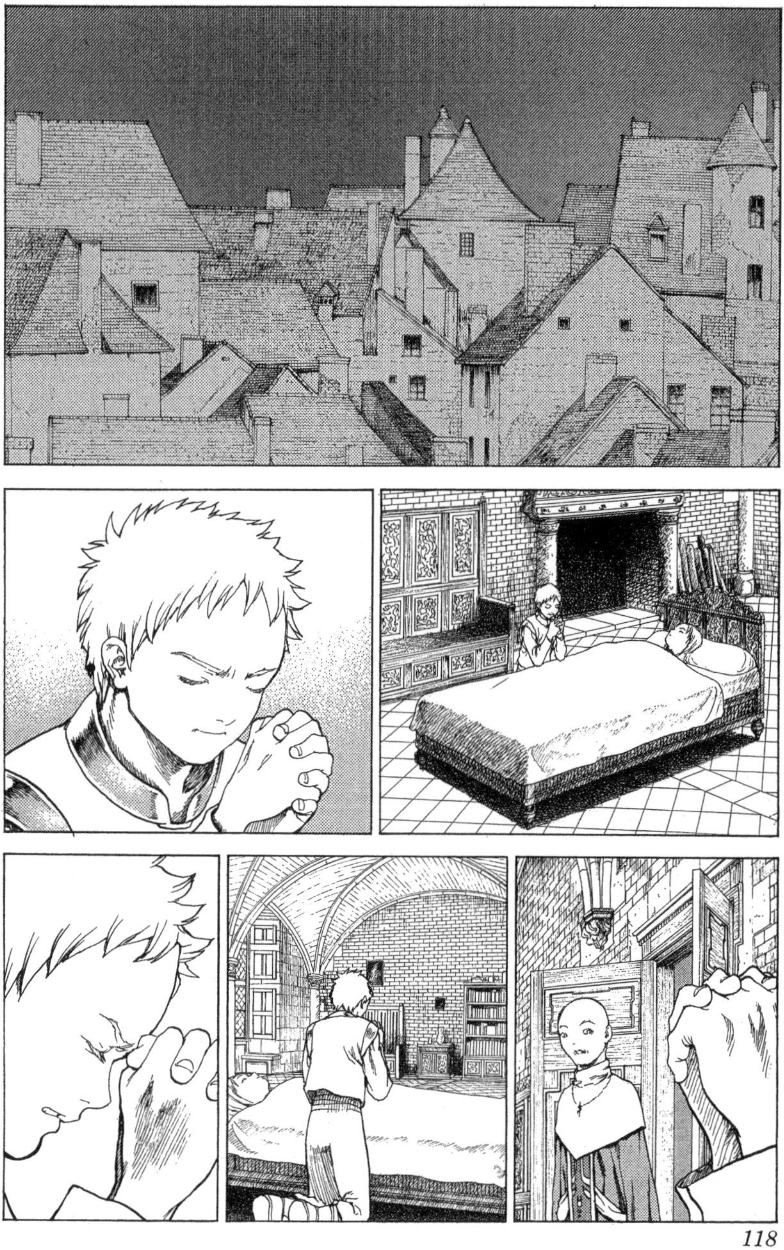

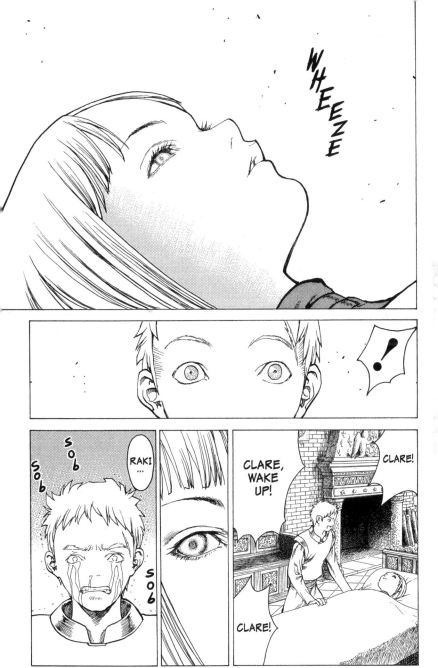

WHEEZE

!

SOB
SOB
SOB

RAKI
...

SOB

CLARE,
WAKE
UP!

CLARE!

CLARE!

119

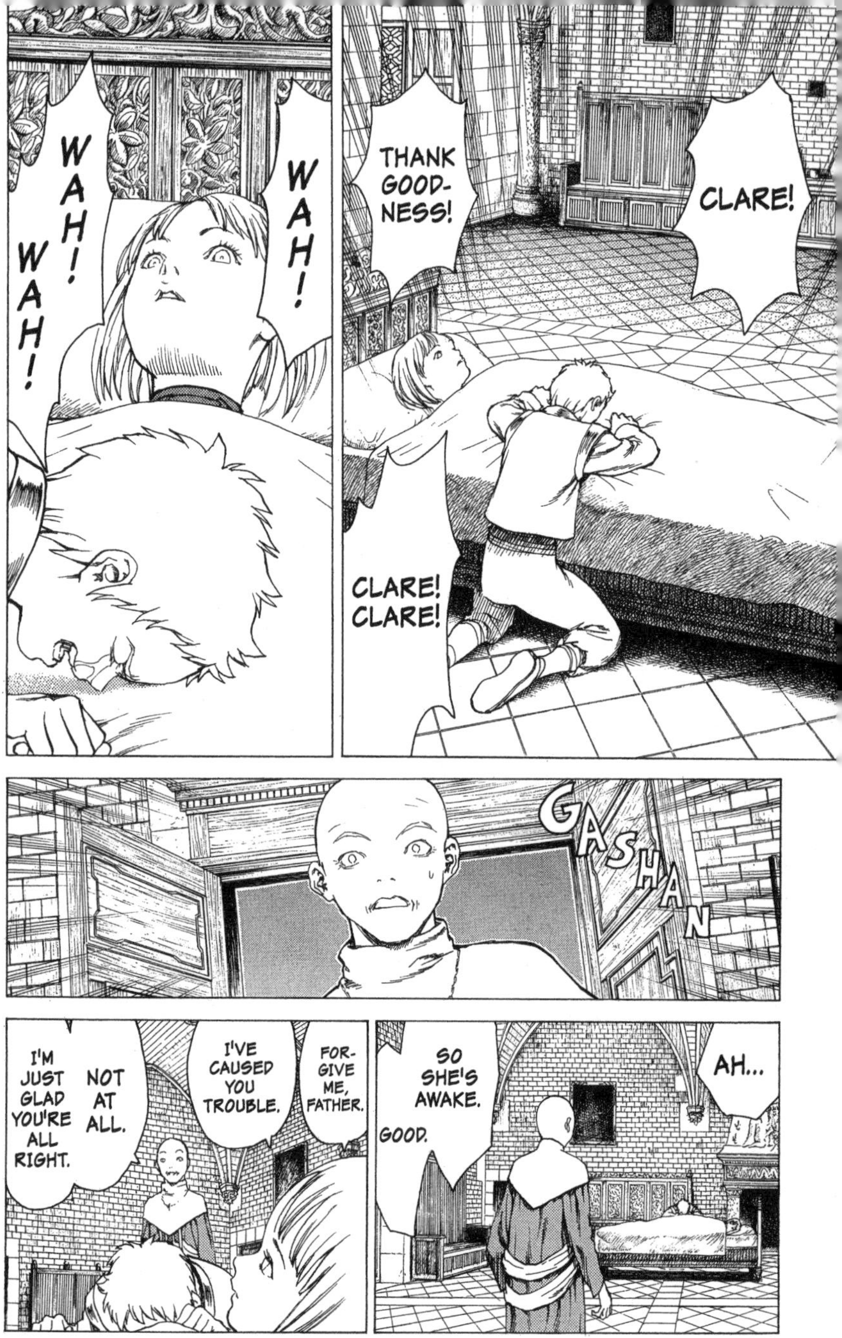
CLARE!
THANK GOOD-NESS!
CLARE! CLARE!
WAH!
WAH! WAH!
GASHAN
AH...
SO SHE'S AWAKE.
GOOD.
FOR-GIVE ME, FATHER.
I'VE CAUSED YOU TROUBLE.
NOT AT ALL.
I'M JUST GLAD YOU'RE ALL RIGHT.

READ THIS WAY

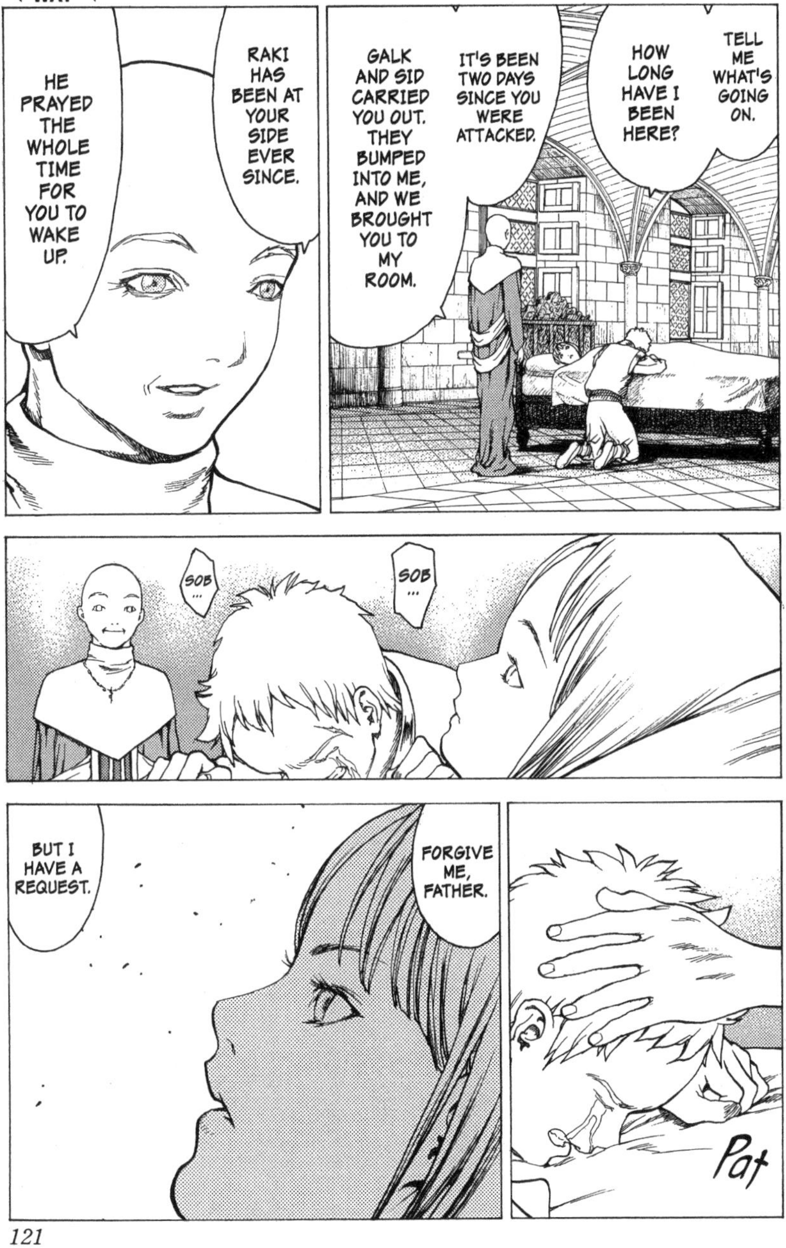
TELL ME WHAT'S GOING ON.
HOW LONG HAVE I BEEN HERE?
IT'S BEEN TWO DAYS SINCE YOU WERE ATTACKED.
GALK AND SID CARRIED YOU OUT. THEY BUMPED INTO ME, AND WE BROUGHT YOU TO MY ROOM.
RAKI HAS BEEN AT YOUR SIDE EVER SINCE.
HE PRAYED THE WHOLE TIME FOR YOU TO WAKE UP.
SOB...
SOB...
Pat
FORGIVE ME, FATHER.
BUT I HAVE A REQUEST.

クレイモア

Claymore™

Scene 8: Darkness in Paradise, Part 4

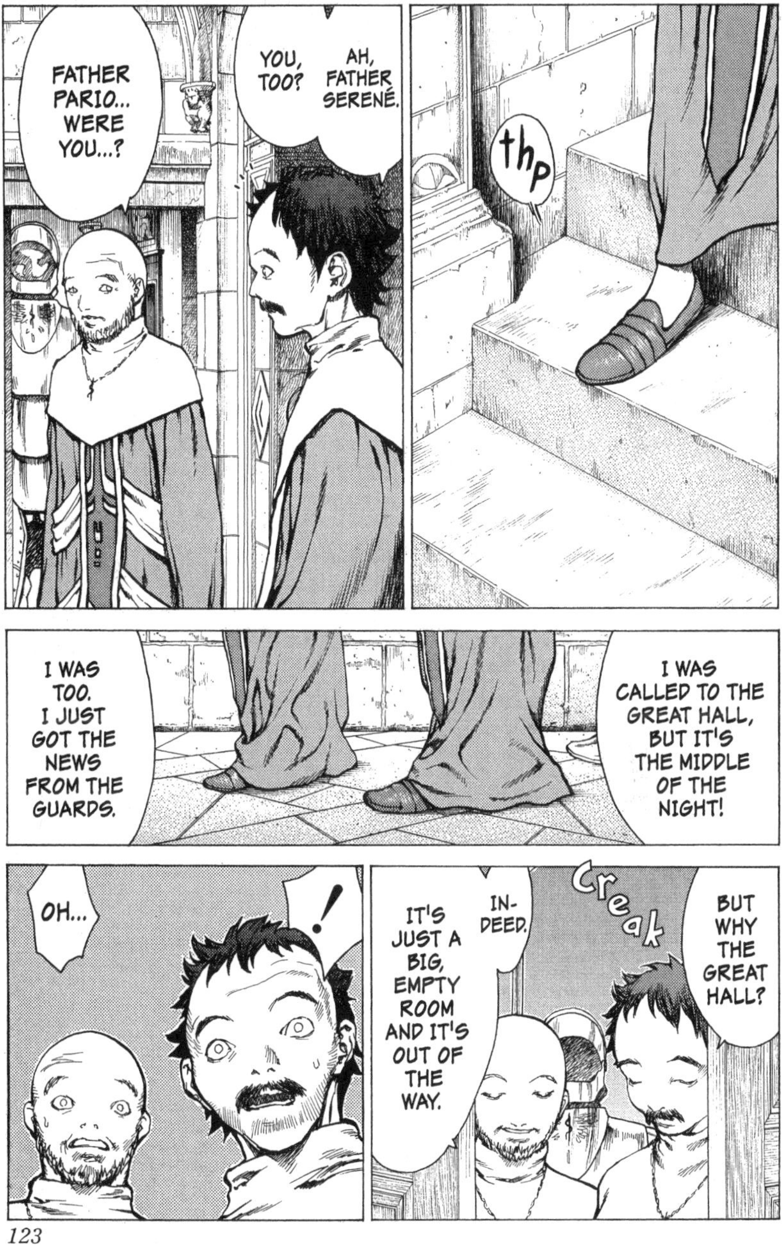
thp
AH, FATHER SERENÉ. YOU, TOO?
FATHER PARIO... WERE YOU...?
I WAS CALLED TO THE GREAT HALL, BUT IT'S THE MIDDLE OF THE NIGHT!
I WAS TOO. I JUST GOT THE NEWS FROM THE GUARDS.
BUT WHY THE GREAT HALL?
Creak
IN-DEED.
IT'S JUST A BIG, EMPTY ROOM AND IT'S OUT OF THE WAY.
!
OH...

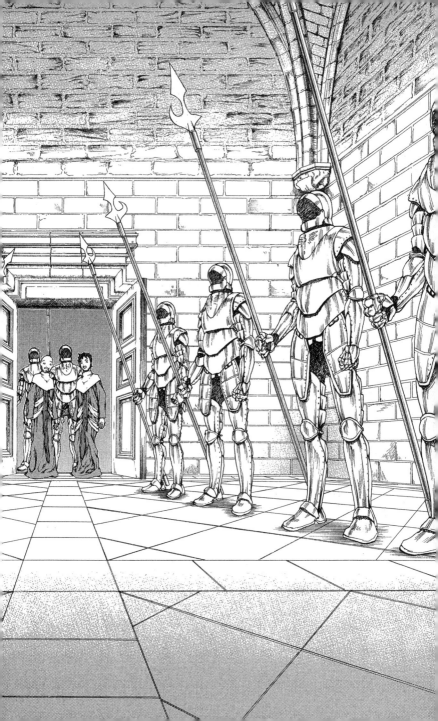

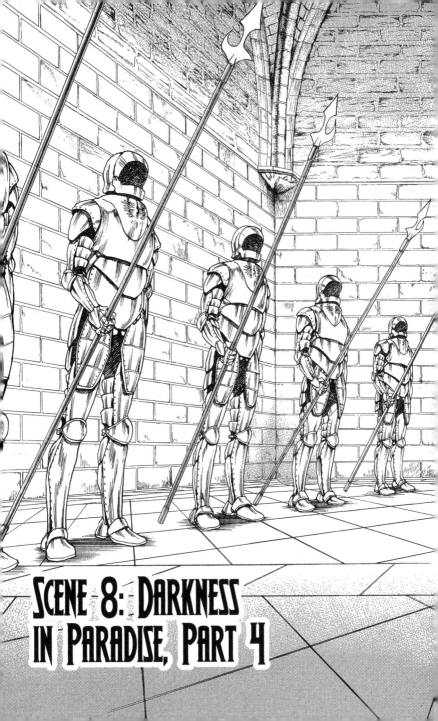

SCENE 8: DARKNESS IN PARADISE, PART 4

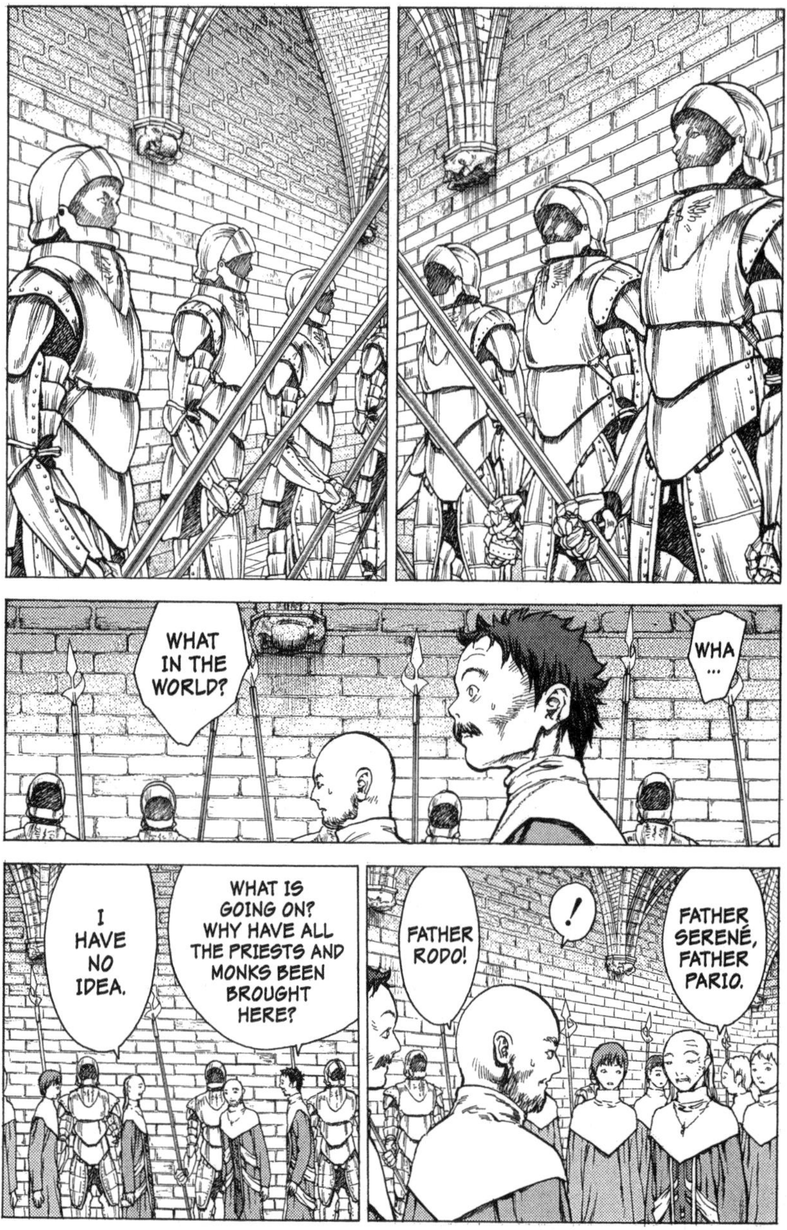
WHA...
WHAT IN THE WORLD?
FATHER SERENÉ, FATHER PARIO.
!
FATHER RODO!
WHAT IS GOING ON? WHY HAVE ALL THE PRIESTS AND MONKS BEEN BROUGHT HERE?
I HAVE NO IDEA.

READ THIS WAY

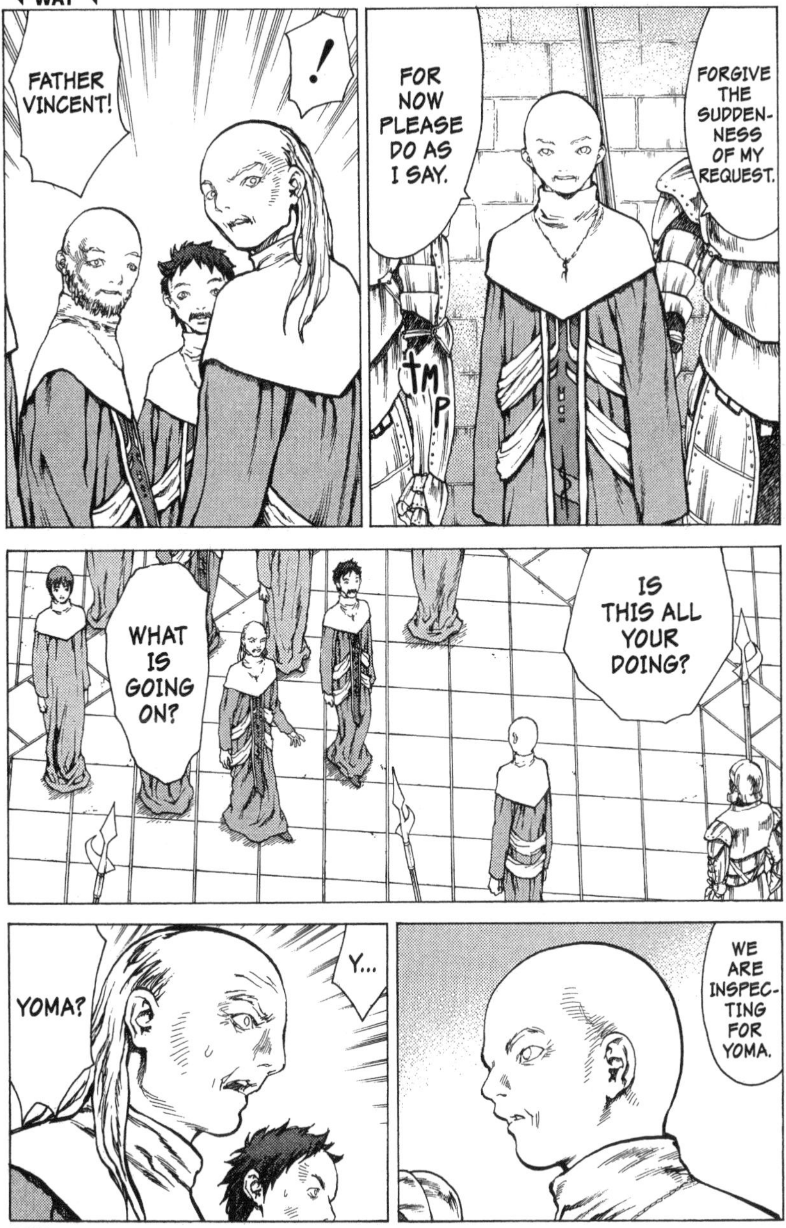
FORGIVE THE SUDDENNESS OF MY REQUEST.
FOR NOW PLEASE DO AS I SAY.
TMP
!
FATHER VINCENT!
IS THIS ALL YOUR DOING?
WHAT IS GOING ON?
WE ARE INSPECTING FOR YOMA.
Y...
YOMA?

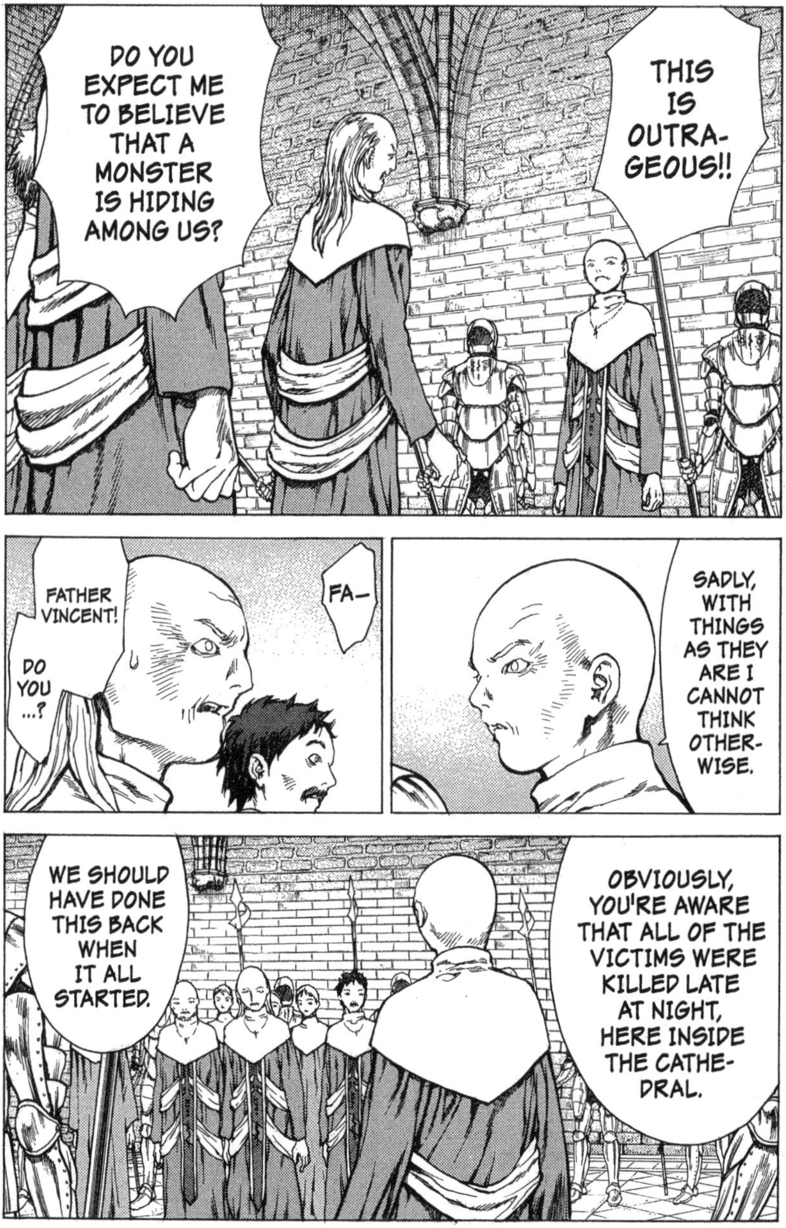
THIS IS OUTRAGEOUS!!
DO YOU EXPECT ME TO BELIEVE THAT A MONSTER IS HIDING AMONG US?
SADLY, WITH THINGS AS THEY ARE I CANNOT THINK OTHERWISE.
FA—
FATHER VINCENT!
DO YOU ...?
OBVIOUSLY, YOU'RE AWARE THAT ALL OF THE VICTIMS WERE KILLED LATE AT NIGHT, HERE INSIDE THE CATHEDRAL.
WE SHOULD HAVE DONE THIS BACK WHEN IT ALL STARTED.

READ THIS WAY

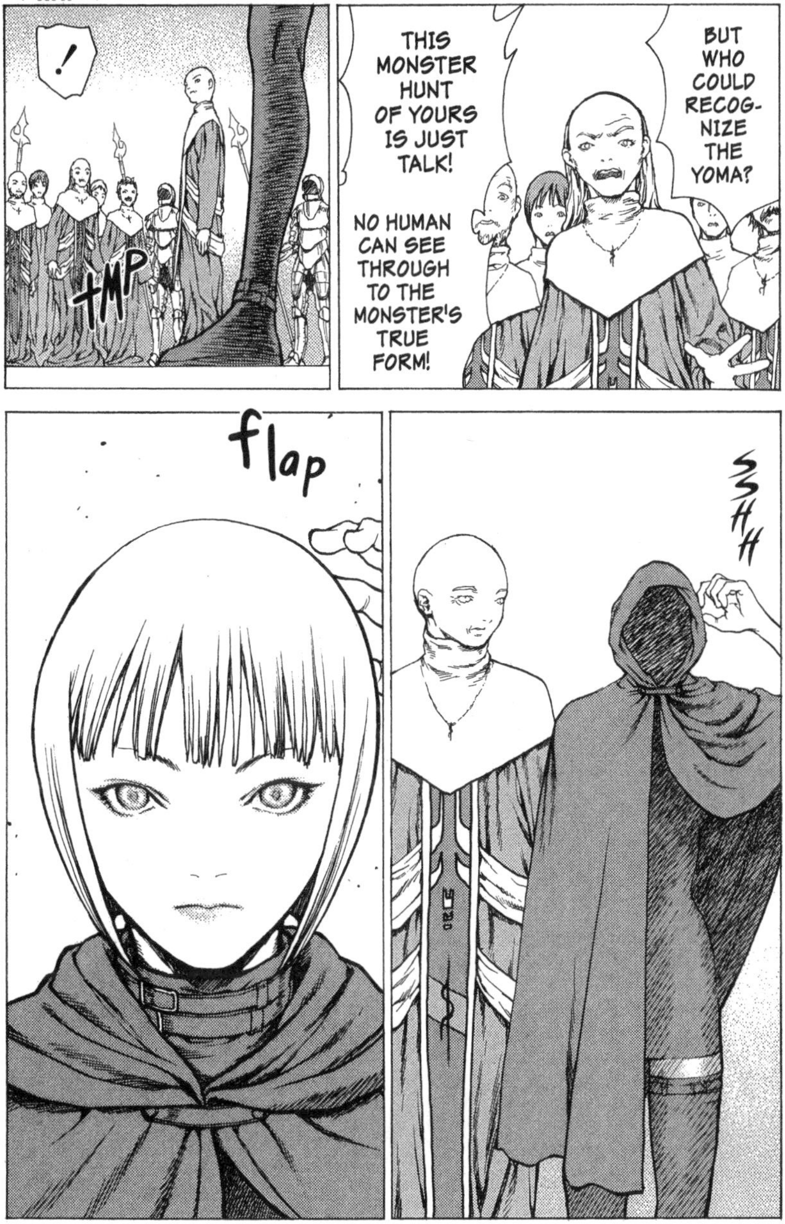
BUT WHO COULD RECOG-NIZE THE YOMA?
THIS MONSTER HUNT OF YOURS IS JUST TALK!
NO HUMAN CAN SEE THROUGH TO THE MONSTER'S TRUE FORM!
!
TMP
SHH
flap

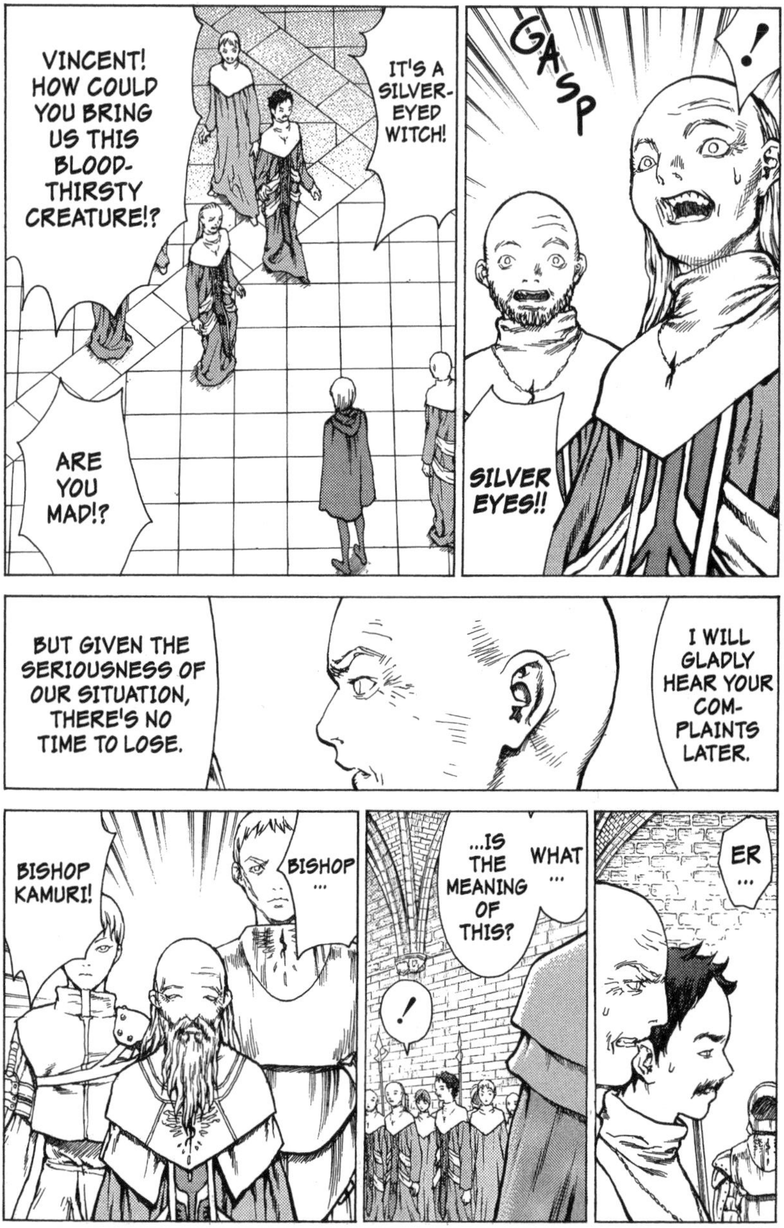
GASP
!
SILVER EYES!!
IT'S A SILVER-EYED WITCH!
VINCENT! HOW COULD YOU BRING US THIS BLOOD-THIRSTY CREATURE!?
ARE YOU MAD!?
I WILL GLADLY HEAR YOUR COM-PLAINTS LATER.
BUT GIVEN THE SERIOUSNESS OF OUR SITUATION, THERE'S NO TIME TO LOSE.
ER ...
WHAT ...
...IS THE MEANING OF THIS?
!
BISHOP ...
BISHOP KAMURI!

READ THIS WAY

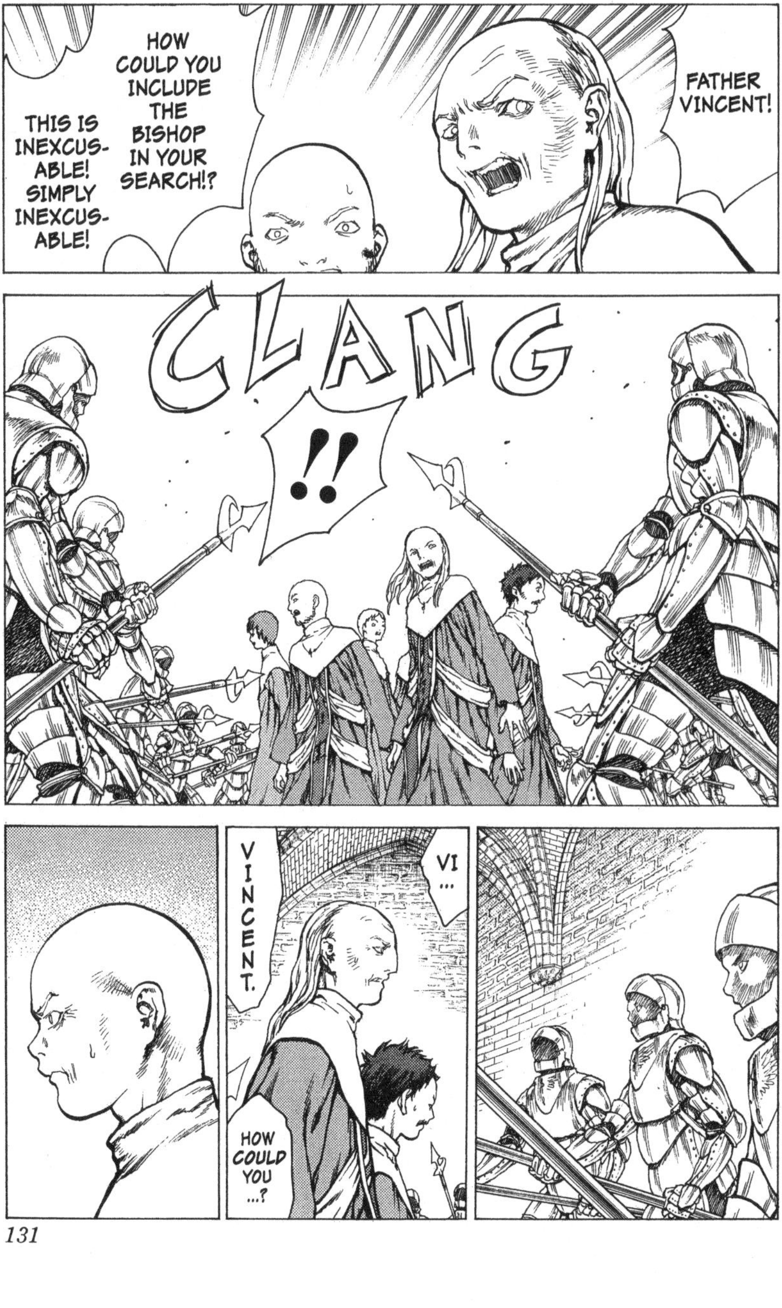
FATHER VINCENT!
HOW COULD YOU INCLUDE THE BISHOP IN YOUR SEARCH!?
THIS IS INEXCUS-ABLE! SIMPLY INEXCUS-ABLE!
CLANG
!!
VI ...
VINCENT.
HOW COULD YOU ...?

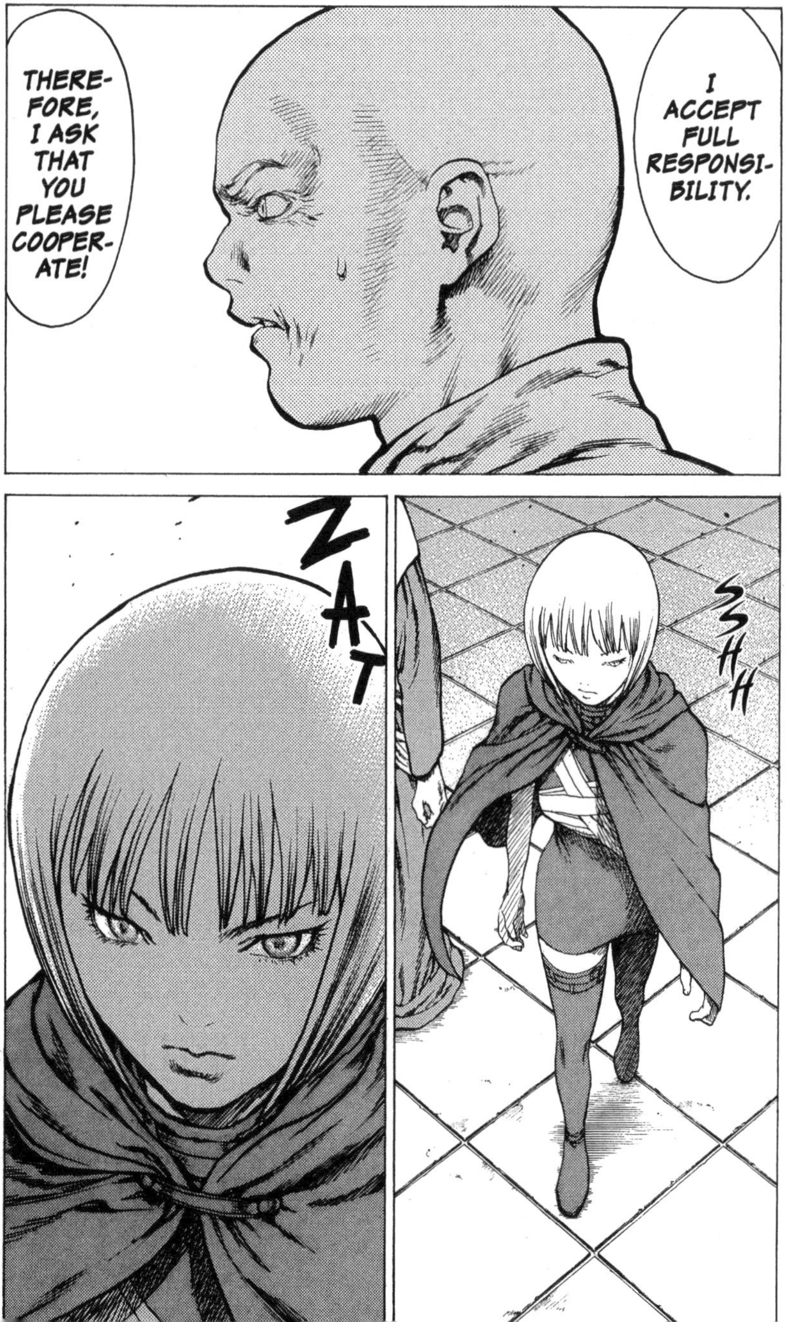
I ACCEPT FULL RESPONSIBILITY.
THEREFORE, I ASK THAT YOU PLEASE COOPERATE!
SSHH
ZAT

READ THIS WAY

UH ...
SSHH
UGH ...

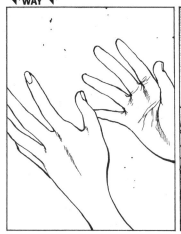

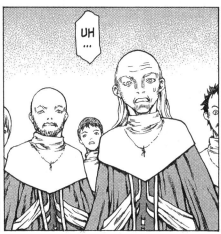

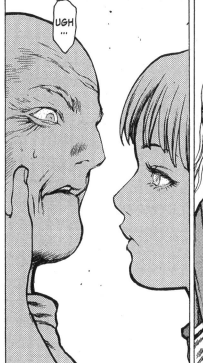

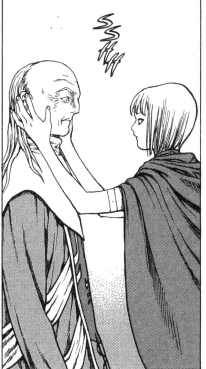

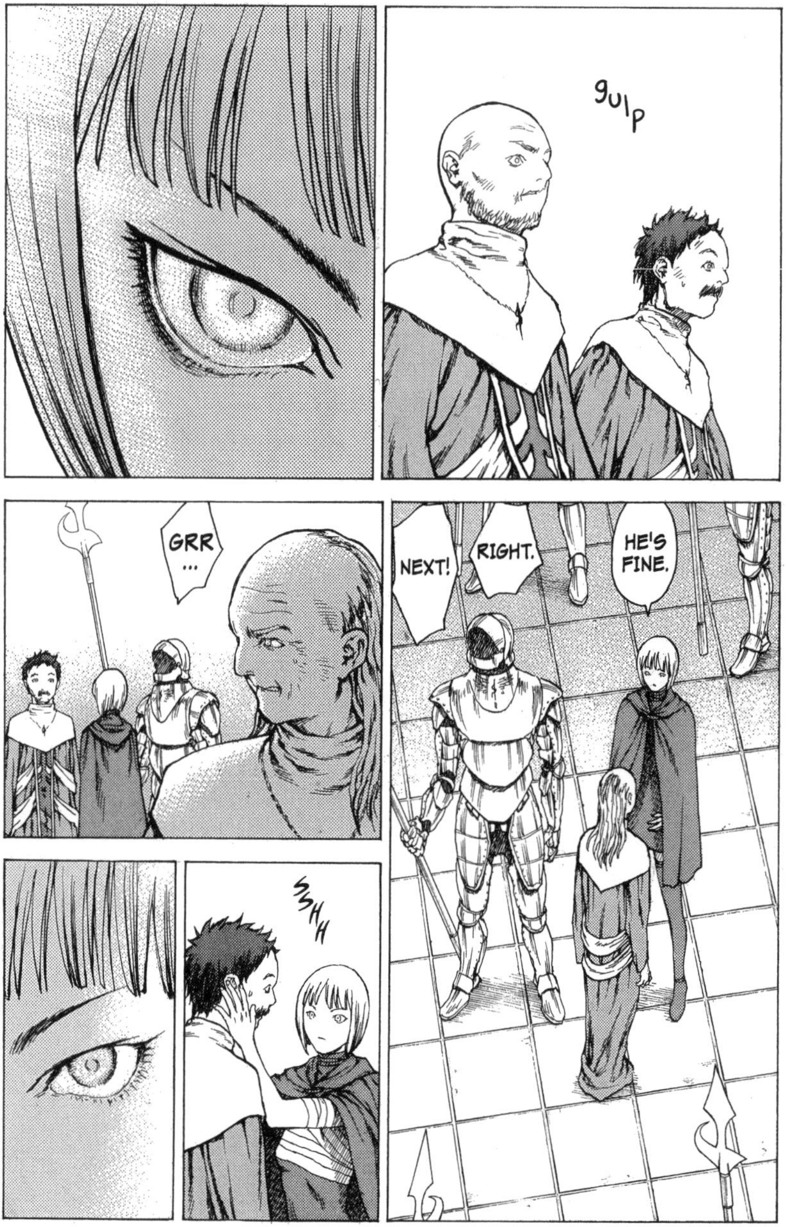
gulp
HE'S FINE.
RIGHT.
NEXT!
GRR ...
SSHH

READ THIS WAY

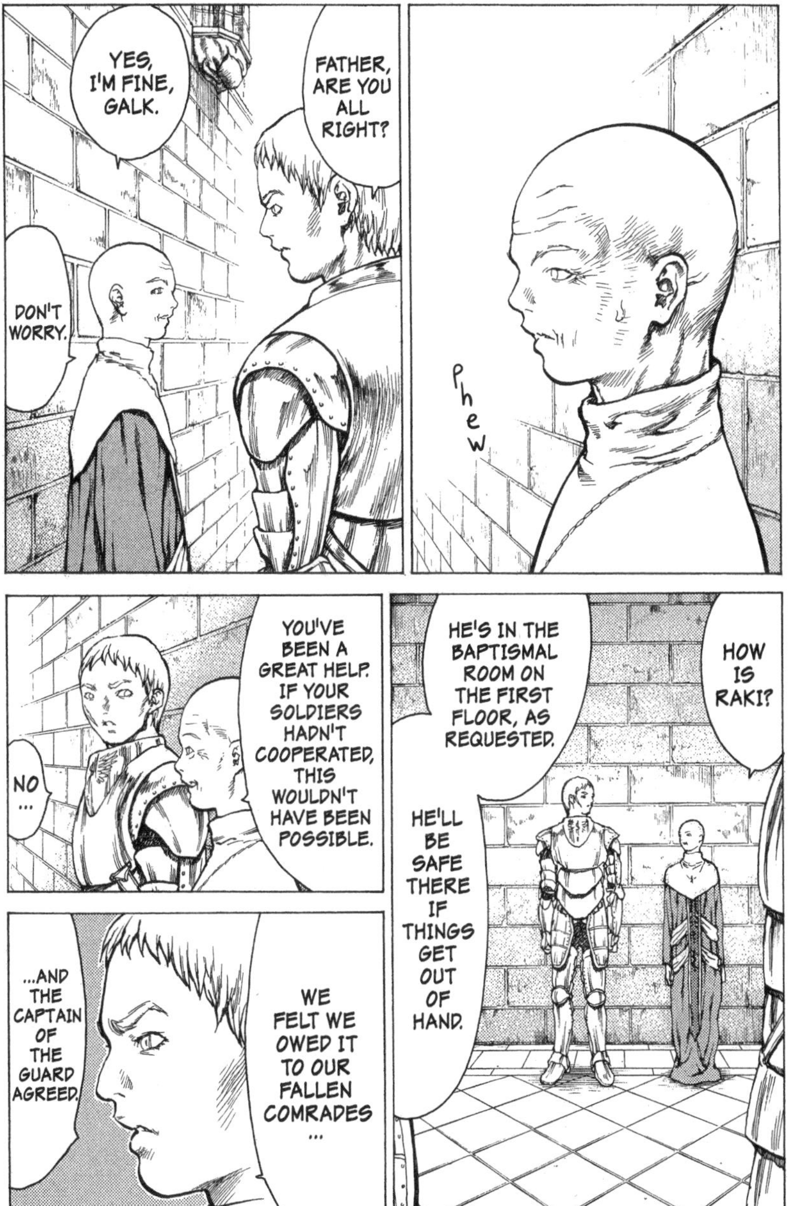
Phew
FATHER, ARE YOU ALL RIGHT?
YES, I'M FINE, GALK.
DON'T WORRY.
HOW IS RAKI?
HE'S IN THE BAPTISMAL ROOM ON THE FIRST FLOOR, AS REQUESTED.
HE'LL BE SAFE THERE IF THINGS GET OUT OF HAND.
YOU'VE BEEN A GREAT HELP. IF YOUR SOLDIERS HADN'T COOPERATED, THIS WOULDN'T HAVE BEEN POSSIBLE.
NO ...
WE FELT WE OWED IT TO OUR FALLEN COMRADES ...
...AND THE CAPTAIN OF THE GUARD AGREED.

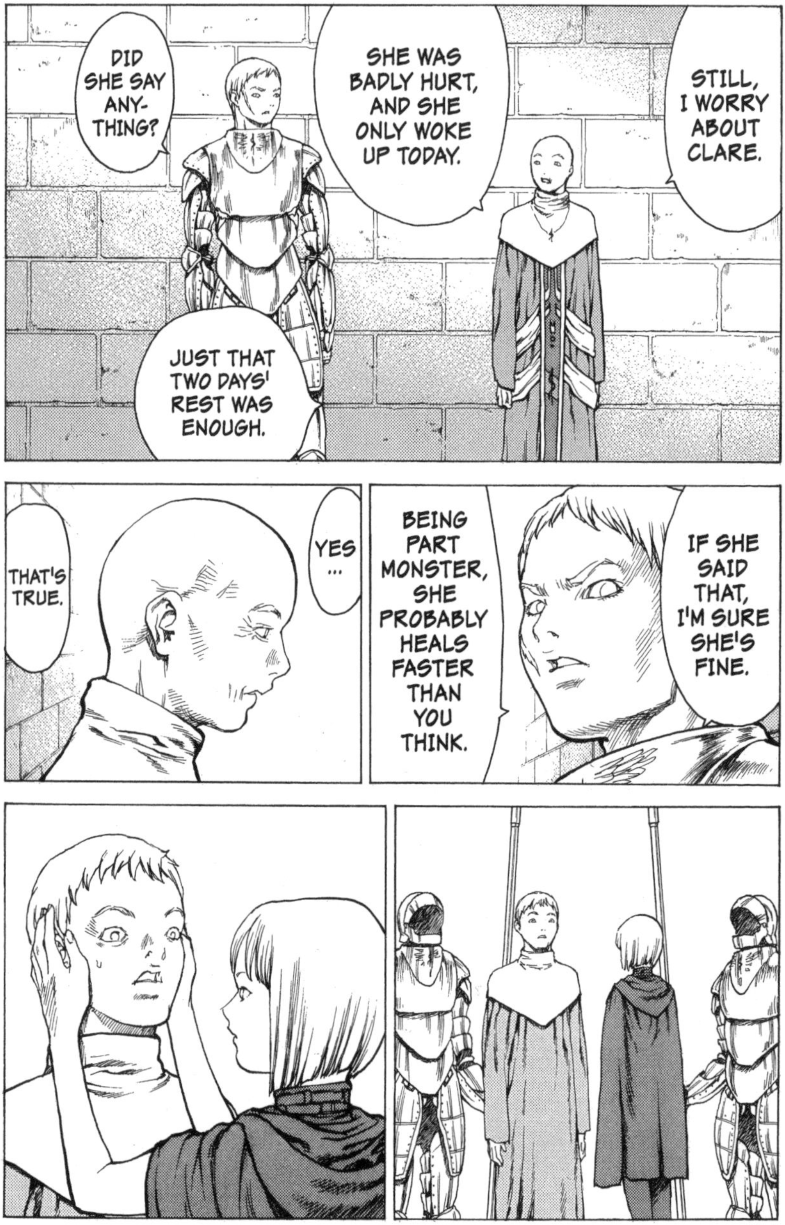
STILL, I WORRY ABOUT CLARE.
SHE WAS BADLY HURT, AND SHE ONLY WOKE UP TODAY.
DID SHE SAY ANY-THING?
JUST THAT TWO DAYS' REST WAS ENOUGH.
IF SHE SAID THAT, I'M SURE SHE'S FINE.
BEING PART MONSTER, SHE PROBABLY HEALS FASTER THAN YOU THINK.
YES ...
THAT'S TRUE.

READ THIS WAY

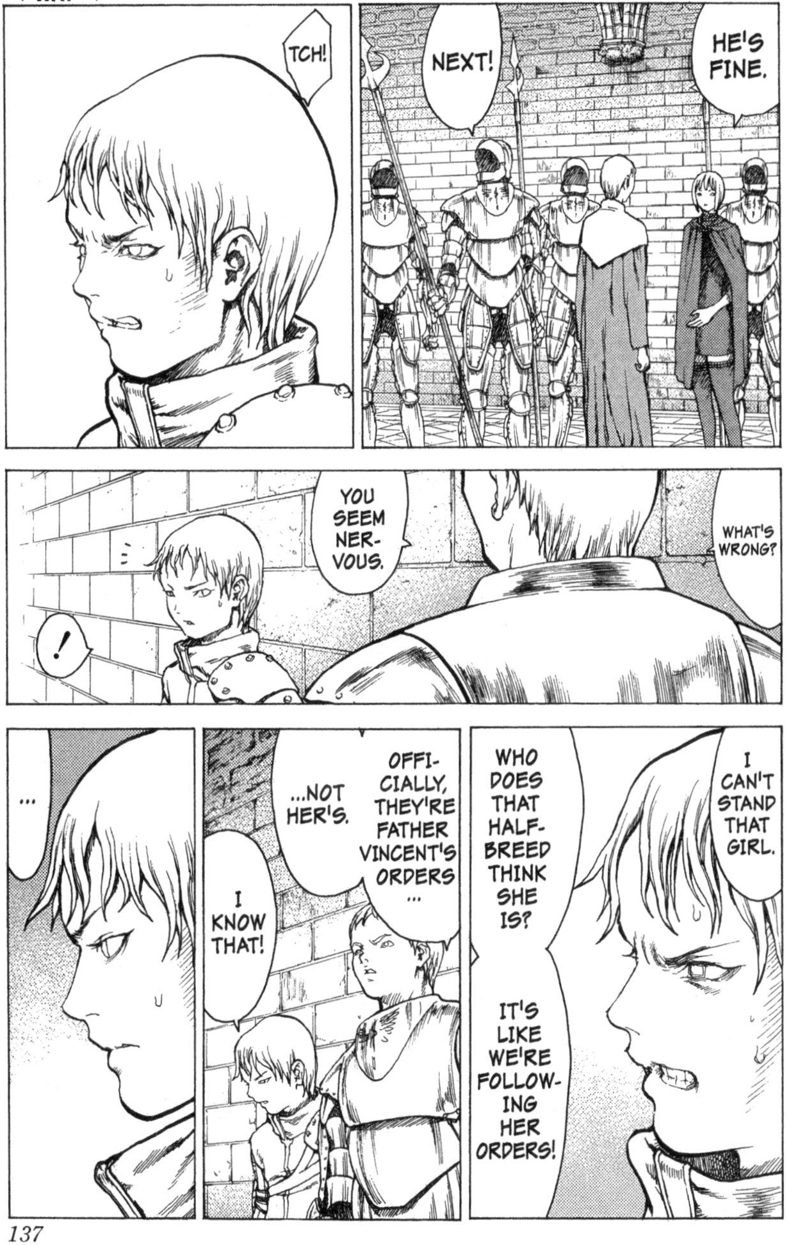

HE'S FINE.
NEXT!
TCH!
WHAT'S WRONG?
YOU SEEM NERVOUS.
!
I CAN'T STAND THAT GIRL.
WHO DOES THAT HALF-BREED THINK SHE IS?
IT'S LIKE WE'RE FOLLOWING HER ORDERS!
OFFICIALLY, THEY'RE FATHER VINCENT'S ORDERS...
...NOT HER'S.
I KNOW THAT!
...

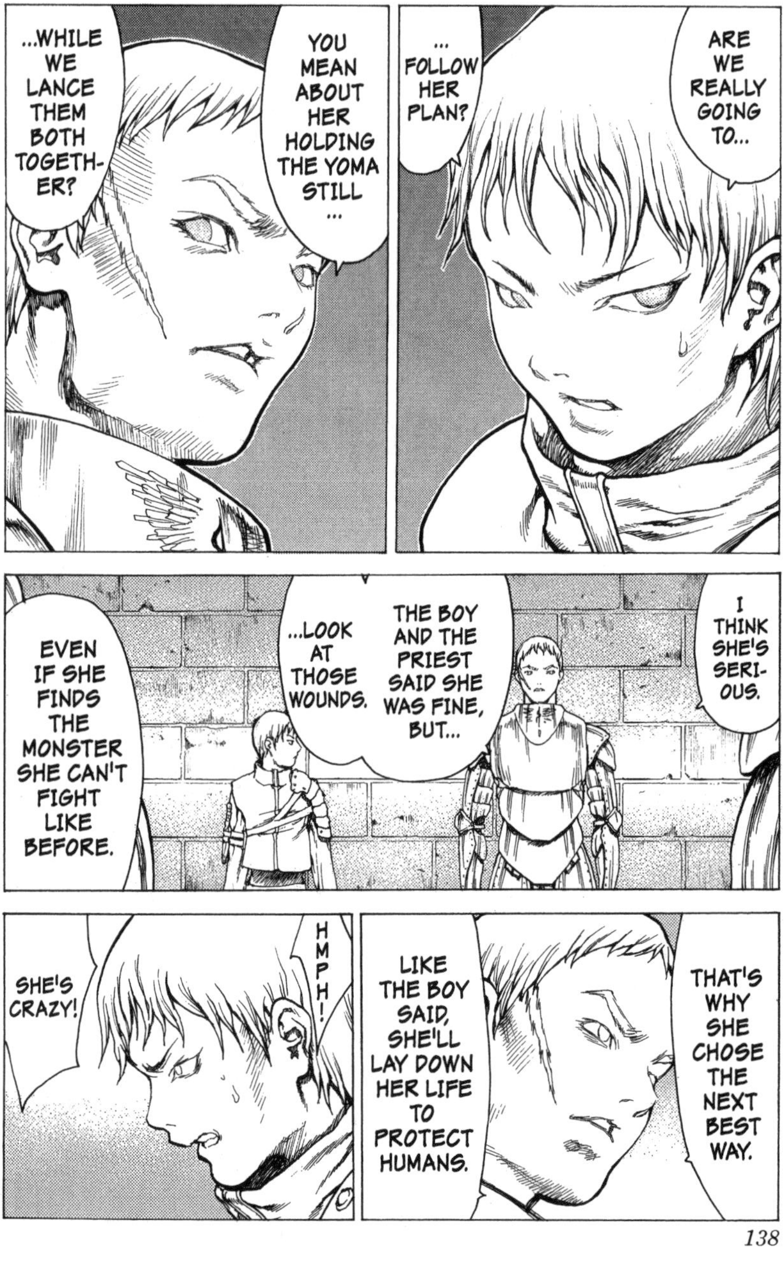
ARE WE REALLY GOING TO...
... FOLLOW HER PLAN?
YOU MEAN ABOUT HER HOLDING THE YOMA STILL ...
...WHILE WE LANCE THEM BOTH TOGETH-ER?
I THINK SHE'S SERI-OUS.
THE BOY AND THE PRIEST SAID SHE WAS FINE, BUT...
...LOOK AT THOSE WOUNDS.
EVEN IF SHE FINDS THE MONSTER SHE CAN'T FIGHT LIKE BEFORE.
THAT'S WHY SHE CHOSE THE NEXT BEST WAY.
LIKE THE BOY SAID, SHE'LL LAY DOWN HER LIFE TO PROTECT HUMANS.
HMPH!
SHE'S CRAZY!

READ THIS WAY

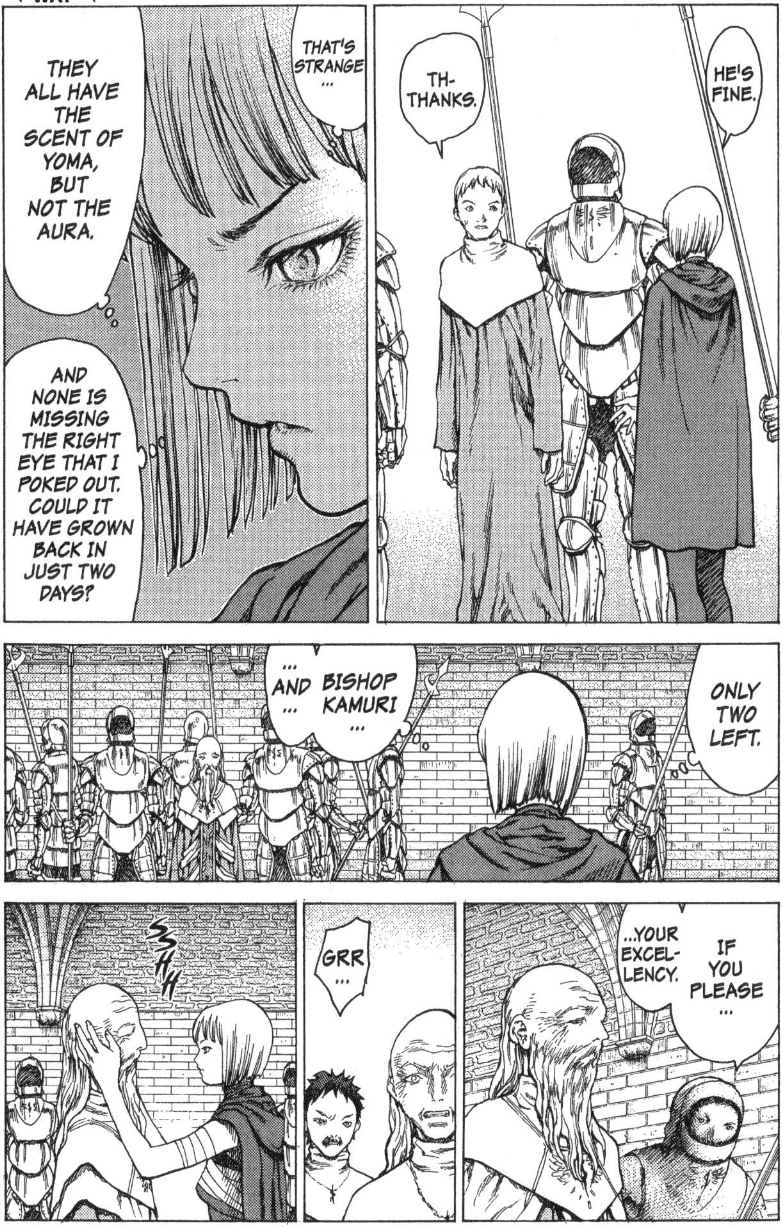
HE'S FINE.
TH- THANKS.
THAT'S STRANGE ...
THEY ALL HAVE THE SCENT OF YOMA, BUT NOT THE AURA.
AND NONE IS MISSING THE RIGHT EYE THAT I POKED OUT. COULD IT HAVE GROWN BACK IN JUST TWO DAYS?
ONLY TWO LEFT.
... AND ... BISHOP KAMURI ...
IF YOU PLEASE ...
...YOUR EXCEL-LENCY.
GRR ...
SHH

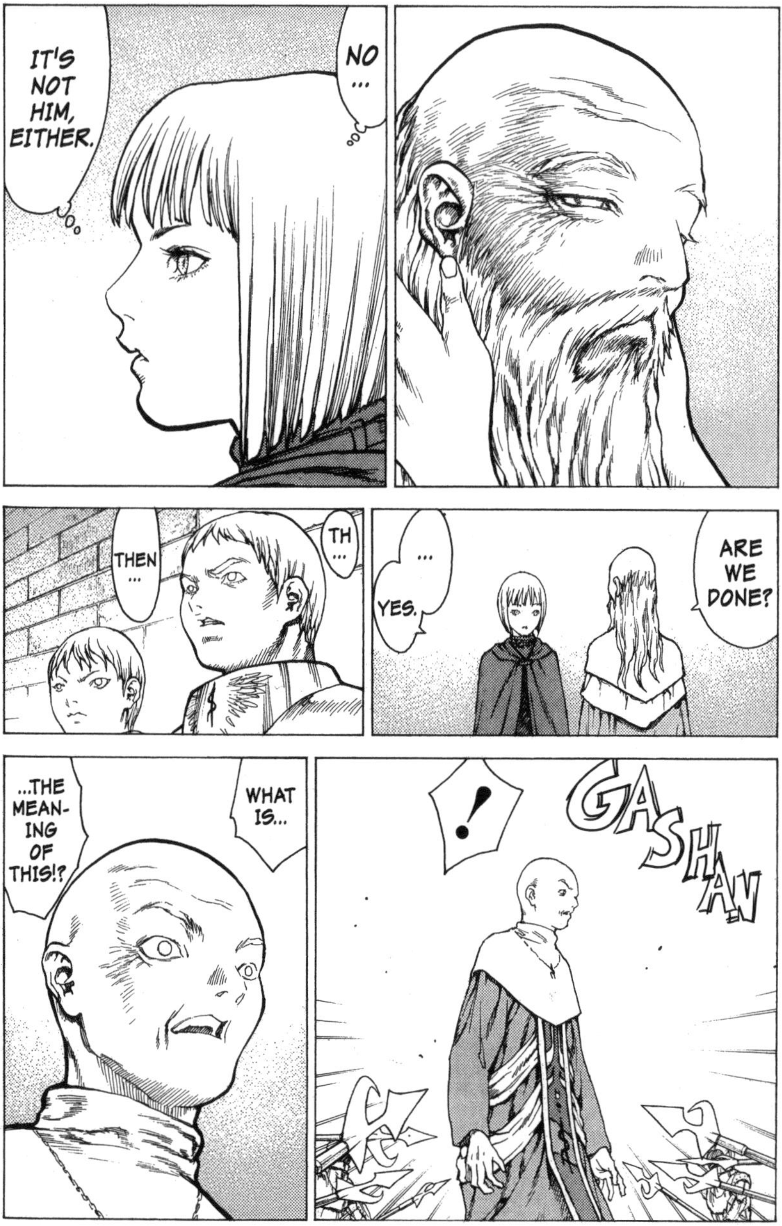
NO ...
IT'S NOT HIM, EITHER.
ARE WE DONE?
...
YES.
TH ...
THEN ...
!
GASHAN
WHAT IS...
...THE MEANING OF THIS!?

READ THIS WAY

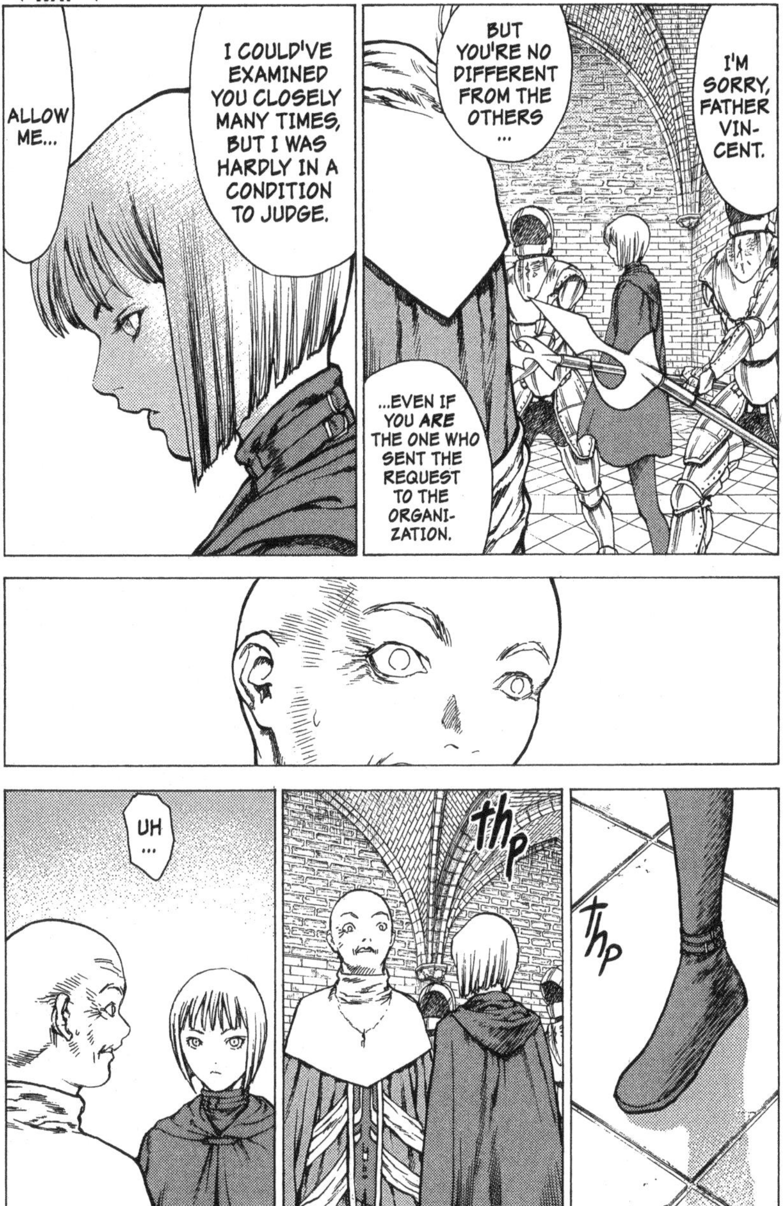

I'M SORRY, FATHER VINCENT.
BUT YOU'RE NO DIFFERENT FROM THE OTHERS...
...EVEN IF YOU ARE THE ONE WHO SENT THE REQUEST TO THE ORGANIZATION.
I COULD'VE EXAMINED YOU CLOSELY MANY TIMES, BUT I WAS HARDLY IN A CONDITION TO JUDGE.
ALLOW ME...
thp
thp
UH...

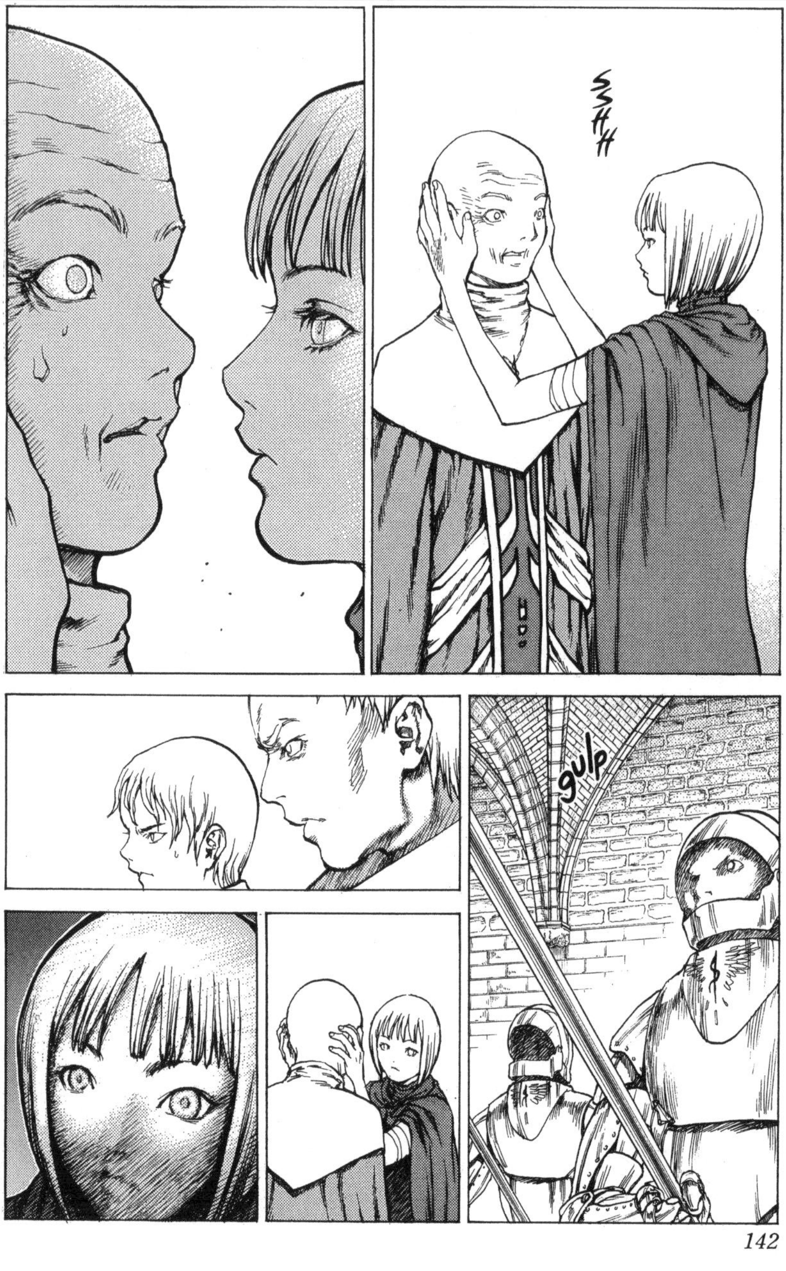
SSHH
gulp

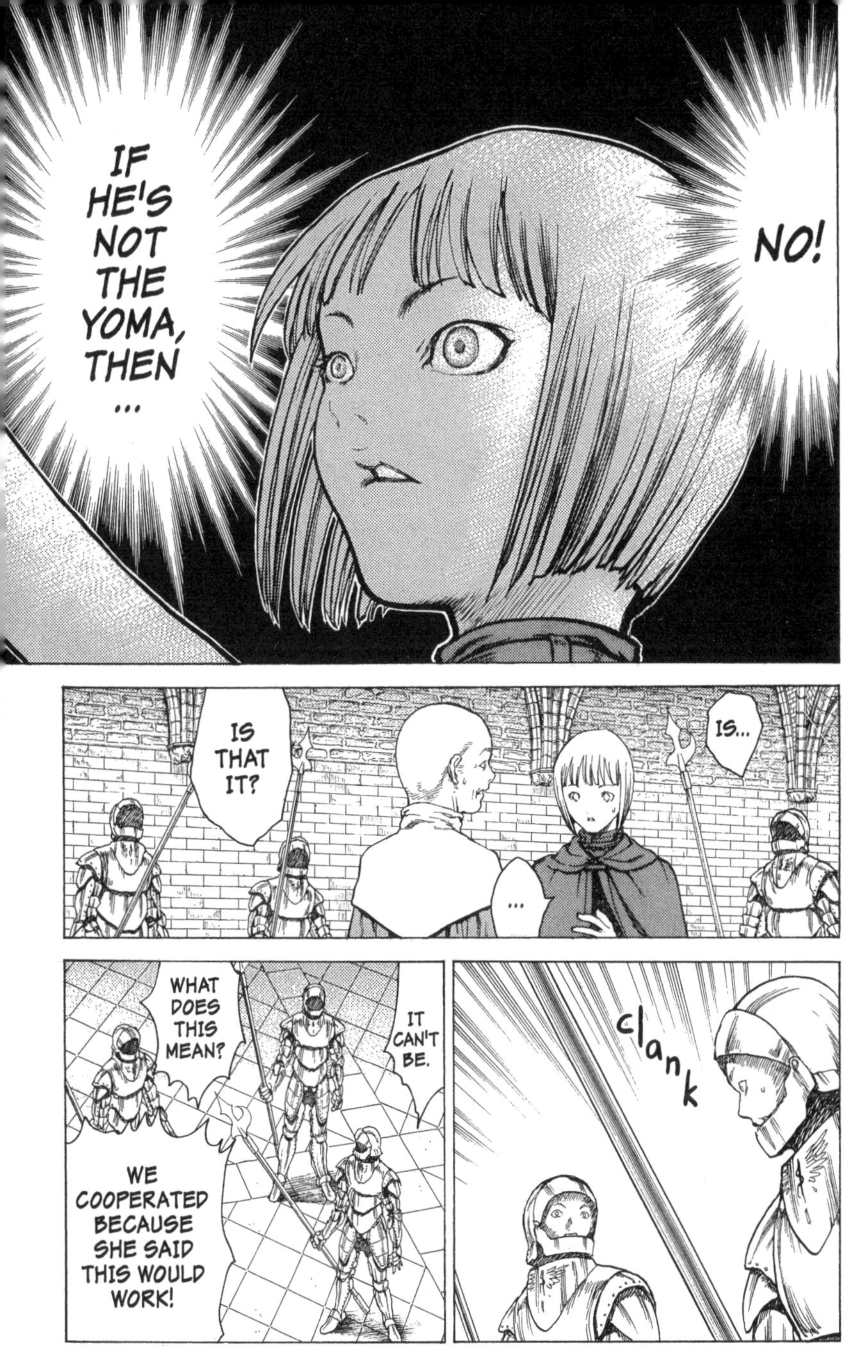
NO!
IF HE'S NOT THE YOMA, THEN ...
IS...
IS THAT IT?
...
clank
IT CAN'T BE.
WHAT DOES THIS MEAN?
WE COOPERATED BECAUSE SHE SAID THIS WOULD WORK!

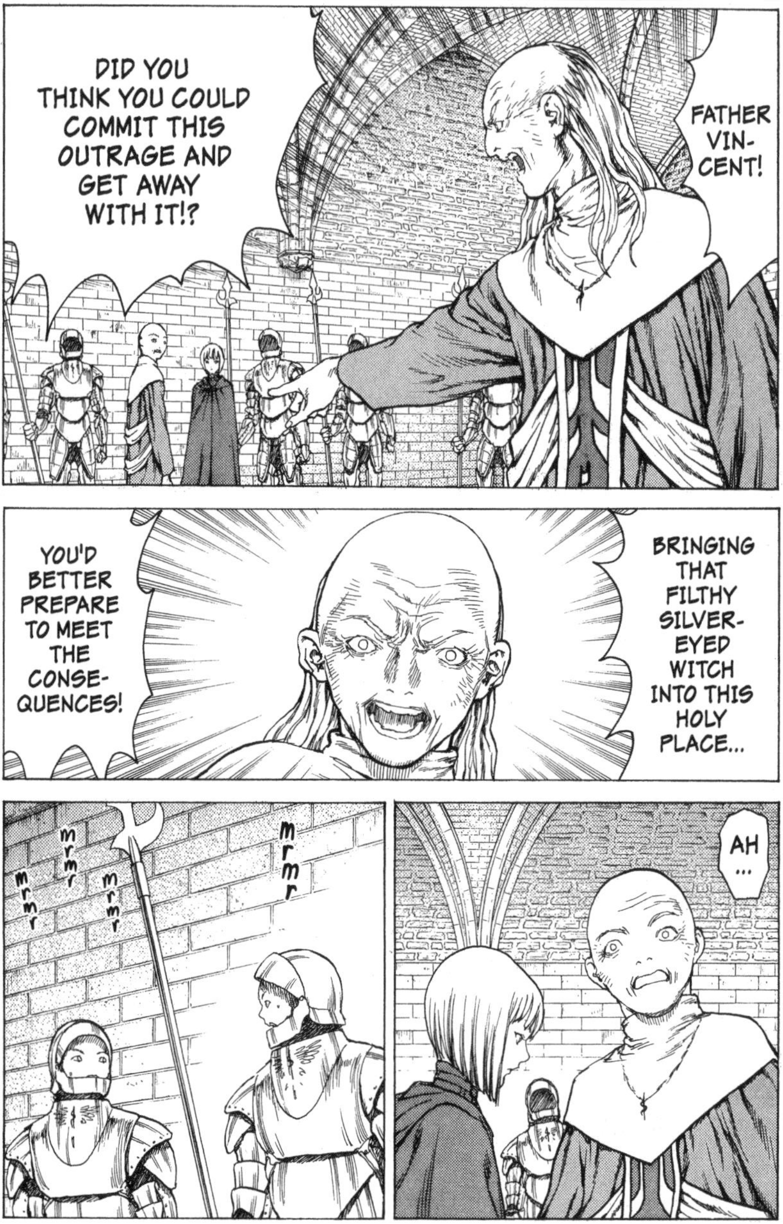
FATHER VIN-CENT!
DID YOU THINK YOU COULD COMMIT THIS OUTRAGE AND GET AWAY WITH IT!?
BRINGING THAT FILTHY SILVER-EYED WITCH INTO THIS HOLY PLACE...
YOU'D BETTER PREPARE TO MEET THE CONSE-QUENCES!
AH ...
mrmr
mrmr
mrmr
mrmr

READ THIS WAY

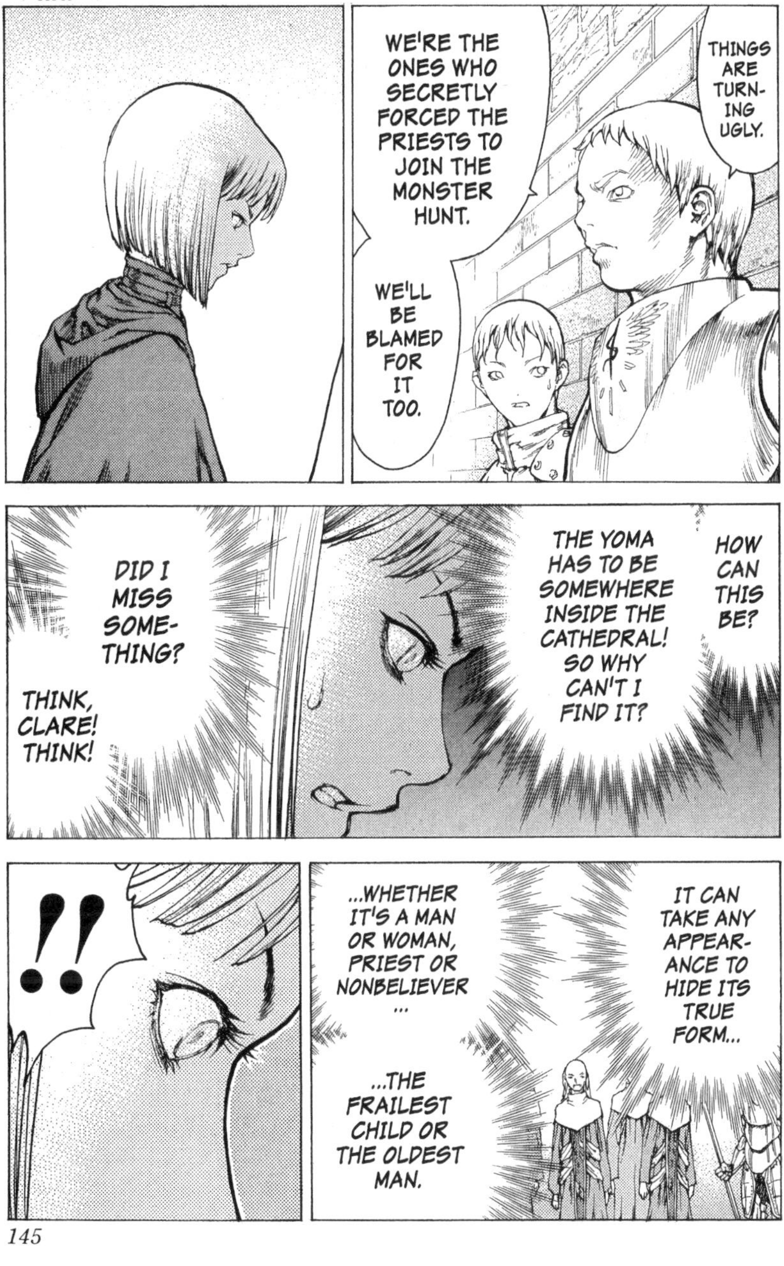
THINGS ARE TURNING UGLY.
WE'RE THE ONES WHO SECRETLY FORCED THE PRIESTS TO JOIN THE MONSTER HUNT.
WE'LL BE BLAMED FOR IT TOO.
HOW CAN THIS BE?
THE YOMA HAS TO BE SOMEWHERE INSIDE THE CATHEDRAL! SO WHY CAN'T I FIND IT?
DID I MISS SOME-THING?
THINK, CLARE! THINK!
IT CAN TAKE ANY APPEAR-ANCE TO HIDE ITS TRUE FORM...
...WHETHER IT'S A MAN OR WOMAN, PRIEST OR NONBELIEVER ...
...THE FRAILEST CHILD OR THE OLDEST MAN.
!!

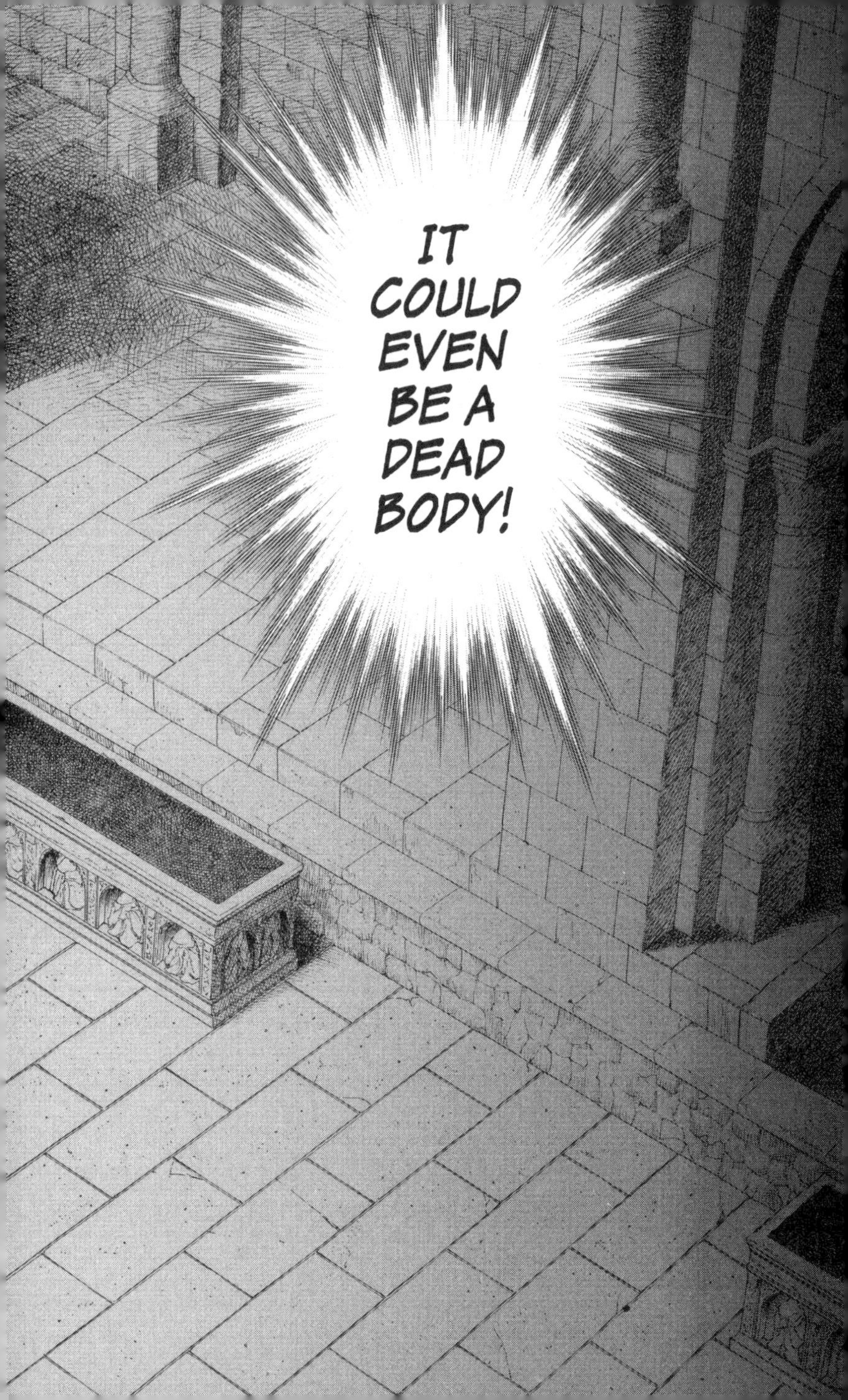
IT COULD EVEN BE A DEAD BODY!

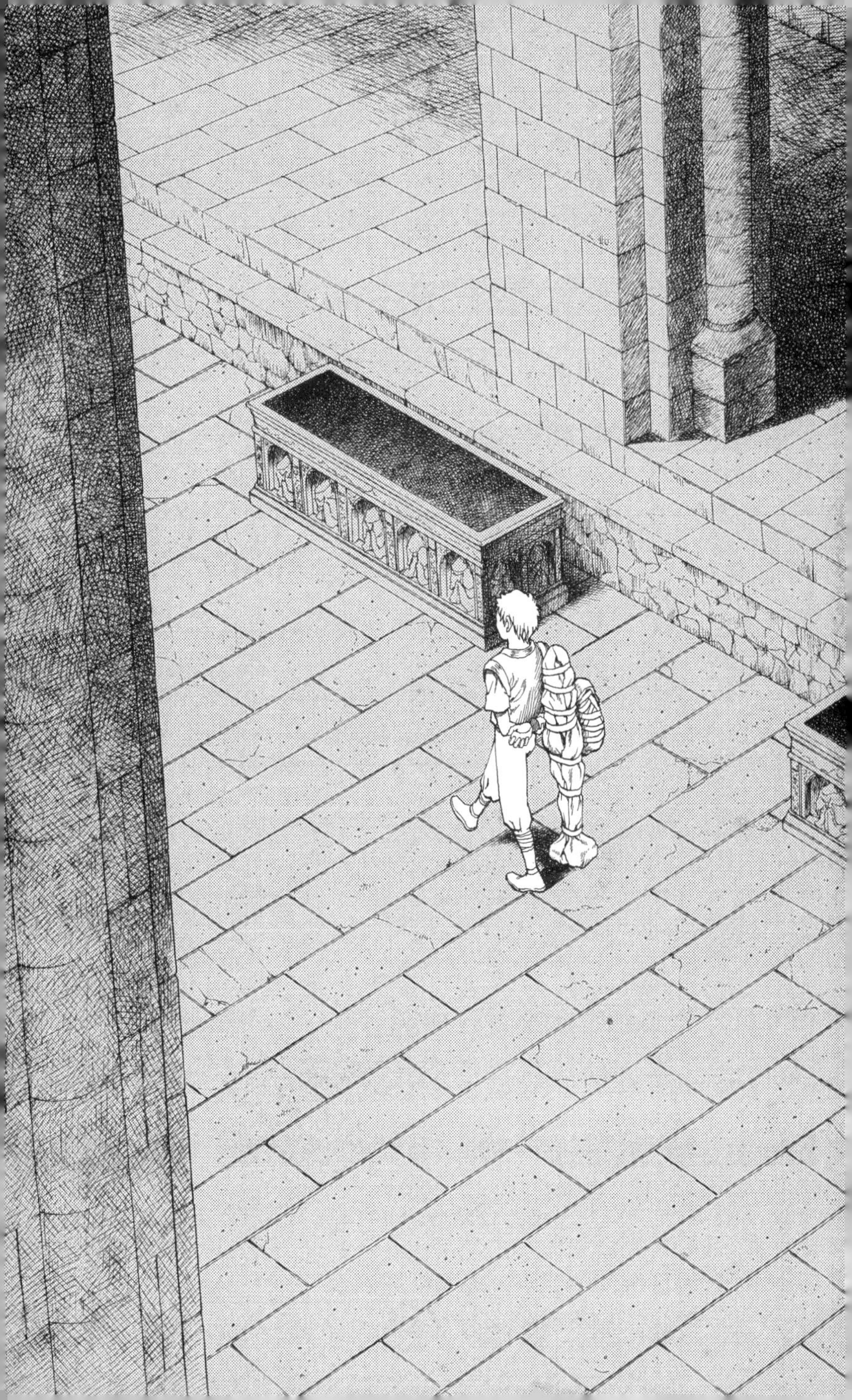

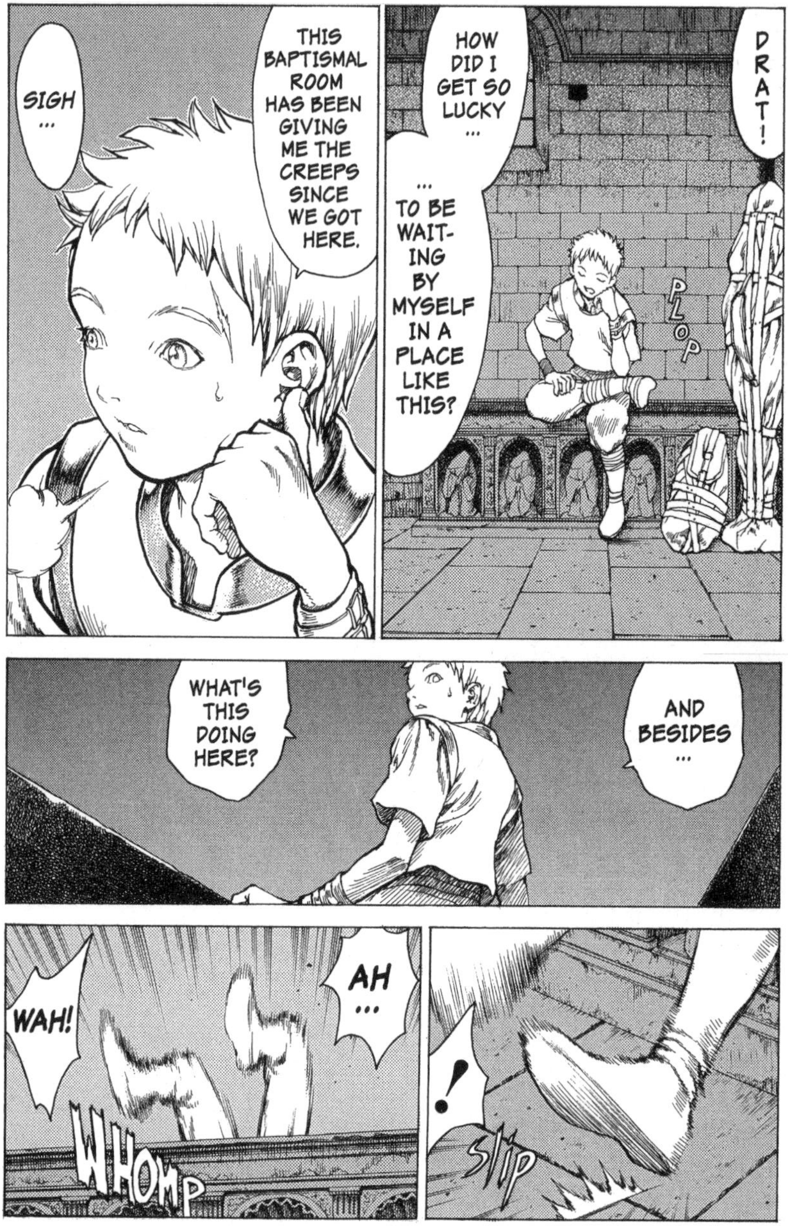
DRAT!
HOW DID I GET SO LUCKY ...
... TO BE WAITING BY MYSELF IN A PLACE LIKE THIS?
PLOP
THIS BAPTISMAL ROOM HAS BEEN GIVING ME THE CREEPS SINCE WE GOT HERE.
SIGH ...
AND BESIDES ...
WHAT'S THIS DOING HERE?
!
SLIP
AH ...
WAH!
WHOMP

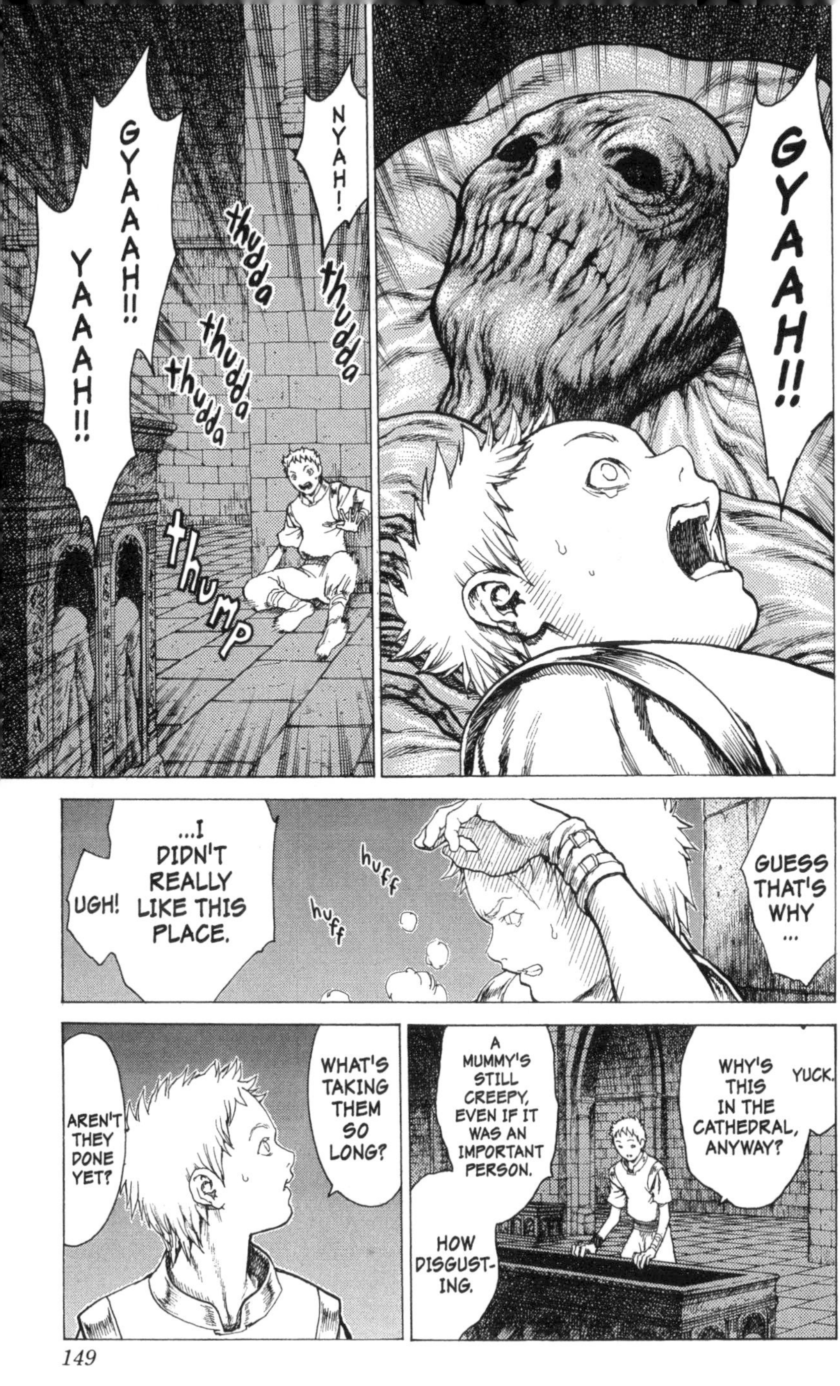
GYAAAH!!
NYAH!
thudda thudda
thudda thudda
GYAAAH!! YAAAAH!!
thump
GUESS THAT'S WHY...
huff
huff
...I DIDN'T REALLY LIKE THIS PLACE.
UGH!
YUCK.
WHY'S THIS IN THE CATHEDRAL, ANYWAY?
A MUMMY'S STILL CREEPY, EVEN IF IT WAS AN IMPORTANT PERSON.
HOW DISGUST-ING.
WHAT'S TAKING THEM SO LONG?
AREN'T THEY DONE YET?

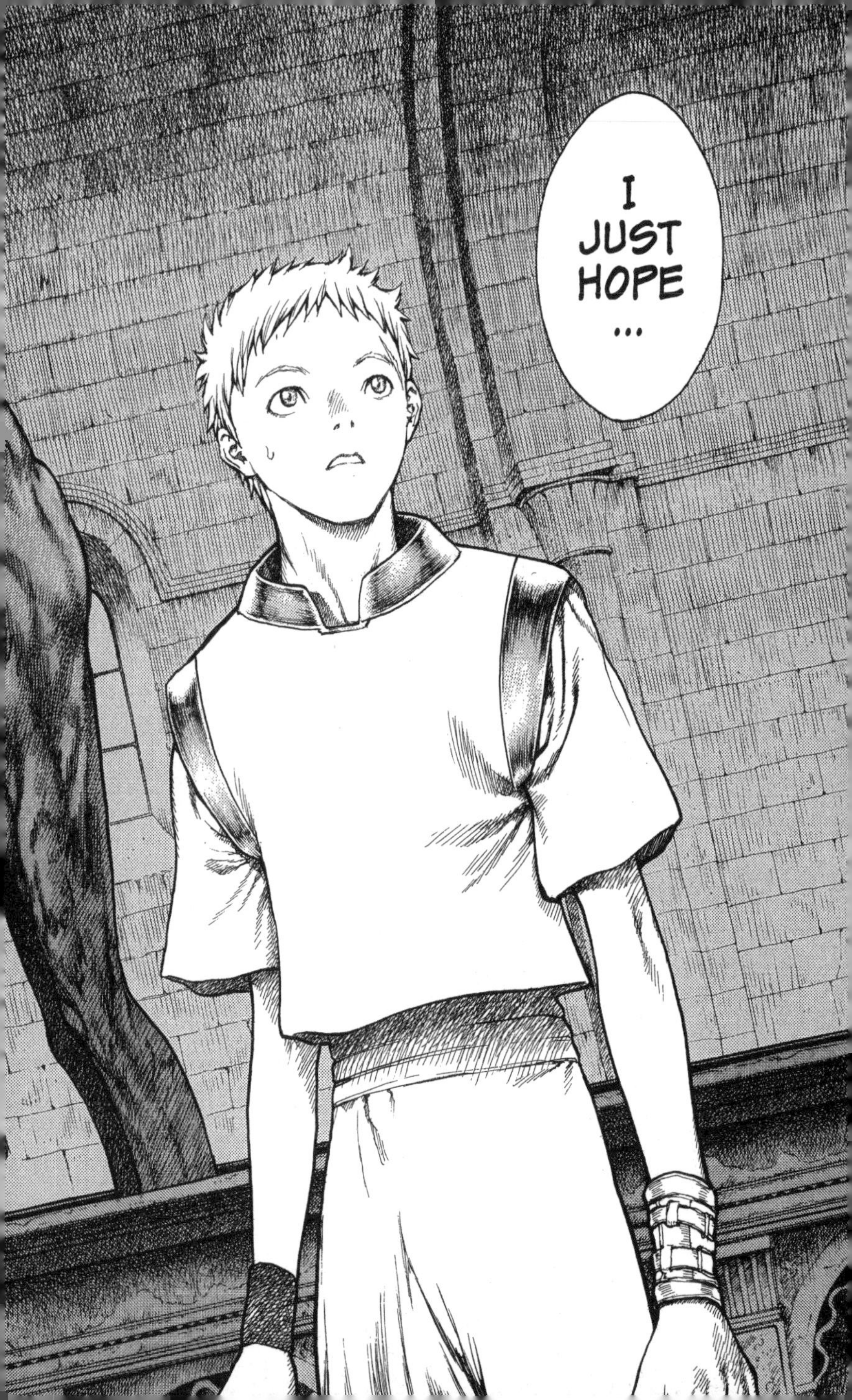
I JUST HOPE ...

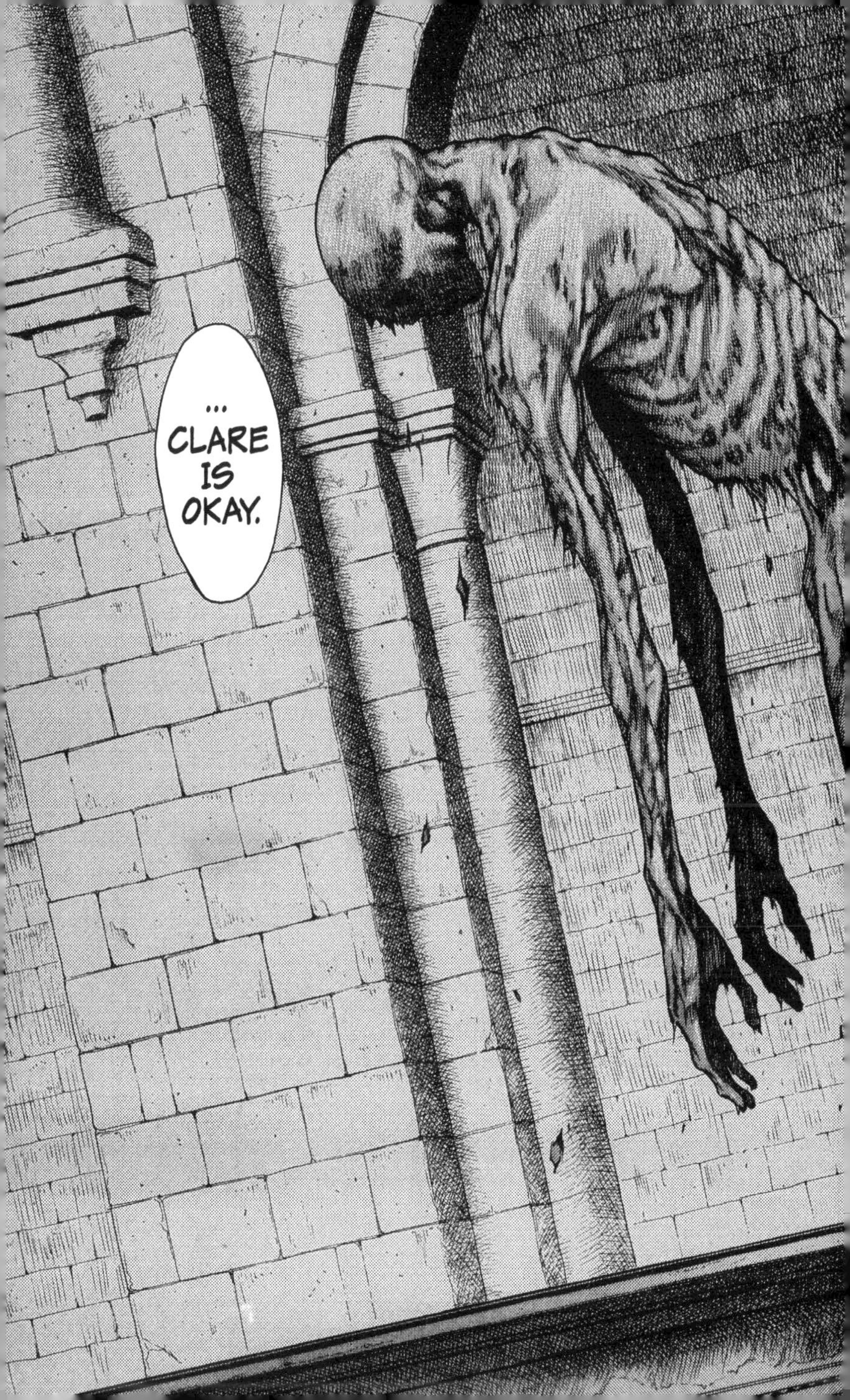
... CLARE IS OKAY.

BIKI
BIKI
BIKI
BIKI
BIKI
BIKI
BIKI
BIKI
BIKI
BIKI
BIKI
BIKI
BIKI
BIKI

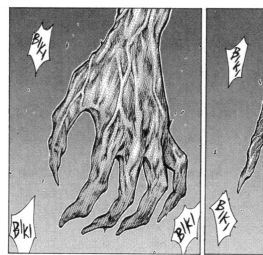

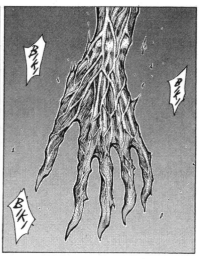

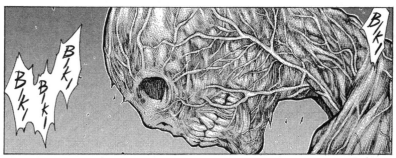

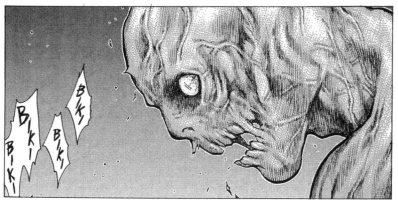

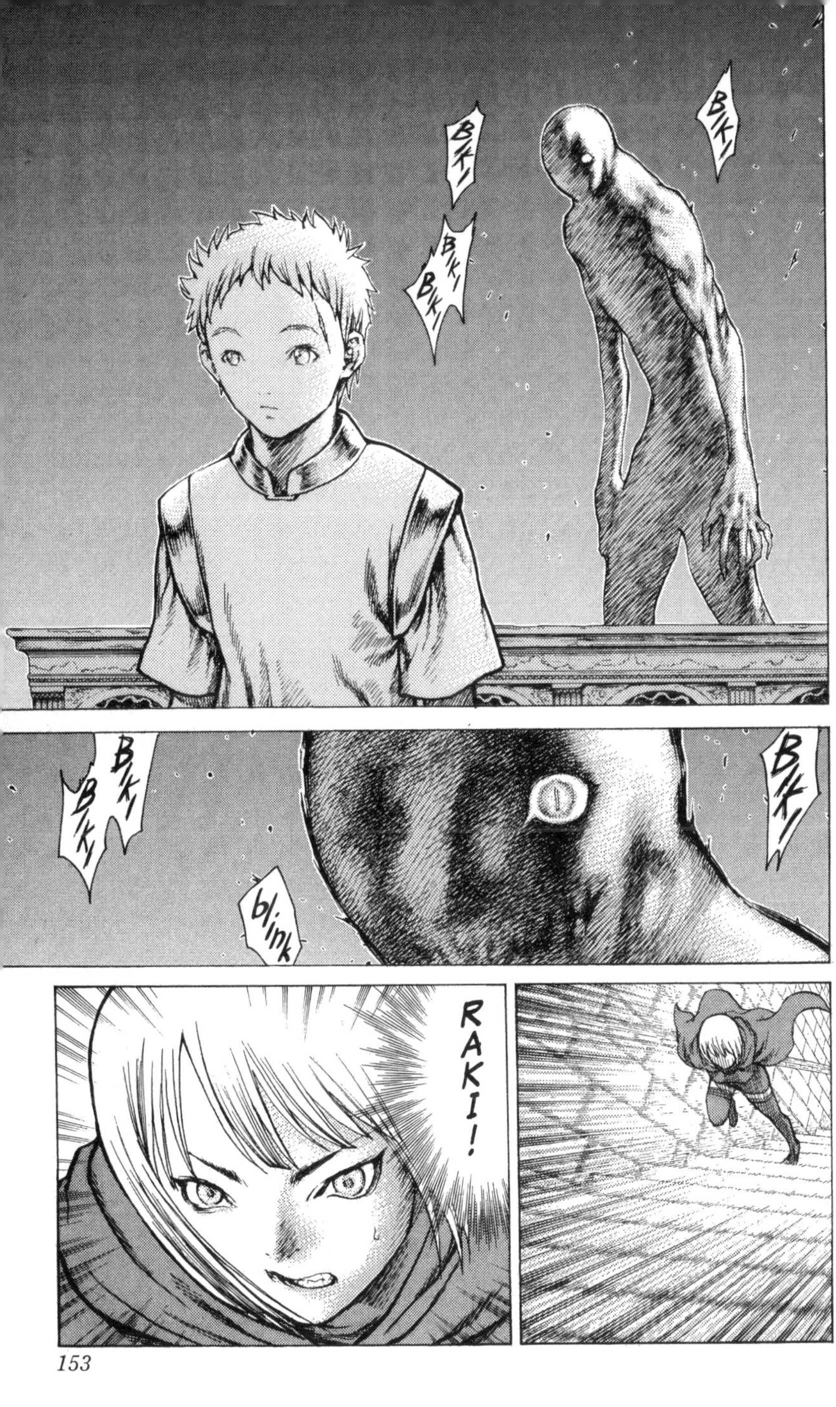
BIKI
BIKI
BIKI
BIKI
BIKI!
BIKI
BIKI
blink
RAKI!

クレイモア

Claymore™

Scene 9: Darkness in Paradise, Part 5

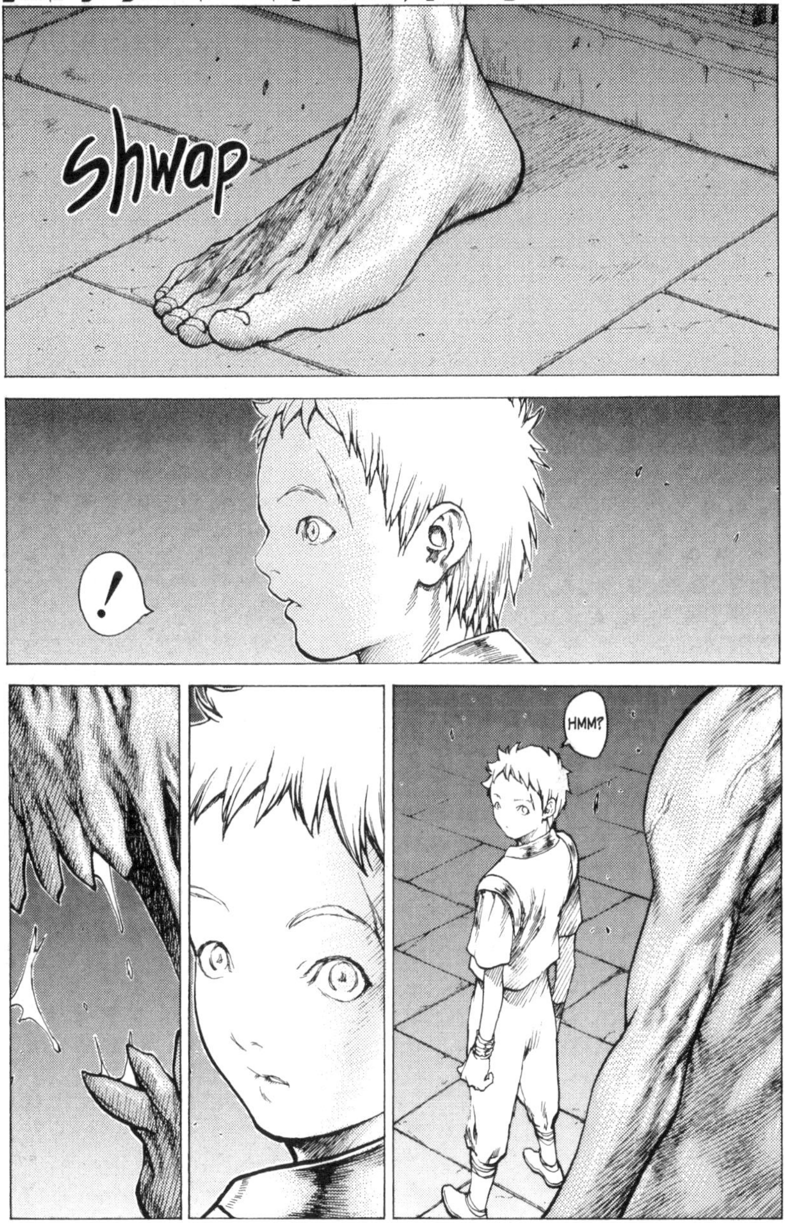
shwap
!
HMM?

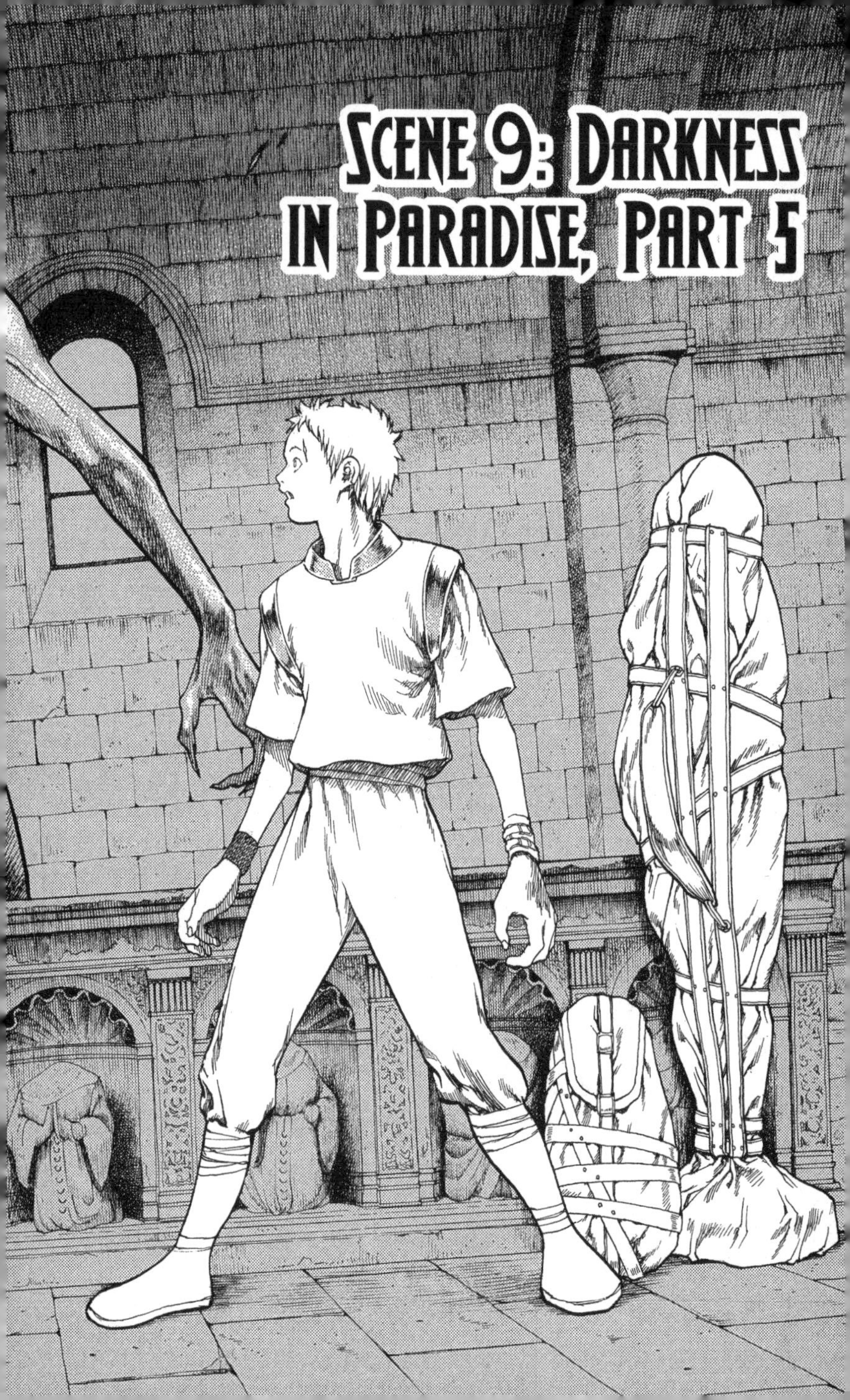
Scene 9: Darkness in Paradise, Part 5

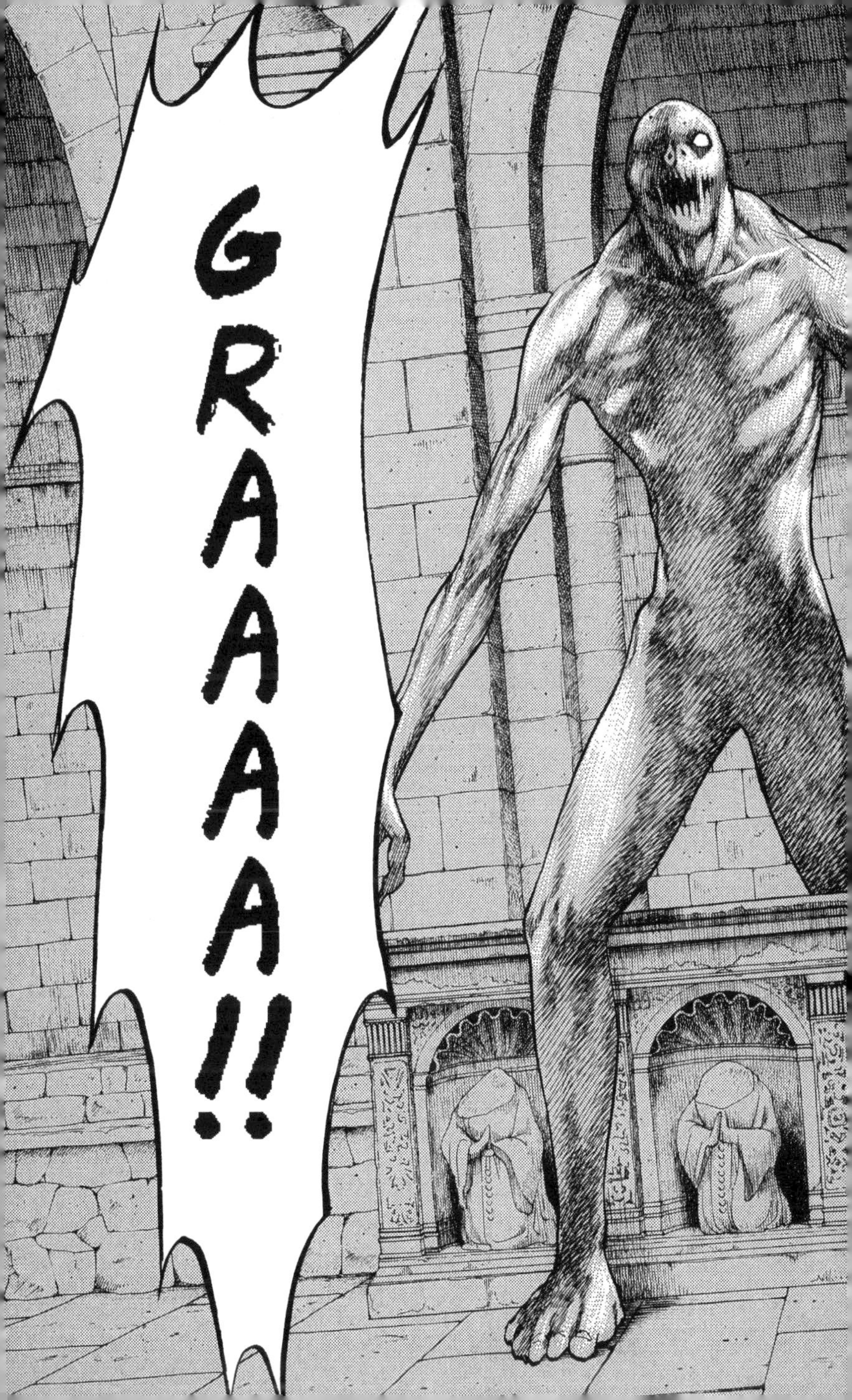
GRAAAA!!

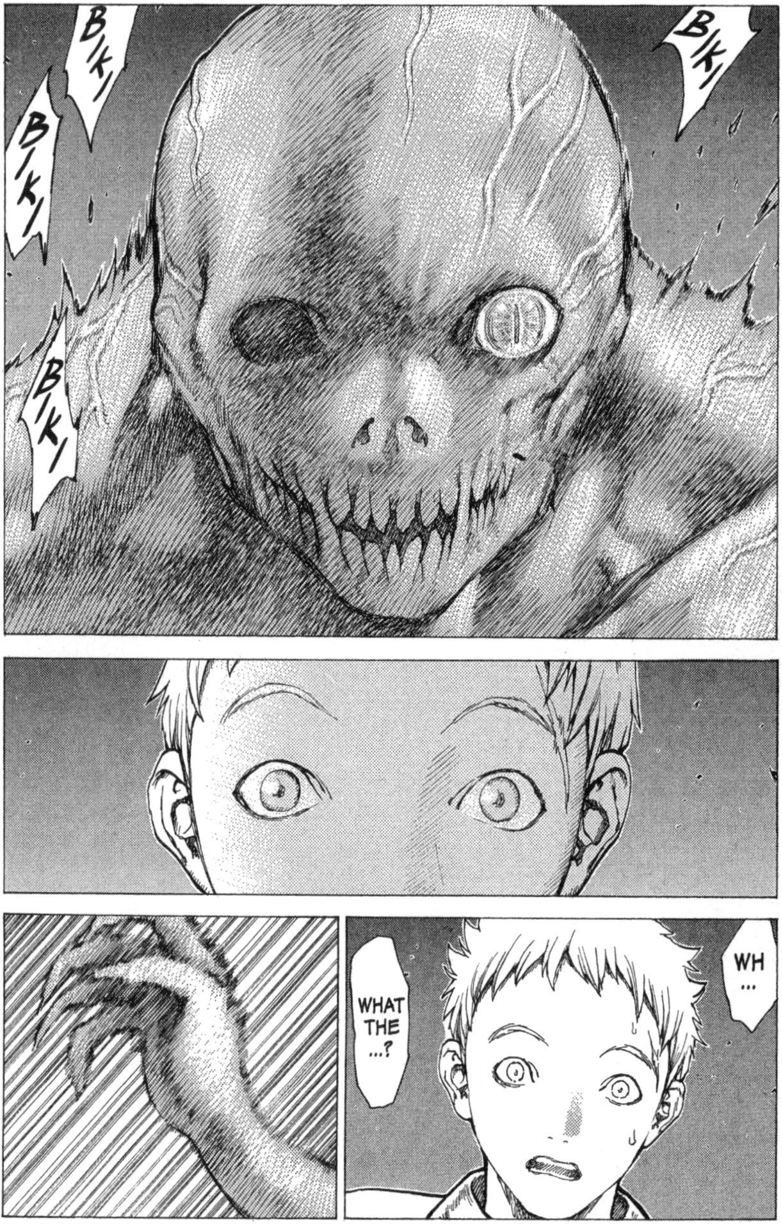
BKI
BKI
BKI
BKI
WH ...
WHAT THE ...?

READ THIS WAY

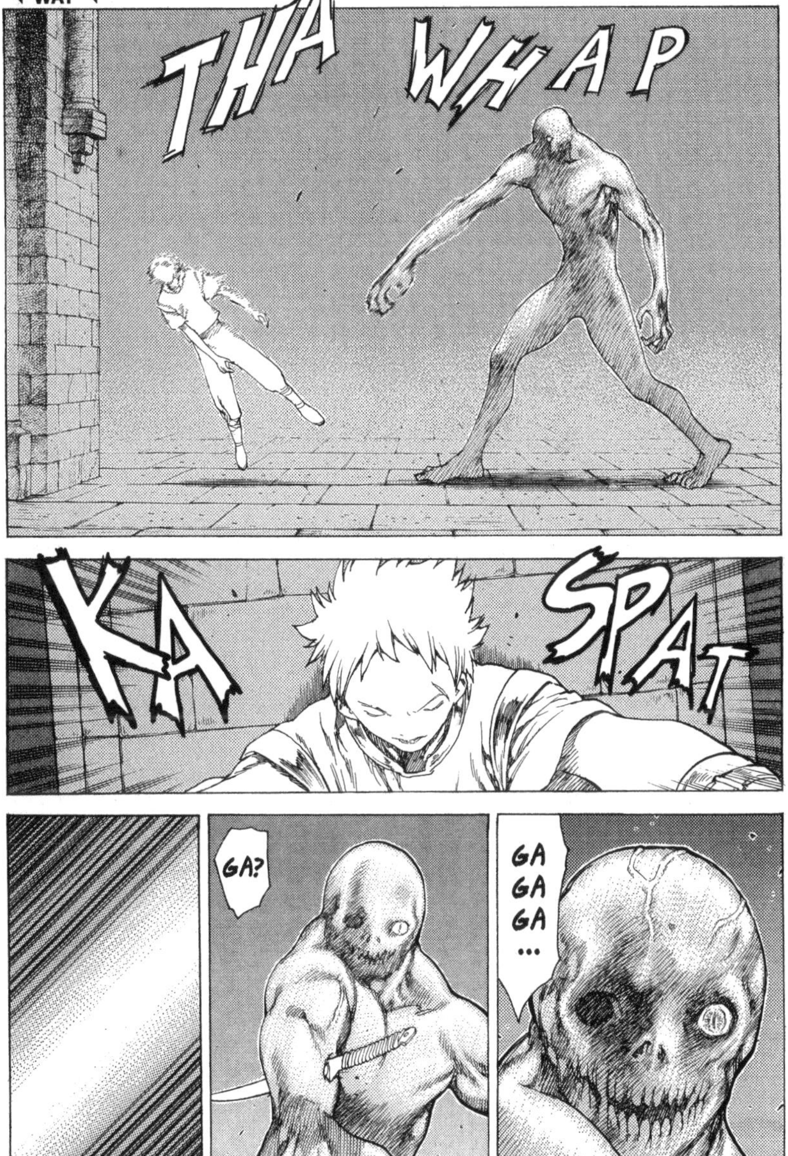
THA WHAP
KA SPAT
GA GA GA ...
GA?

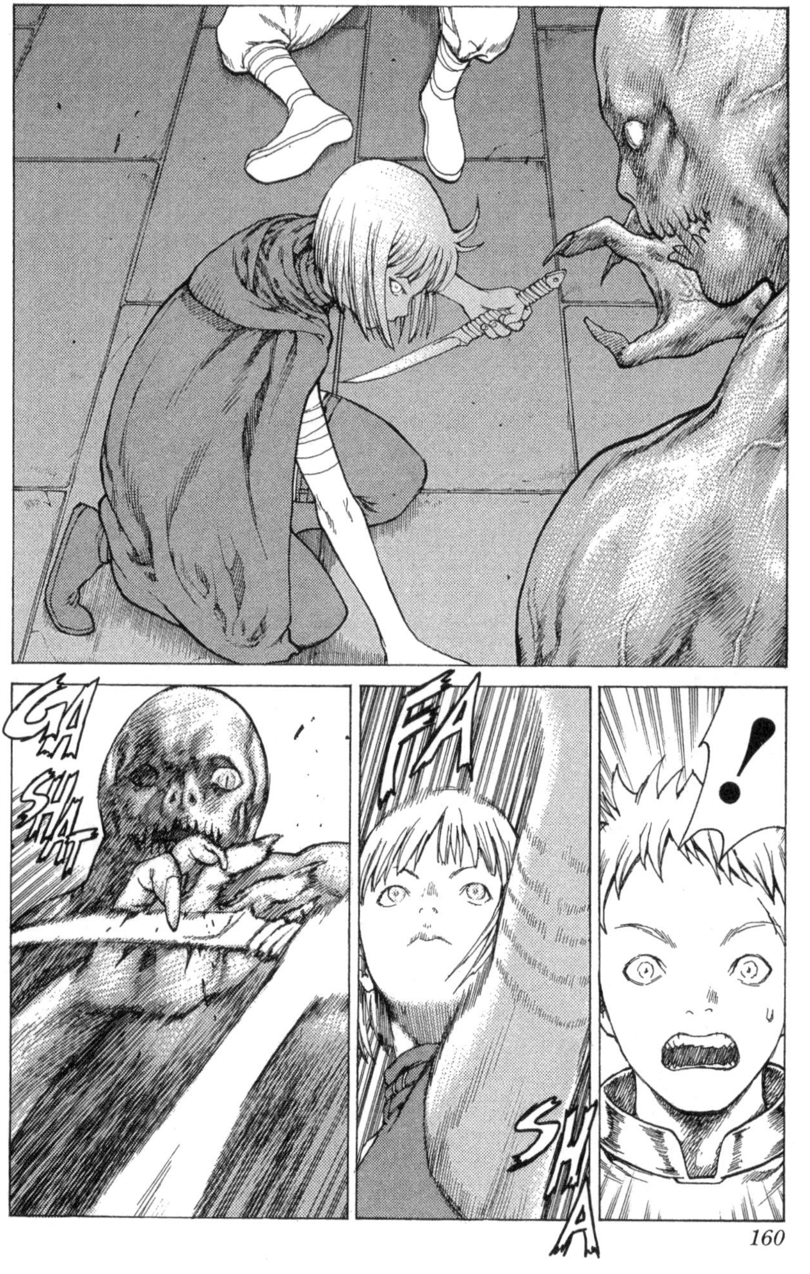
!
FA
SHA
GASUHAT

READ THIS WAY

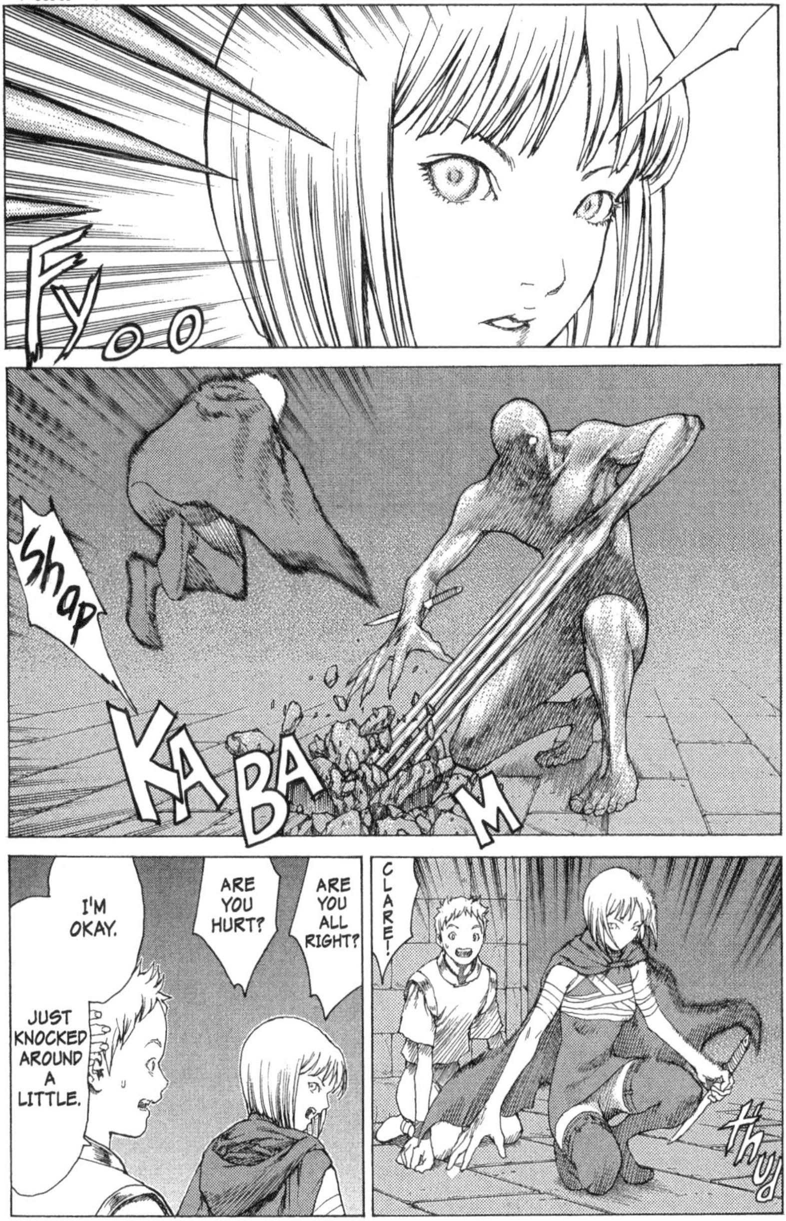
FYOO
SHAP
KABAM
CLARE!
THUD
ARE YOU ALL RIGHT?
ARE YOU HURT?
I'M OKAY.
JUST KNOCKED AROUND A LITTLE.

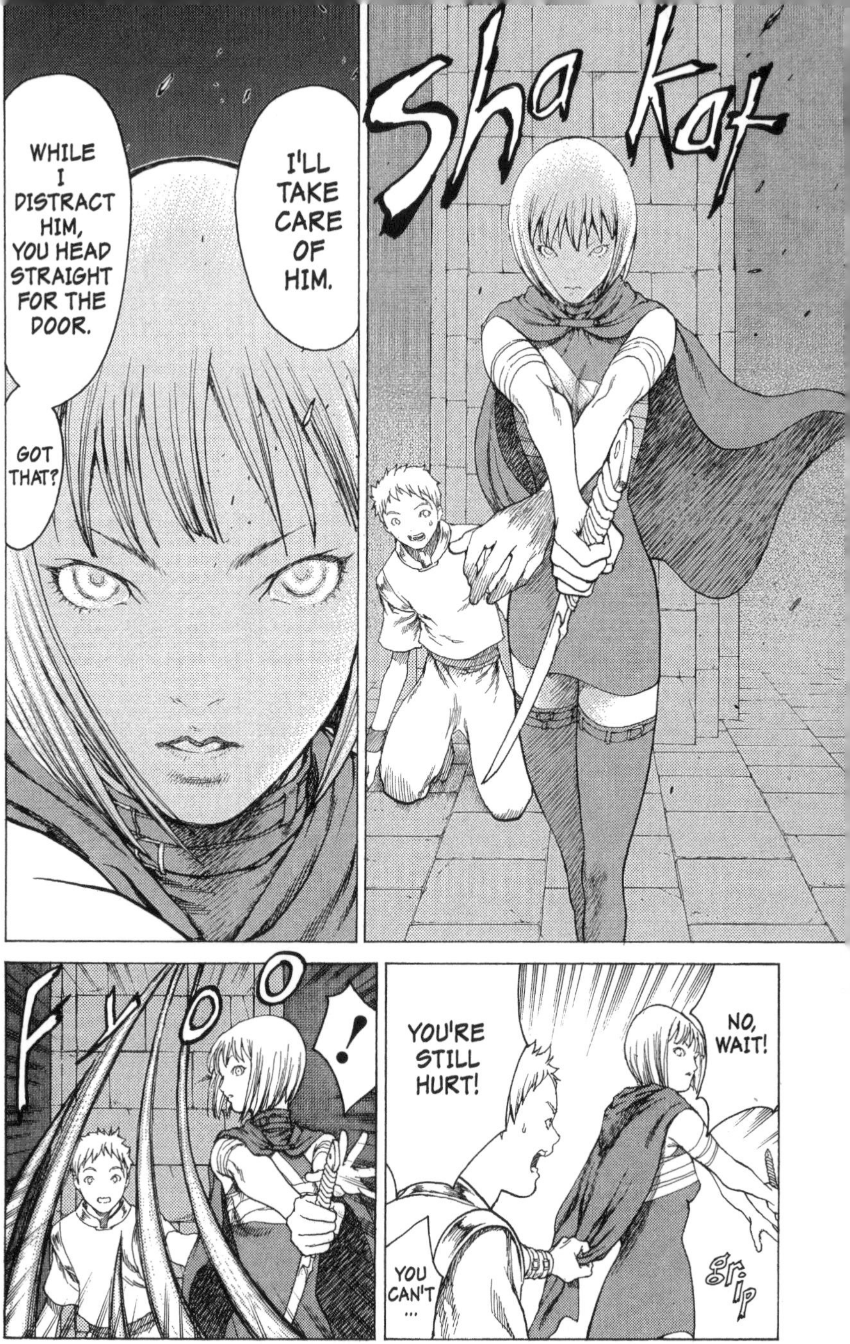
Sha Kat
I'LL TAKE CARE OF HIM.
WHILE I DISTRACT HIM, YOU HEAD STRAIGHT FOR THE DOOR.
GOT THAT?
NO, WAIT!
YOU'RE STILL HURT!
grip
YOU CAN'T ...
!
Fyoo

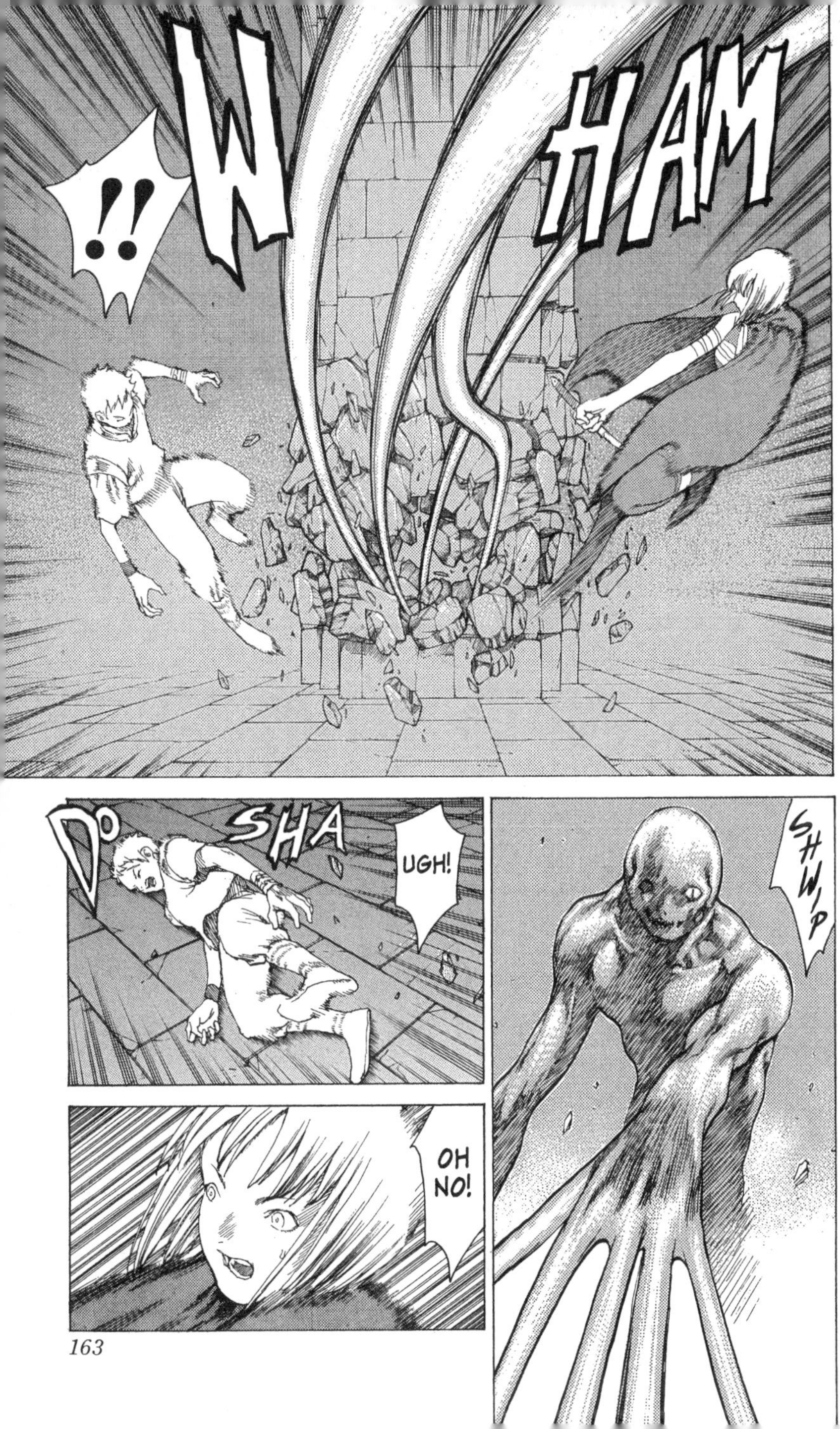
WHAM
!!
SHWIP
UGH!
DOSHA
OH NO!

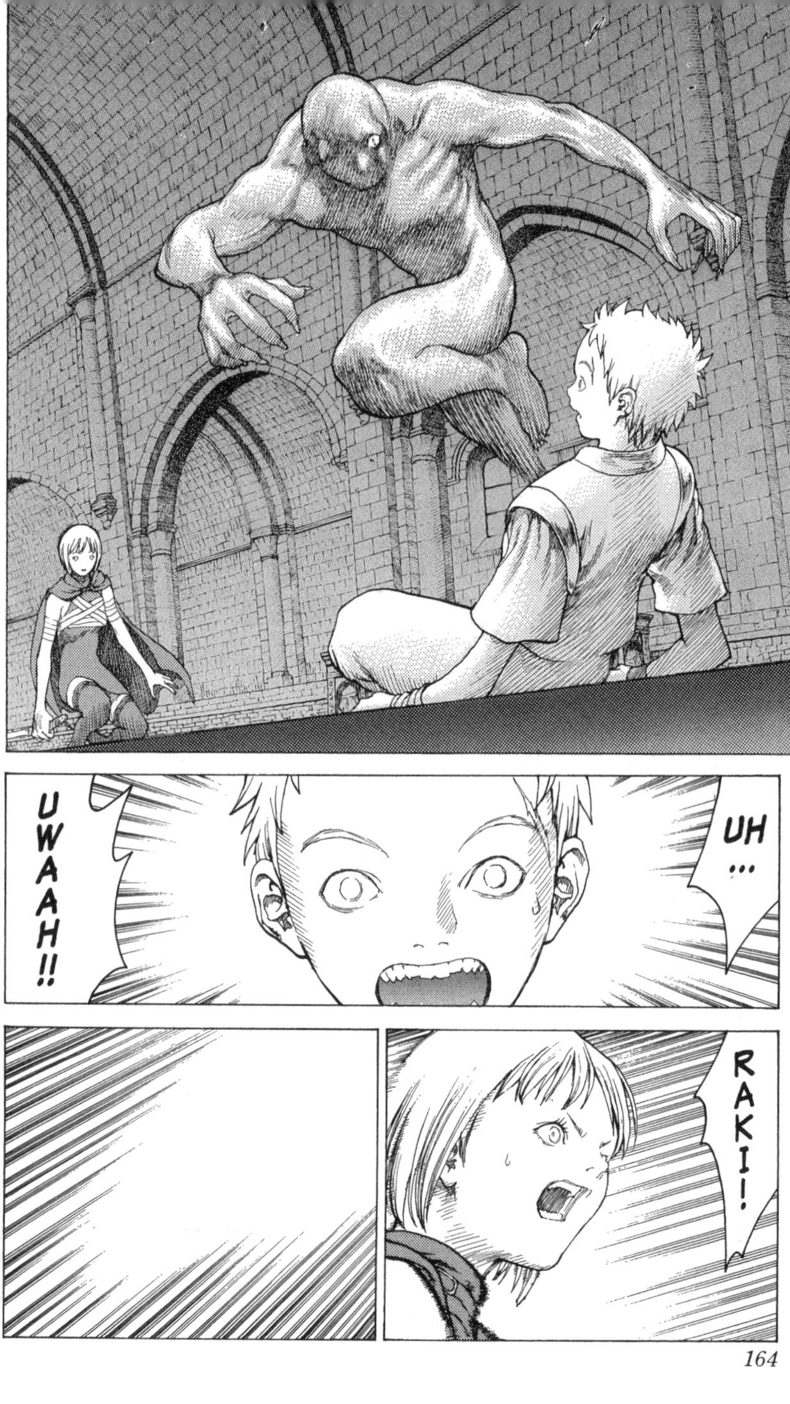
UH...
UWAAAH!!
RAKI!

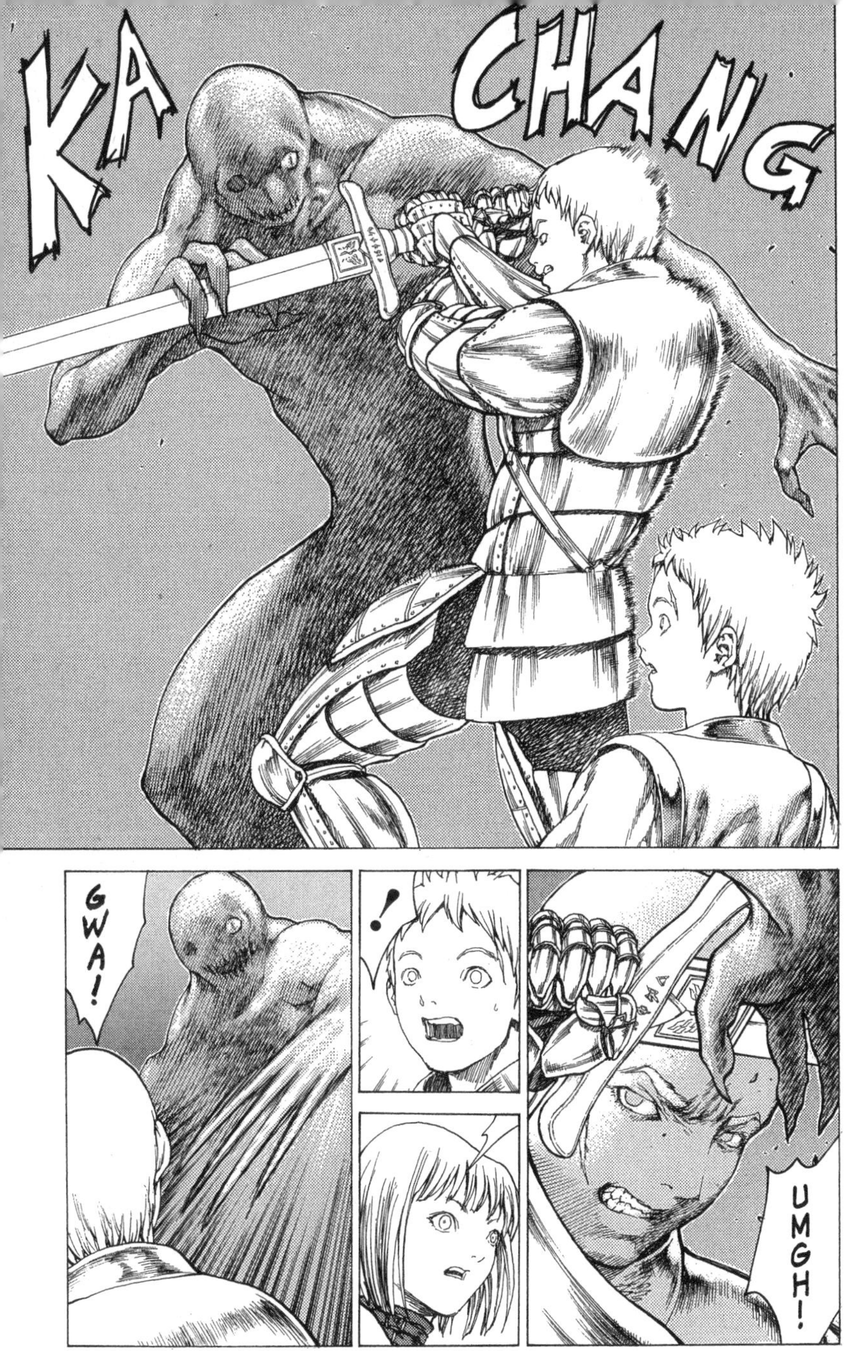
KA CHANG
UMGH!
!
GWA!

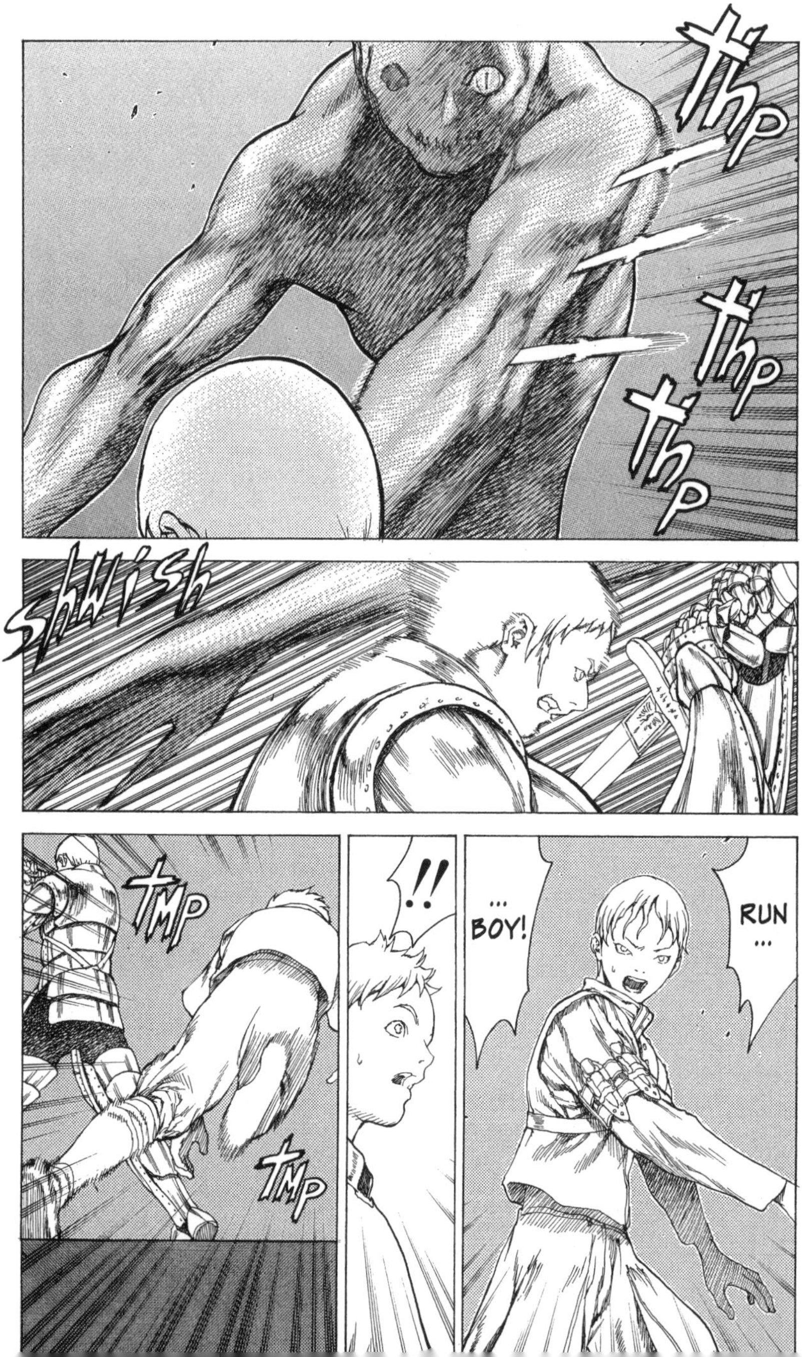
thp
thp
thp
shwish
RUN ...
... BOY!
!!
TMP
TMP

READ THIS WAY

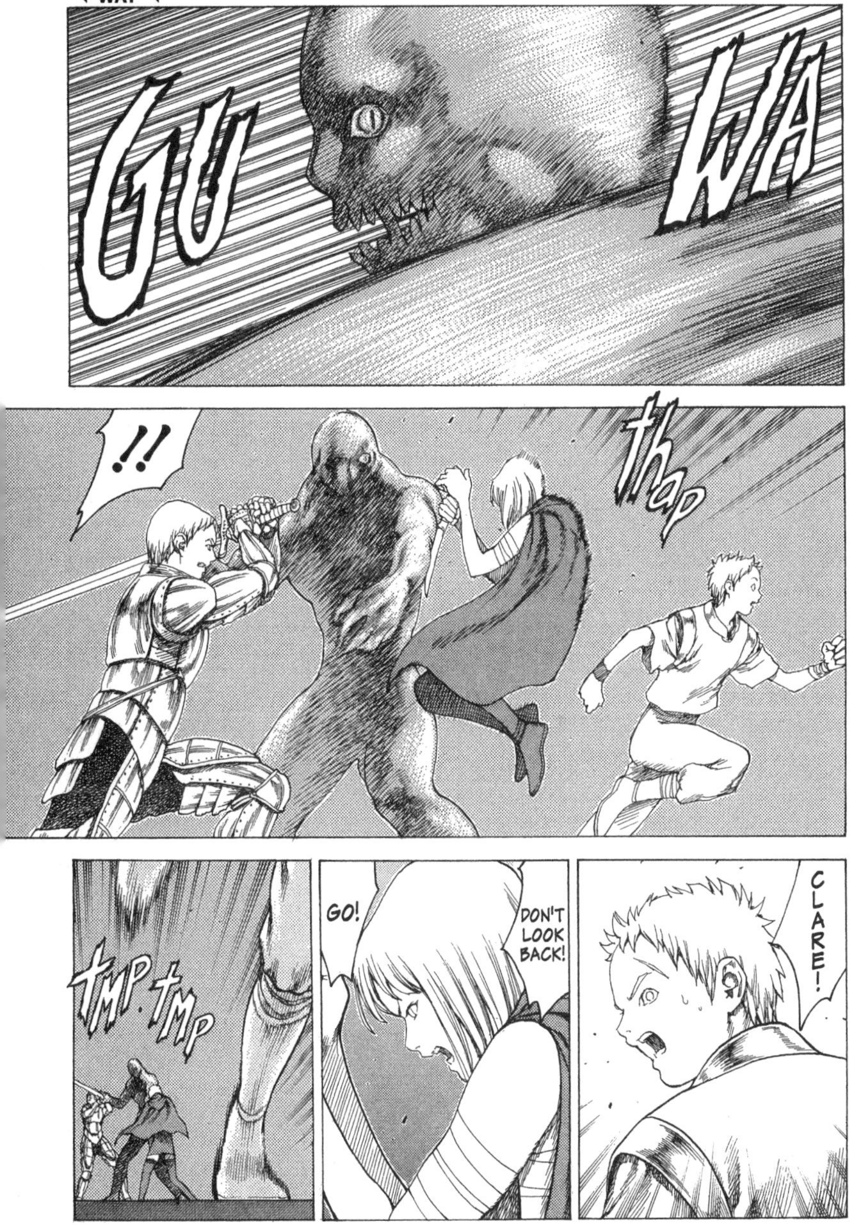
GU WA
thap
!!
CLARE!
DON'T LOOK BACK!
GO!
TMP TMP

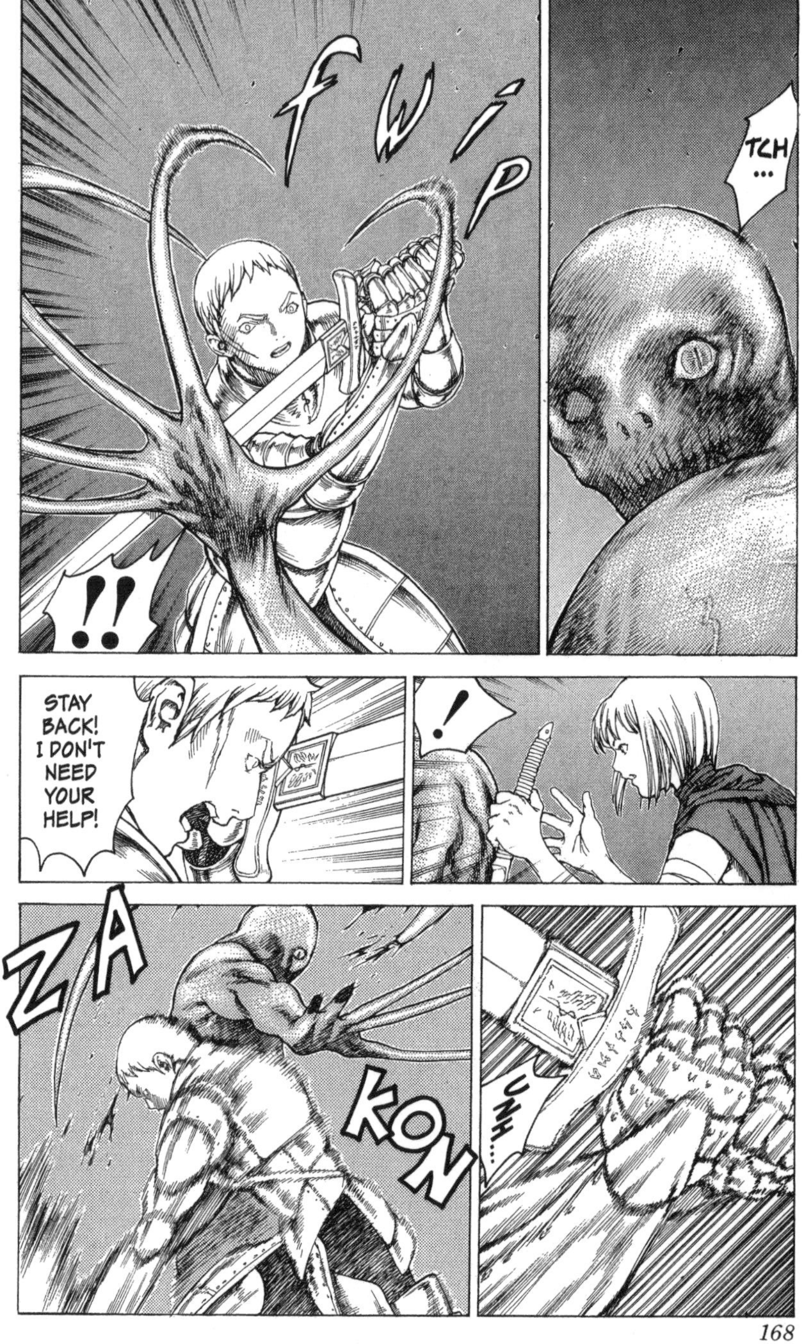
TCH ...
FWIP
!!
!
STAY BACK! I DON'T NEED YOUR HELP!
UNH...
ZA
KON

READ THIS WAY

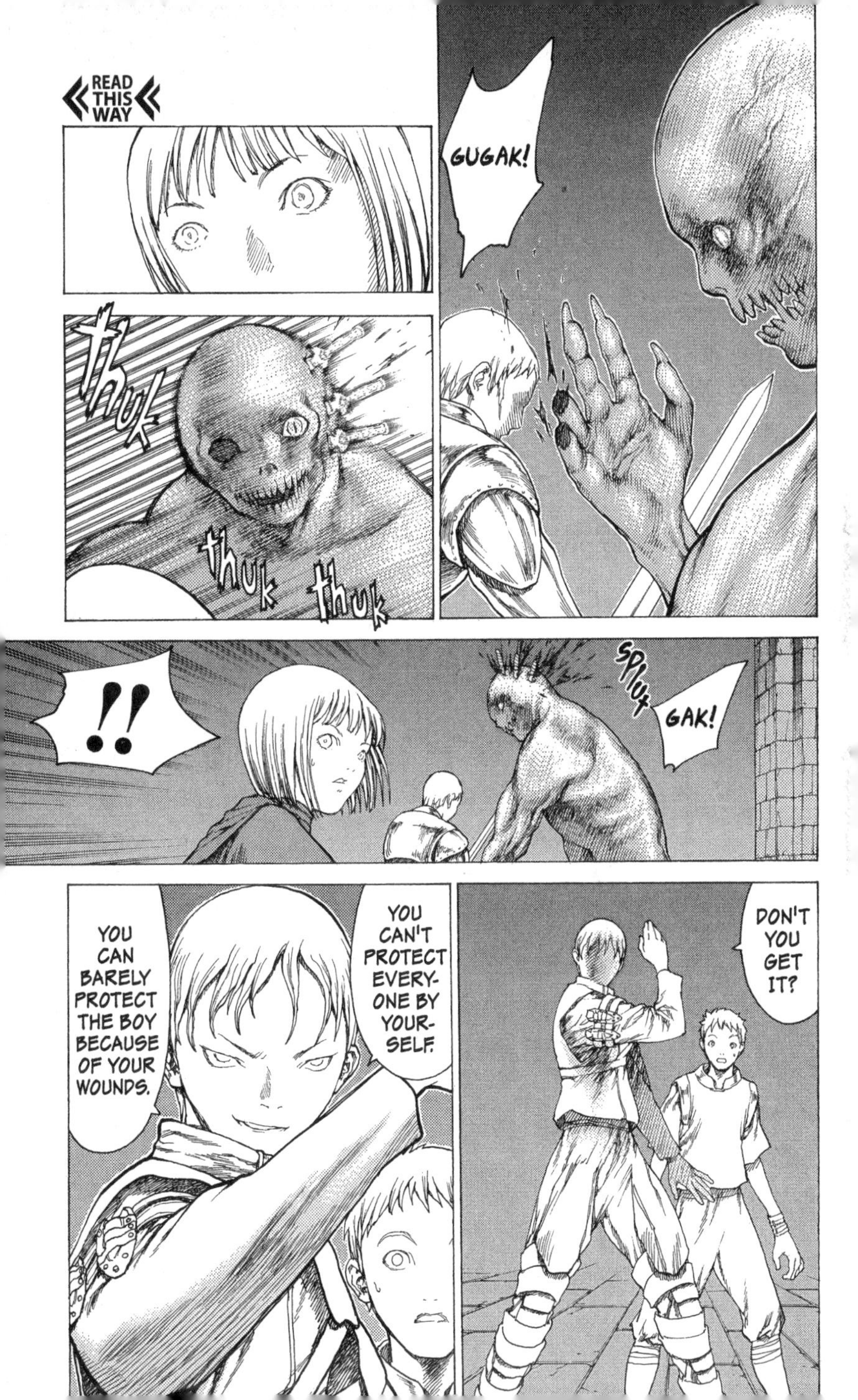
GUGAK!
thuk
thuk
thuk
SPLUT
GAK!
!!
DON'T YOU GET IT?
YOU CAN'T PROTECT EVERY-ONE BY YOUR-SELF.
YOU CAN BARELY PROTECT THE BOY BECAUSE OF YOUR WOUNDS.

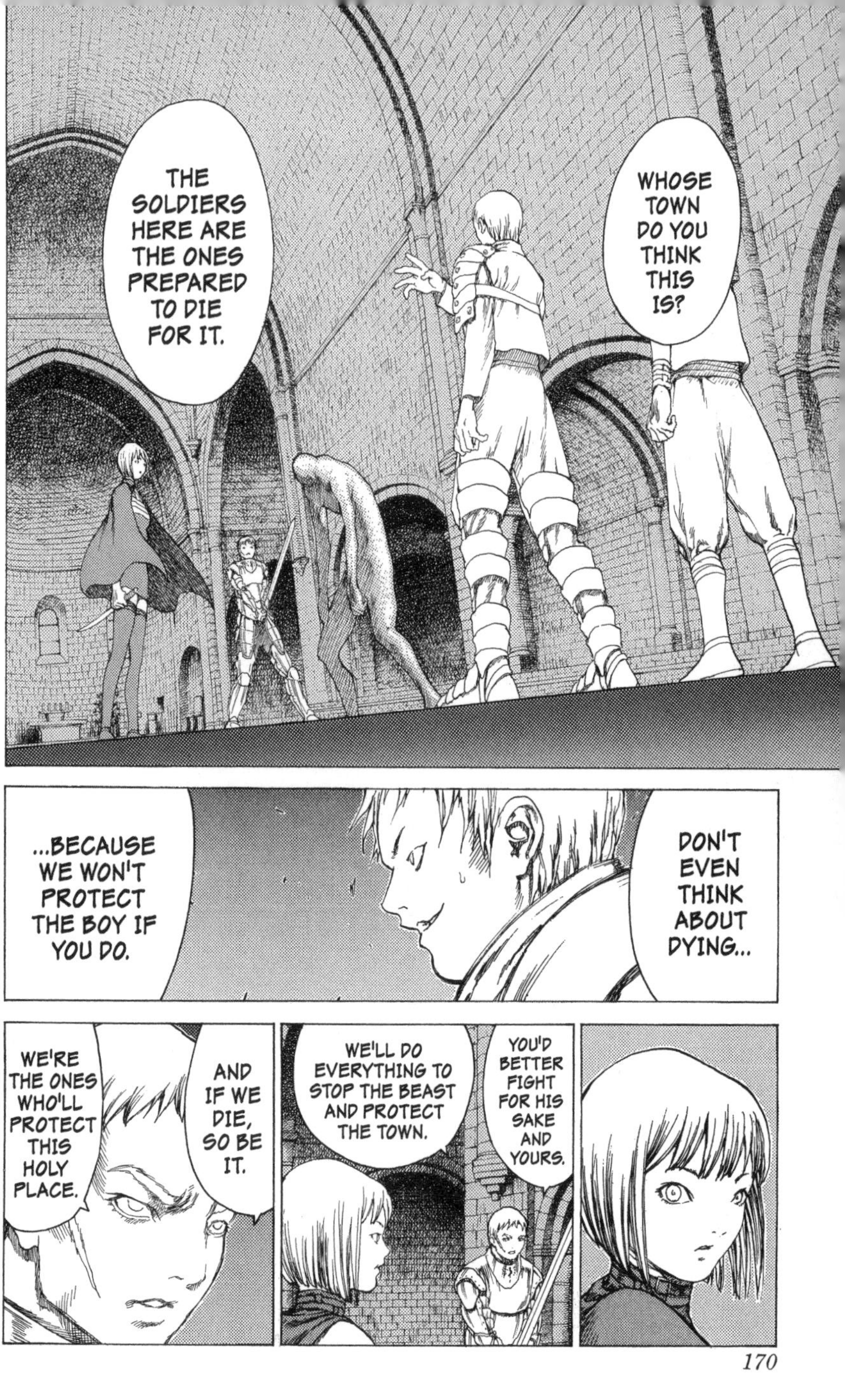
WHOSE TOWN DO YOU THINK THIS IS?
THE SOLDIERS HERE ARE THE ONES PREPARED TO DIE FOR IT.
DON'T EVEN THINK ABOUT DYING...
...BECAUSE WE WON'T PROTECT THE BOY IF YOU DO.
YOU'D BETTER FIGHT FOR HIS SAKE AND YOURS.
WE'LL DO EVERYTHING TO STOP THE BEAST AND PROTECT THE TOWN.
AND IF WE DIE, SO BE IT.
WE'RE THE ONES WHO'LL PROTECT THIS HOLY PLACE.

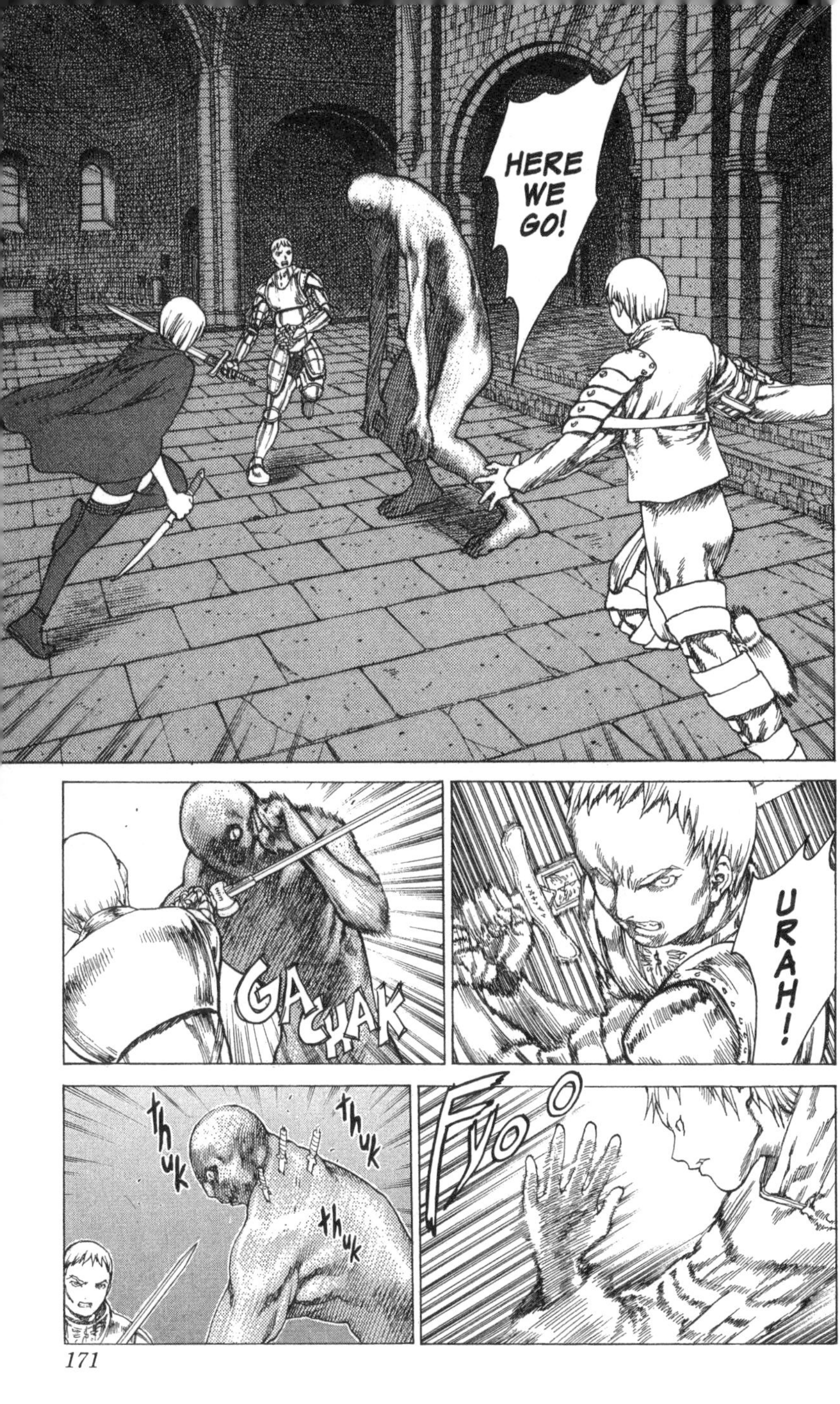
HERE WE GO!
URAH!
GACHAK
FVOO
thuk
thuk
thuk

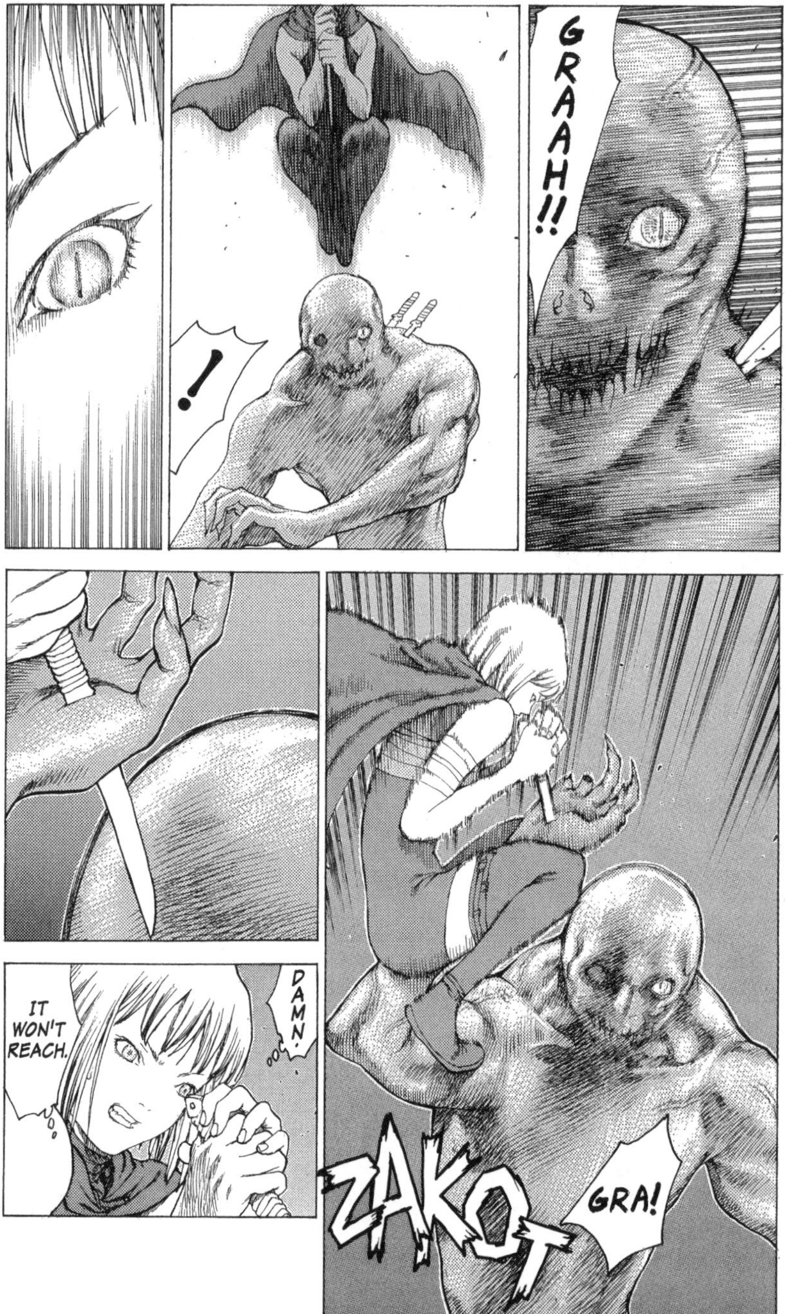
GRAAAH!!
!
GRA!
ZAKOT
DAMN.
IT WON'T REACH.

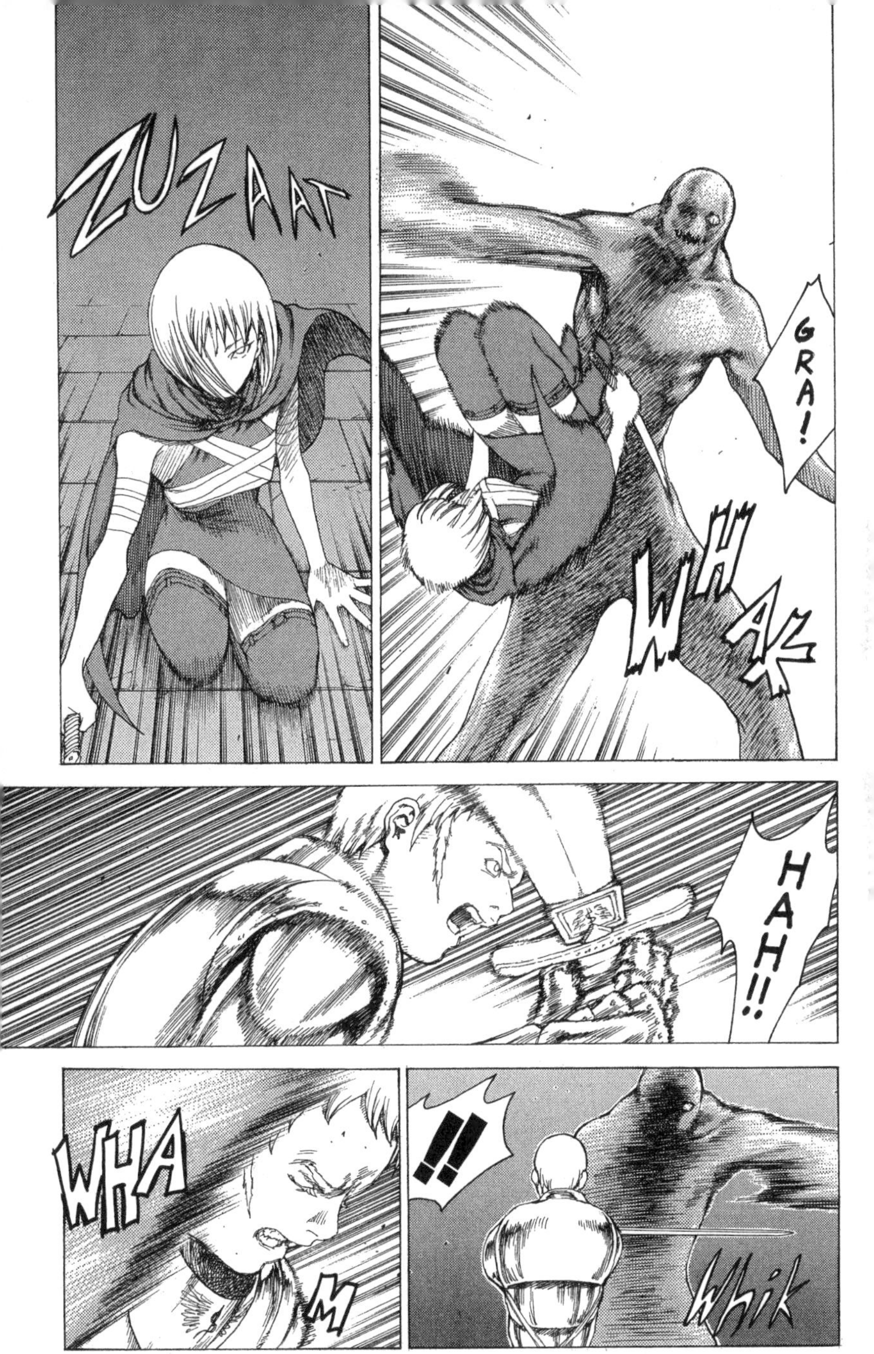
GRA!
WHAK
ZUZAAT
HAH!!
!!
Whik
WHAM

BAP
BAP

NO!

CLANG

WHABAM

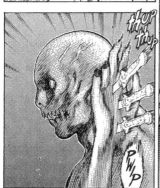

THUP
THP
THP

PWP

!!

GUK

SLAK

Whish

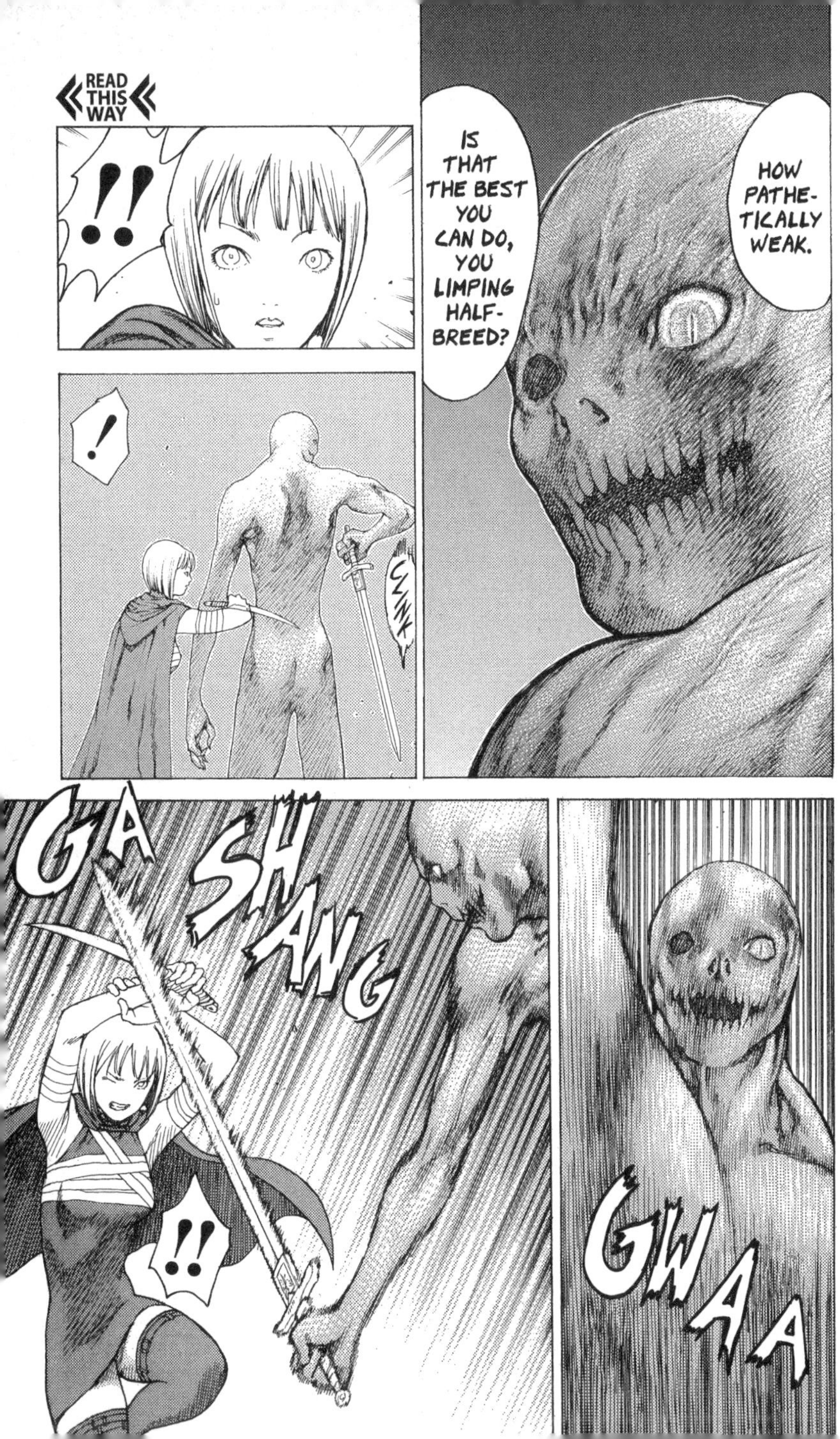
READ THIS WAY
HOW PATHETICALLY WEAK.
IS THAT THE BEST YOU CAN DO, YOU LIMPING HALF-BREED?
!!
!
CLINK
GWAA
GASHANG
!!

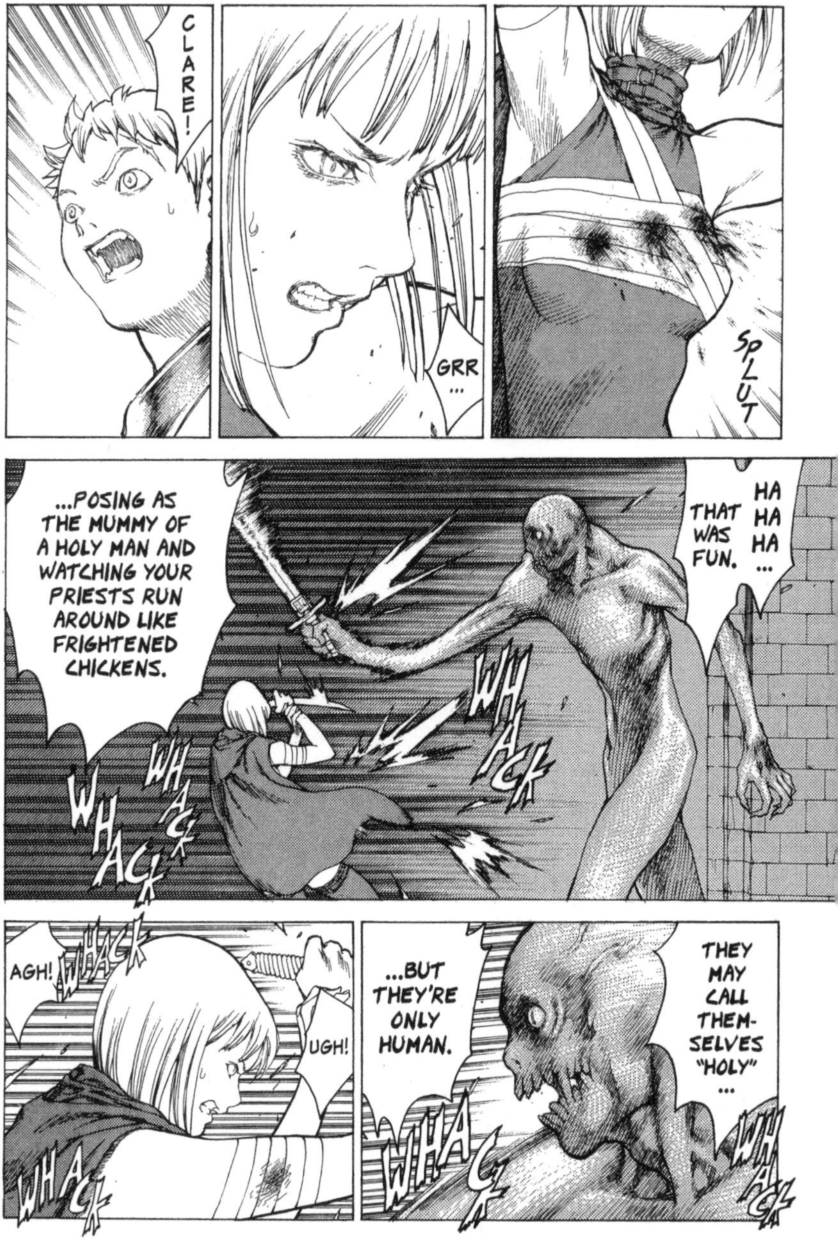
SPLUT
GRR...
CLARE!
HA HA HA ...
THAT WAS FUN.
...POSING AS THE MUMMY OF A HOLY MAN AND WATCHING YOUR PRIESTS RUN AROUND LIKE FRIGHTENED CHICKENS.
WHACK
WHACK
WHACK
THEY MAY CALL THEM-SELVES "HOLY" ...
...BUT THEY'RE ONLY HUMAN.
WHACK
WHACK
UGH!
WHACK
AGH!
WHACK

READ THIS WAY

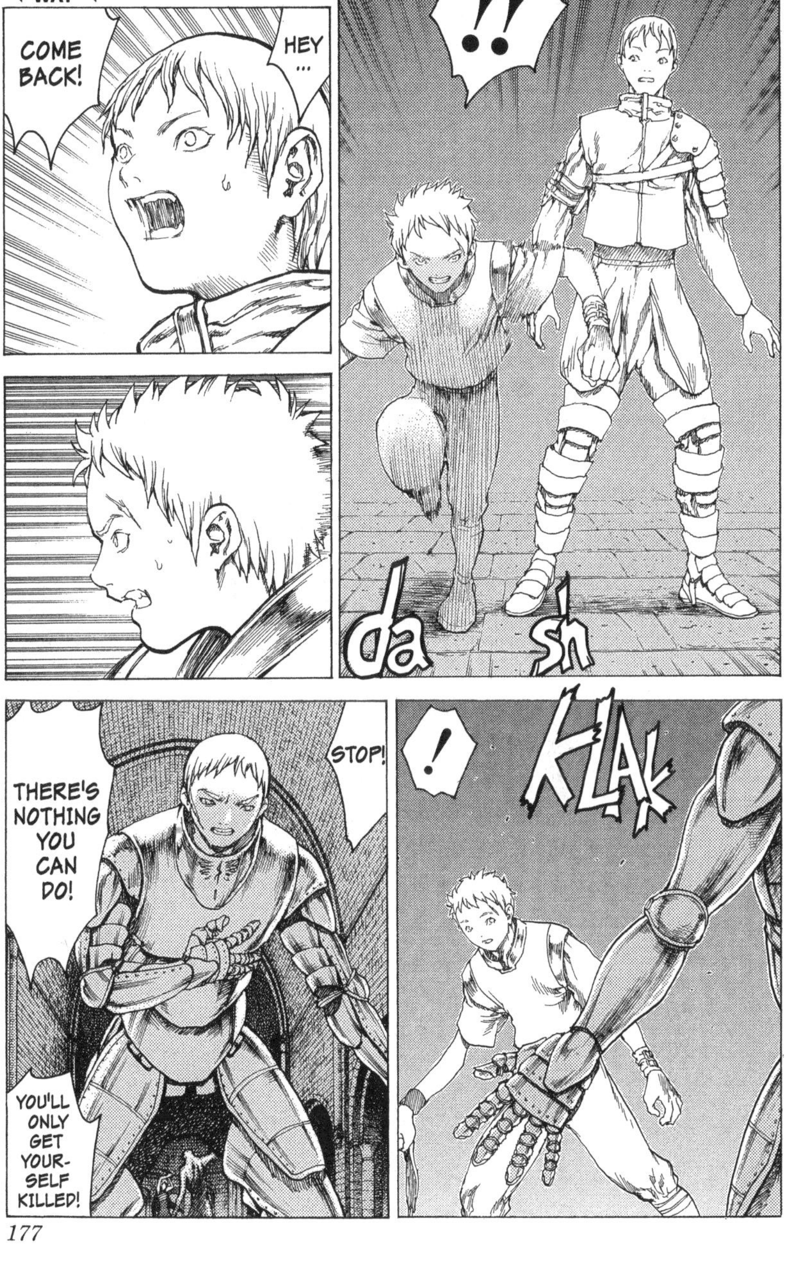
!!
dash
HEY ...
COME BACK!
!
KLAK
STOP!
THERE'S NOTHING YOU CAN DO!
YOU'LL ONLY GET YOUR-SELF KILLED!

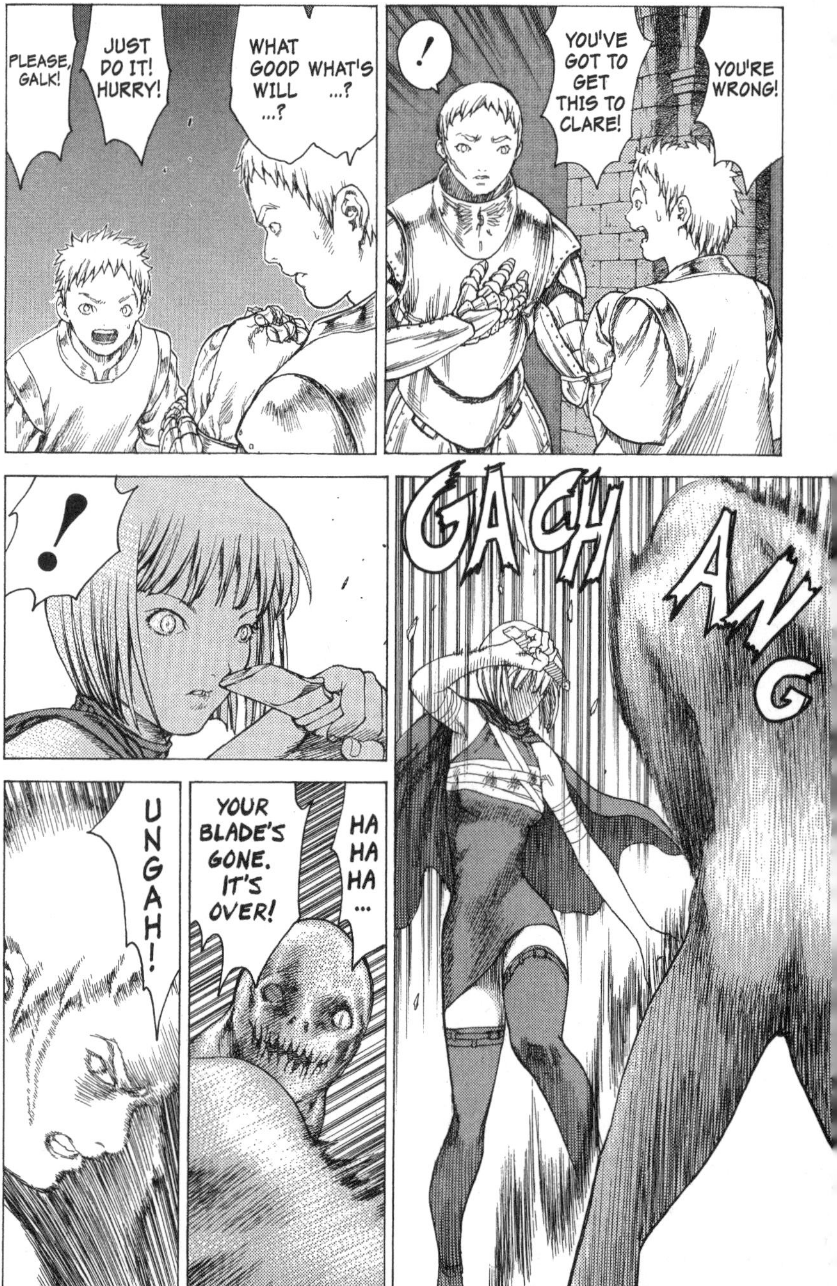
YOU'RE WRONG!
YOU'VE GOT TO GET THIS TO CLARE!
!
WHAT'S ...?
WHAT GOOD WILL ...?
JUST DO IT! HURRY!
PLEASE, GALK!
GACHANG
!
HA HA HA ...
YOUR BLADE'S GONE. IT'S OVER!
UNGAH!

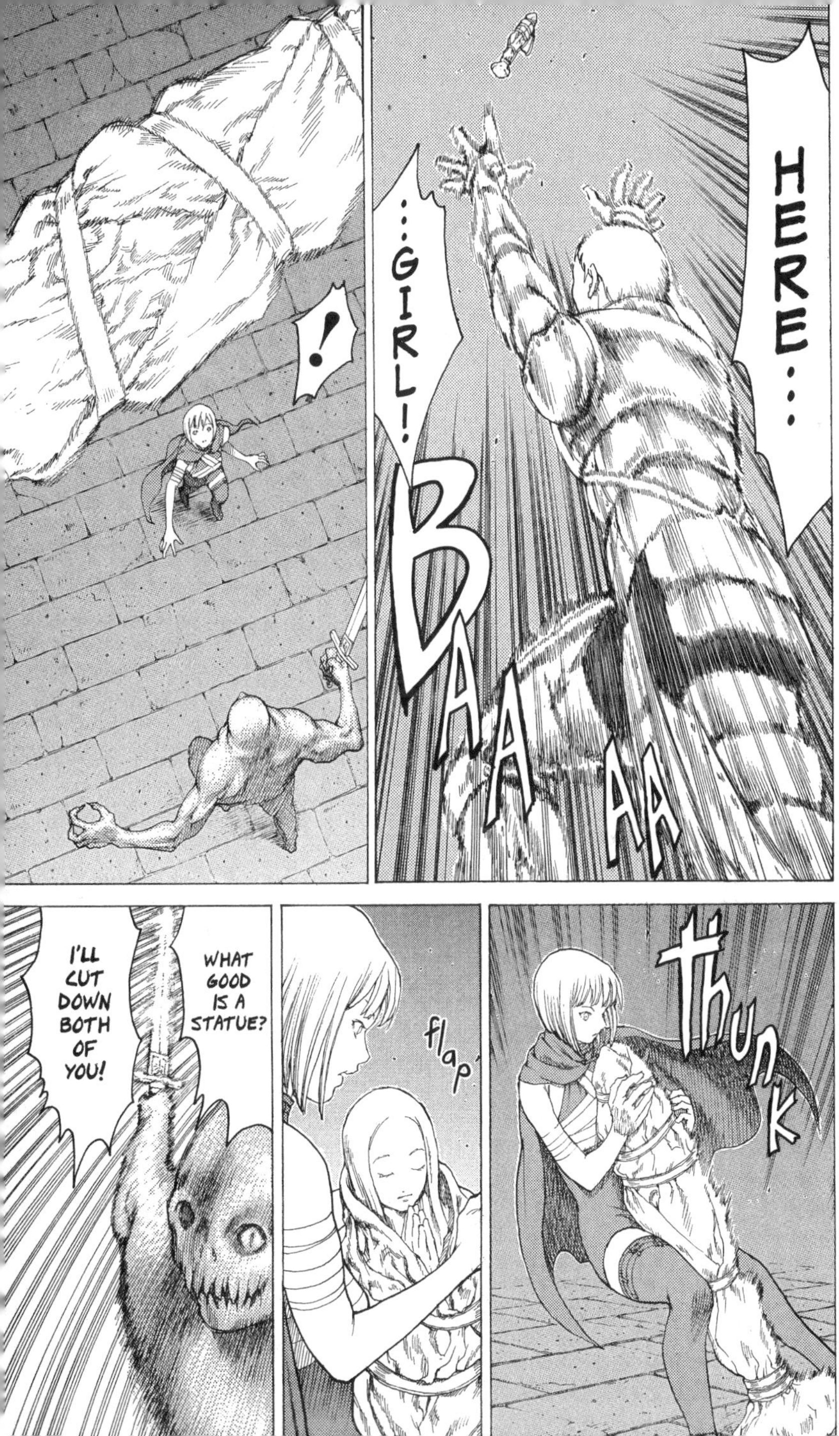

HERE...
...GIRL!
BAAAA
!
thunk
flap
WHAT GOOD IS A STATUE?
I'LL CUT DOWN BOTH OF YOU!

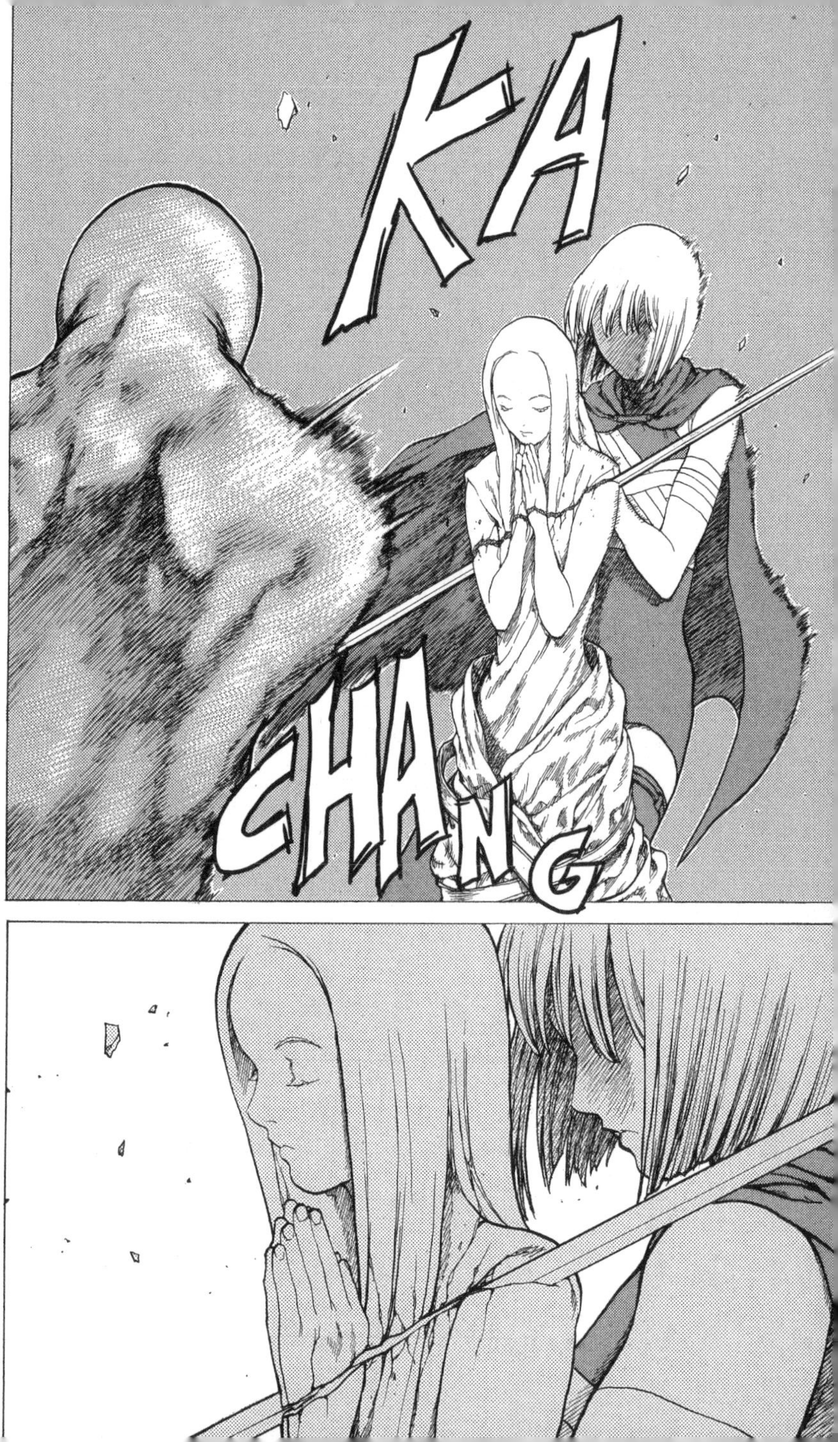
KA CHANG

READ THIS WAY

WHA ...!?
CRACK
BIKI
BIKI
BIKI
BIKI
BIKI
BIKI
BIKI
BIKI
BIKI
BIKI
BIKI
CRACK
CRACK

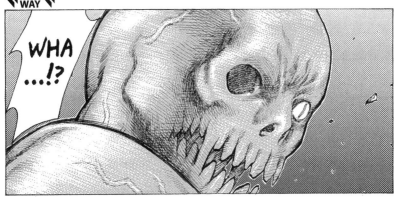

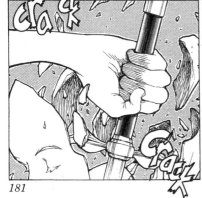

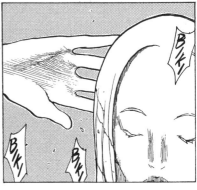

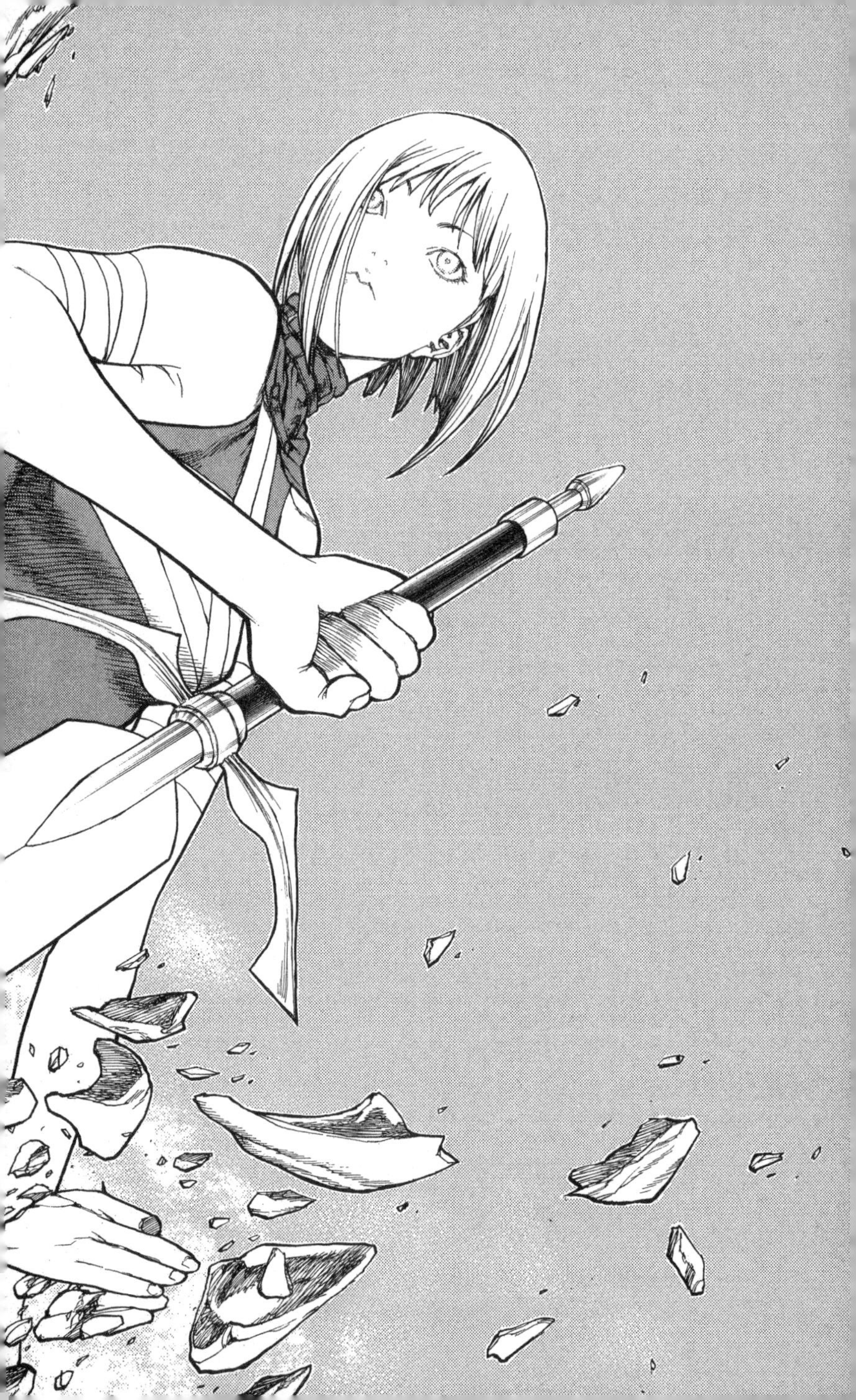

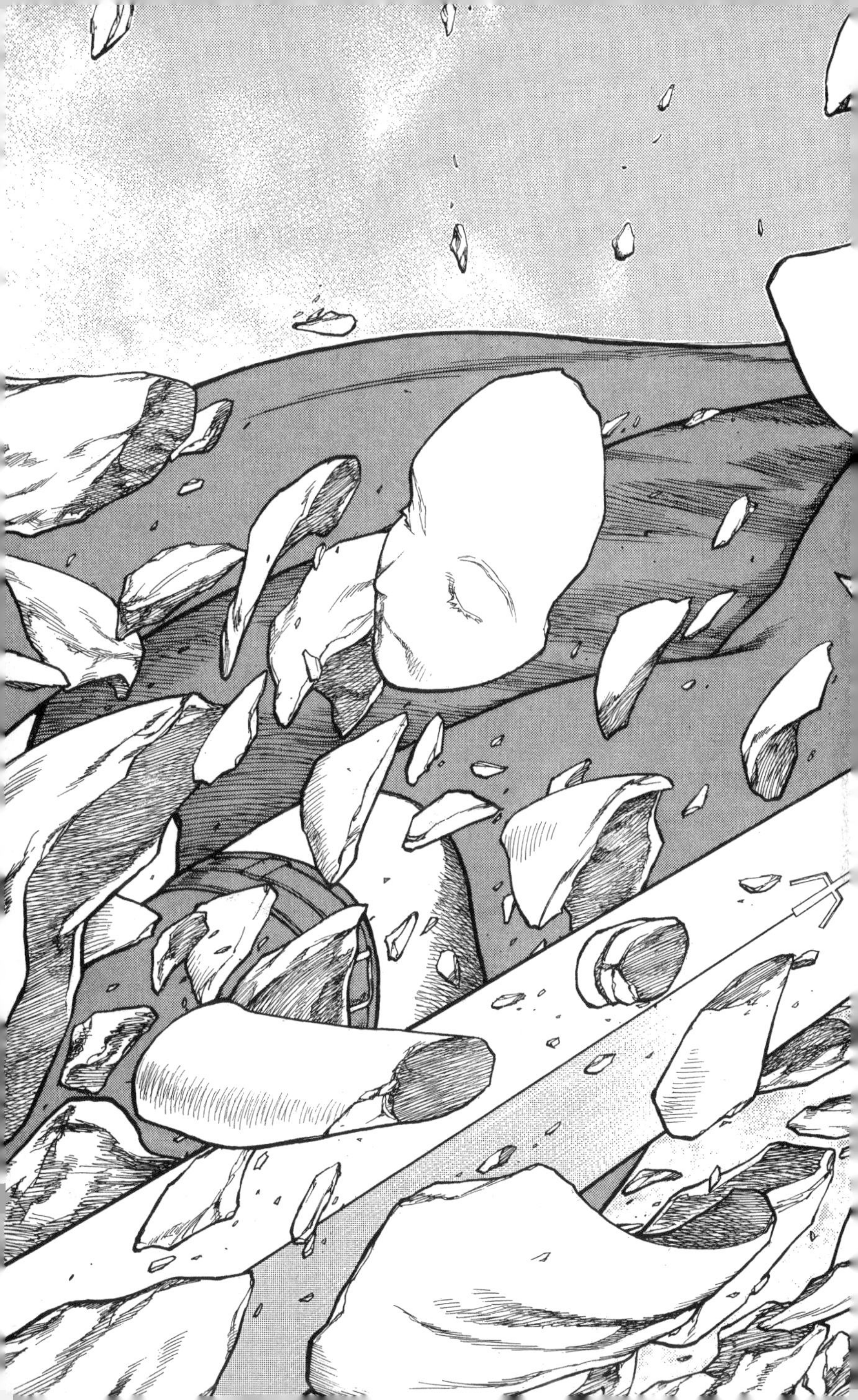

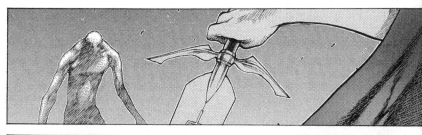

...CLAY-MORE...

A...

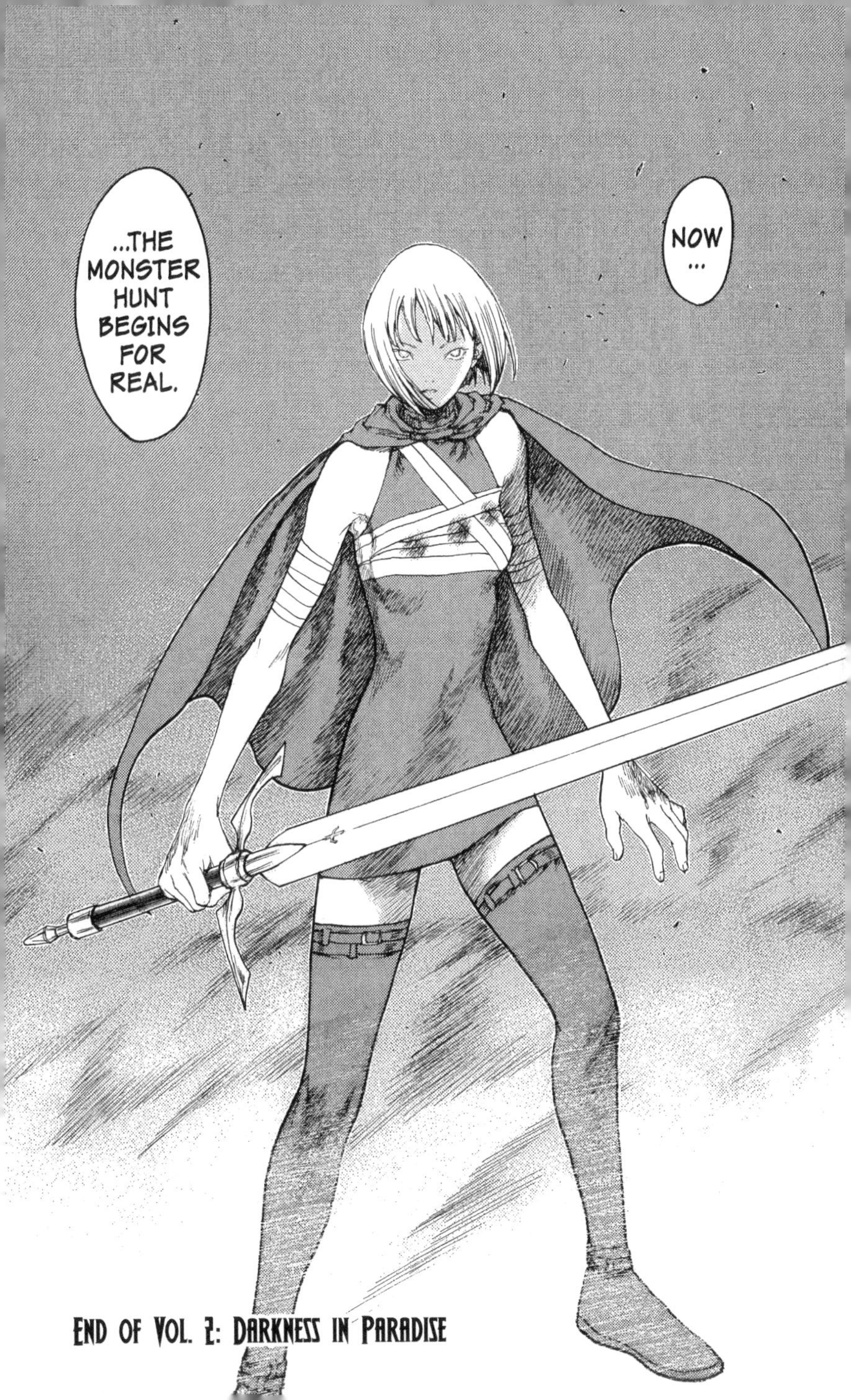
NOW ...
...THE MONSTER HUNT BEGINS FOR REAL.
End of Vol. 2: Darkness in Paradise

IN THE NEXT VOLUME

The Yoma that has been terrorizing the cathedral of Rabona finally shows itself, and it's bigger and stronger than anyone expected. Clare has a fighting chance of defeating the creature, now that she has her Claymore sword, but there's more to this wily Yoma than meets the eye.

Available now!

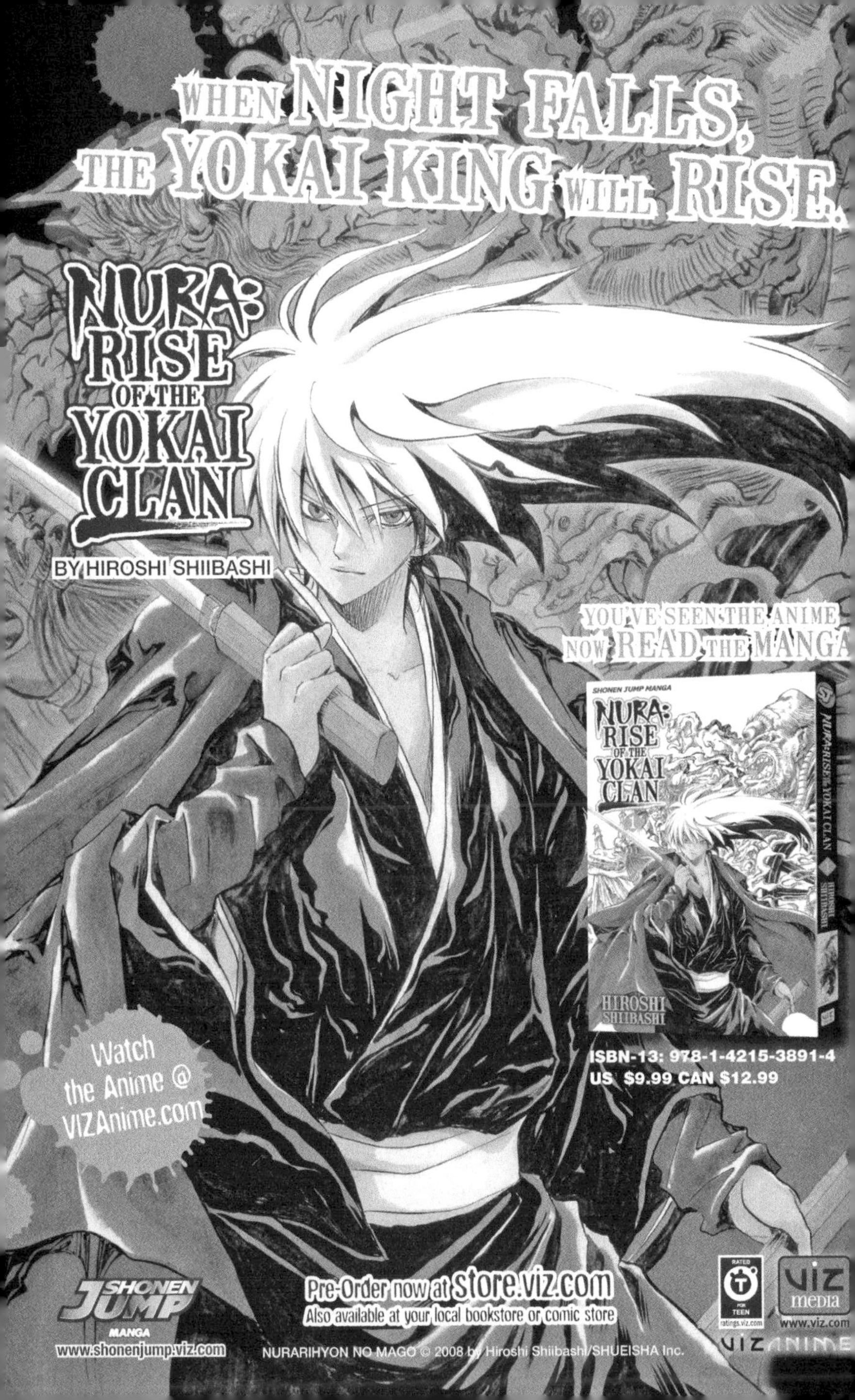
WHEN NIGHT FALLS, THE YOKAI KING WILL RISE.
NURA: RISE OF THE YOKAI CLAN
BY HIROSHI SHIIBASHI
YOU'VE SEEN THE ANIME NOW READ THE MANGA
SHONEN JUMP MANGA
NURA: RISE OF THE YOKAI CLAN
1
NURA: RISE OF THE YOKAI CLAN
HIROSHI SHIIBASHI
HIROSHI SHIIBASHI
ISBN-13: 978-1-4215-3891-4
US $9.99 CAN $12.99
Watch the Anime @ VIZAnime.com
SHONEN JUMP MANGA
www.shonenjump.viz.com
Pre-Order now at store.viz.com
Also available at your local bookstore or comic store
RATED T FOR TEEN
ratings.viz.com
VIZ media
www.viz.com
NURARIHYON NO MAGO © 2008 by Hiroshi Shiibashi/SHUEISHA Inc.
VIZ ANIME

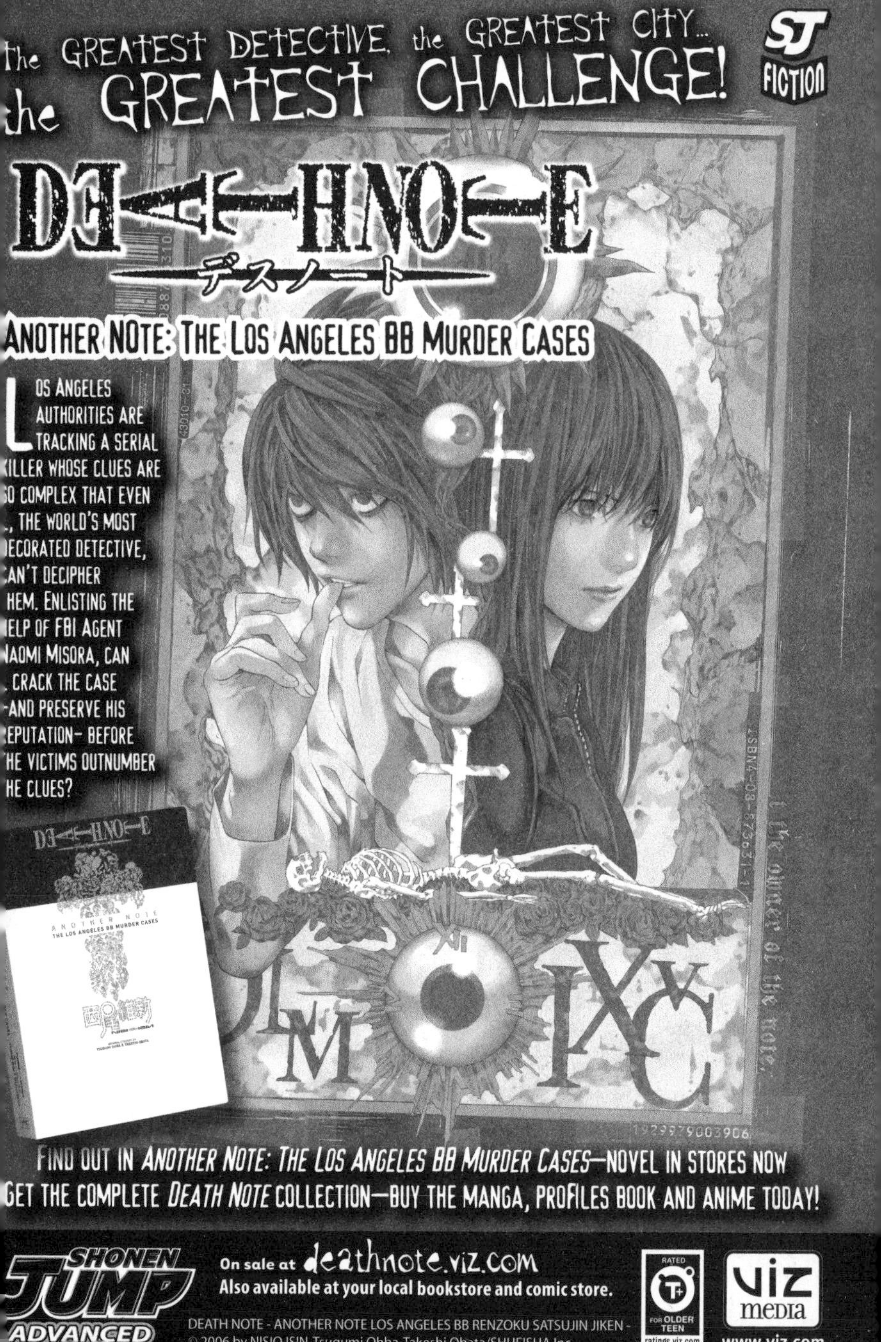
the GREATEST DETECTIVE, the GREATEST CITY...
the GREATEST CHALLENGE!
SJ FICTION
DEATH NOTE
デスノート
ANOTHER NOTE: THE LOS ANGELES BB MURDER CASES
LOS ANGELES AUTHORITIES ARE TRACKING A SERIAL KILLER WHOSE CLUES ARE SO COMPLEX THAT EVEN L, THE WORLD'S MOST DECORATED DETECTIVE, CAN'T DECIPHER THEM. ENLISTING THE HELP OF FBI AGENT NAOMI MISORA, CAN L CRACK THE CASE —AND PRESERVE HIS REPUTATION— BEFORE THE VICTIMS OUTNUMBER THE CLUES?
FIND OUT IN ANOTHER NOTE: THE LOS ANGELES BB MURDER CASES—NOVEL IN STORES NOW
GET THE COMPLETE DEATH NOTE COLLECTION—BUY THE MANGA, PROFILES BOOK AND ANIME TODAY!
SHONEN JUMP ADVANCED
On sale at deathnote.viz.com
Also available at your local bookstore and comic store.
DEATH NOTE - ANOTHER NOTE LOS ANGELES BB RENZOKU SATSUJIN JIKEN -
RATED T+ FOR OLDER TEEN ratings.viz.com
viz media
www.viz.com

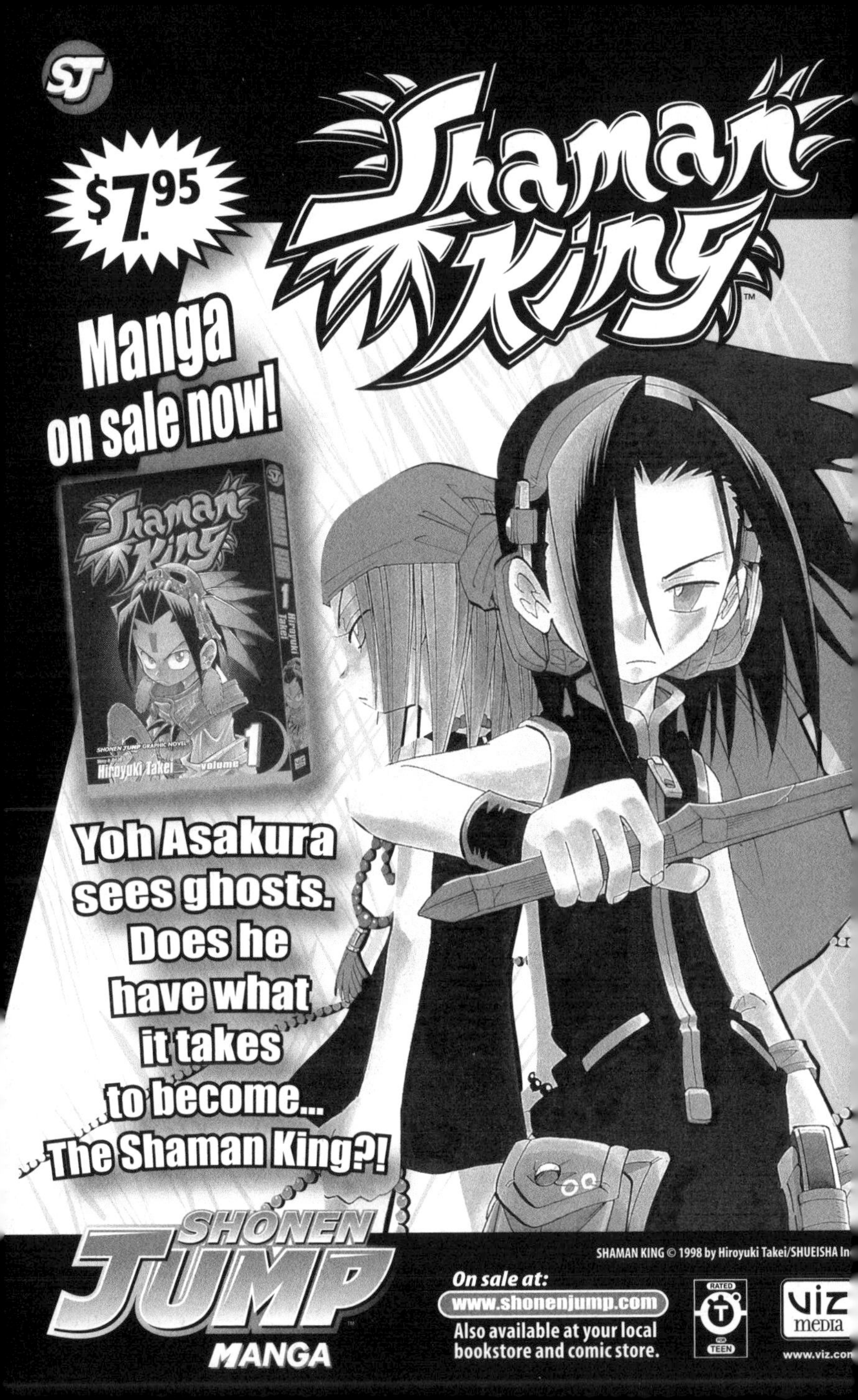

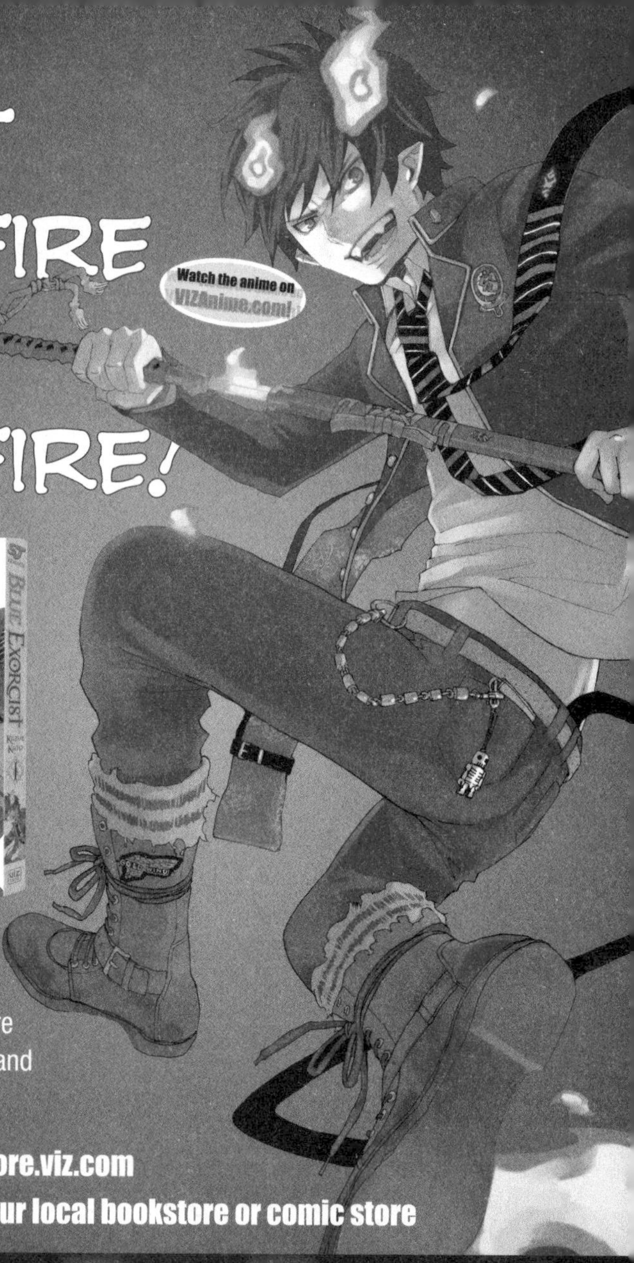

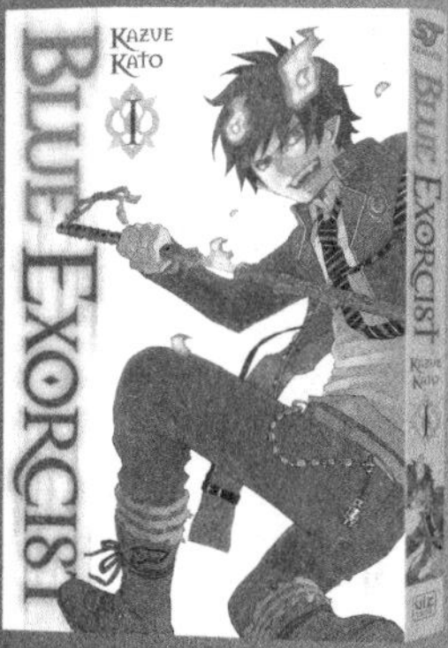
Kazue Kato
Blue Exorcist
1

The World's Greatest Manga
Now available on your iPad

**Full of FREE previews and tons of
new manga for you to explore**

From legendary manga like *Dragon Ball*
to *Bakuman*₀ the newest series from the
creators of *Death Note*, the best manga
in the world is now available on the iPad
through the official VIZ Manga app.

- **Free App**
- **New content weekly**
- **Free chapter 1 previews**